Deborah Cezal

September / 1986

ANALYSIS, REPAIR AND
INDIVIDUATION

The Library of Analytical Psychology

Edited by

MICHAEL FORDHAM
ROSEMARY GORDON
JUDITH HUBBACK
KENNETH LAMBERT

1. Analytical Psychology: a Modern Science*
2. Technique in Jungian Analysis*
3. The Self and Autism *Michael Fordham**
4. Dying and Creating: a Search for Meaning
   *Rosemary Gordon**
5. Analysis, Repair and Individuation
   Kenneth Lambert

These volumes are now distributed by Academic Press

THE LIBRARY OF ANALYTICAL PSYCHOLOGY
Volume 5

ANALYSIS, REPAIR AND INDIVIDUATION

KENNETH LAMBERT

1981

Published for
THE SOCIETY OF ANALYTICAL PSYCHOLOGY, LONDON
by
ACADEMIC PRESS
London   New York   Toronto   Sydney   San Francisco

ACADEMIC PRESS INC. (LONDON) LTD
24/28 Oval Road, London NW1 7DX

United States Edition published by
ACADEMIC PRESS INC.
111 Fifth Avenue, New York, New York, 10003

British Library Cataloguing in Publication Data

Lambert, Kenneth
Analysis repair and individuation.—(The
library of analytical psychology; v.5)
1. Individuality
I. Title   II. Series
155.2   BF697

ISBN 0-12-434640-5

LCCCN 81-66383

Typeset by
Reproduction Drawings Ltd,
Sutton, Surrey

Printed by
Page Bros (Norwich) Ltd

Contents

Editorial introduction		vii
Preface		ix
Introduction		xiii
1.	Individuation and the mutual influence of psychoanalysis and analytical psychology	1
2.	Personal psychology and the choice of analytic school	14
3.	Individuation and the personality of the analyst	20
4.	Resistance and counter-resistance	52
5.	Archetypes, object-relations and internal objects	88
6.	Reconstruction	106
7.	Transference, counter-transference and interpersonal relations	133
8.	Dreams and dreaming	168
9.	The individuation process	188
Postscript		200
Glossary		202
References		218
Index		225

Editorial introduction

Analysis, Repair and Individuation is undoubtedly a most valuable, informative and thought-provoking addition to the Library of Analytical Psychology. Kenneth Lambert describes here in great detail and with case material—yet without obscuring the general patterns—the process of analysis and its relation to Jung's concept of individuation. For those who have been curious to know what the actual work and procedure of Jungian analysts in London might be he opens a window into their consulting rooms. His capacity to explore, to analyse and to put into words the complex interactions between analyst and analysand is likely to strike his own colleagues also as wise and very helpful.

Lambert, like Jung, emphasizes the importance of the person of the analyst for the course of any analysis, which includes the analyst's development in the course of his own analysis and all further personal growth; for all this inevitably determines the kind of patient, and the sort of problem he can—or cannot—work with. Lambert also suggests ways in which the analyst's psycho–social–cultural background may be a factor in deciding with which school of analysis he may choose to train. And so he brings together his own theoretical and clinical evolution with the fact of his being Anglo–Irish; with his interest in the history of ideas and practices whereby he can seek to demonstrate an historical continuum between the clinical attitudes of contemporary psychotherapy and those expressed in the Hippocratic Oath and St Paul's concept of agape; and with his willingness to expose himself to and allow himself to be stimulated by the work of his colleagues, not least of those in the Freud–Jung group founded in London by Dr William Kraemer in 1964.

Whatever the relative influence and importance of these various factors and historical strands, Kenneth Lambert has woven from them a most impressive tapestry. He shows a deep grasp and understanding of the clinical concepts developed in the Freudian, Kleinian and Jungian schools, and he can trace with much clarity their interdependence and how they can—and do—affect and guide analytic practice. He defines and describes in his book those Jungian concepts that are particularly relevant to our clinical work, but he also shows how some of them have been refined as a result of the constantly increasing experience of an ever wider variety of patients, each of whom is not only our patient but also our teacher.

I believe that this book arrives in the series of the Library of Analytical Psychology at just the right moment, for it informs precisely, in depth and with much humanity, on what Jungians in London do with their patients—and with themselves in relation to their patients—and describes the various sources and influences that have brought them to their present position and to their present way of working.

As in the four previous volumes of the Library of Analytical Psychology, all the references to Jung's writings are taken from the Collected Works, abbreviated as *Coll. Wks*, followed by the volume number. The dates refer to the first publication in whatever language and not to the English translation. This volume, like Volume 4, contains a glossary.

Rosemary Gordon

Preface

Many working analysts, when they move from the consulting room to the study to make a book of their writings, tend, perforce, to produce something less coherent and less of a piece than professional writers could tolerate. Their lives are lived under pressure from the insistent and needy demands of their patients, whose plight requires of their analysts a reliability and continuity that is supported mercifully by the interesting and challenging nature of their work. Out of working hours, meetings, clinical and administrative, abound. Furthermore the maintenance of personal integrity and the life of family and friendship, together with some awareness of and relationship to the intellectual, politico–social and artistic environment, represent involvements that are more than legitimate. These, plus practical life, money, even sport, constitute much of the stuff of life within which psychological knowledge can develop and illuminate. Analytic work and analytic writing had better arise within a life style that grapples with such a complexity, but it means that writing tends to take place in odd hours through snatched time. Continuity of thought and attention can suffer in a way that well-meaning conscious and ordered planning cannot fully overcome. This can, however, be said without very much apology, for the subject matter of the book is itself concerned with multifariousness, chaos, disintegration and the conflict of opposites out of which various kinds of integration can arise. Such integrations can happen within a person spontaneously, but not by contrivance, and only at the cost of becoming free from perfectionism. The book then, a pale parallel to a human being, likewise goes into the world palpably partial, for better or for worse, to contribute what it can.

The completion and publication of this book are necessarily accompanied by an expression of gratitude on my part to my family, friends, and colleagues, for their forbearance over what may well have been experienced as my neglect, unavailability and absent-mindedness in my dealings with them at the time of bringing the book together. To my wife, especially, gratitude is due for more than forbearance and is immense for her understanding and support in listening, reading and uncovering the obscurities of style and thought that so easily invade psycho–dynamic discourse.

Furthermore, deep gratitude is due—and felt by me to be due—to my analysts for taking me into and exposing me to the analytic process and to my patients for allowing me to work with them. They have all made contributions that are for myself—it must be the same for every analyst—essential to the long process of experiencing, learning and digesting. It is this alone that can lead a person to begin to feel competent to practise analysis and perhaps ultimately to write about it.

That gratitude extends to what is indeed a generous giving of their knowledge and experience on the part of many London colleagues whose contributions, during three decades, to the cut and thrust, if not the love and hate, of the scientific debate, have made a great deal of difference to my knowledge and, indeed, to a sense of security in my working life. The shared intimacy and the possession of a common language, despite the misunderstandings that arise out of the multifarious communication difficulties of the English language in matters psychological and philosophical, represent a benefit that, though nearly essential, is sometimes taken for granted, if not unappreciated. My debt to them extends from their personal communications to their writings in *The Journal of Analytical Psychology*. In addition there is a background of books by Michael Fordham and, in particular, one published in 1978 and surely a landmark in the growth of analytical psychology in London, entitled *Jungian Psychotherapy*. That book has already been widely read and appreciated and covers a much more comprehensive range of topics than I have attempted in mine. Specific gratitude in respect of the book is due to Olive Polge and Hazel Capal for typing; to Rosemary Gordon, especially, among my co-editors for much time spent upon editorial comment and criticism; to Diana Riviere for literary editing; to Nicholas Collins for indexing; to the staff of Academic Press for courtesy and long suffering.

Chapters 3 to 8 draw upon papers I have already published in varying amounts with considerable revision and, in any case, slanted to illustrate ways in which the clinical work of analysis and repair can release a spontaneous development of individuation that is appropriate to age and circumstance. Chapter 3 is based upon a paper originally published in the *Journal of Analytical Psychology*, **18**, 1 under the title "Agape as a therapeutic factor in analysis" and later in Volume 2 of

The Library of Analytical Psychology under the title "The personality of the analyst in interpretation and therapy". Chapter 4 is a revised version of "Resistance and counter–resistance" published in *The Journal of Analytical Psychology*, **21**, 2. Chapter 5 is a revised version in English of a paper published in German entitled "Die Bedeutung von archetypischen Functionen Objektbeziehunger und internalisierten Objekten für die individuellen Erfahrungen des kindes an der Mutter" in the *Zeitschrift für Analytische Psychologie und ihre Grenzgebiete*, **8**, 1. Chapter 6 uses some material from a paper entitled "Some notes on the process of reconstruction" first published in *The Journal of Analytical Psychology*, **15**, 1 and also in Volume 2 of The Library of Analytical Psychology. Chapter 7 uses material from a paper entitled "Transference/counter–transference; talion law and gratitude" first published in the *Journal of Analytical Psychology*, **17**, 1 and also in Volume 2 of The Library of Analytical Psychology. Chapter 8 is a slightly revised version of a paper entitled "The use of the dream in contemporary analysis" published in *The Journal of Analytical Psychology*, **24**, 2 and in *Methods of Treatment in Analytical Psychology* edited Ian F. Baker, 1980, Fellbach, Verlag Adolf Bonz, being the papers presented at the VIIth International Congress for The International Association for Analytical Psychology. A version in Italian was published in *Oggi Jung* edited by Aldo Carotenuto, 1978, Rome. Marsilio editori.

Acknowledgements are due to the Editors of *The Journal of Analytical Psychology*, the *Zeitschrift für Analytische Psychology* and the *Rivista di Psicologia Analitica* for permission to use material already published by them, and to Verlag Adolf Bonz for the same reason.

London and Cambridge   *Kenneth Lambert*
May 1981

Author's introduction

During the past thirty years, analytical psychologists in London and elsewhere have been attending to phenomena that have involved them in a certain revision and elaboration of Jung's concept of individuation. One of the foremost results of this work has been Michael Fordham's theory of the original self that progressively deintegrates and reintegrates at various points during the life-span of an individual. Thus inner archetypal potentialities are progressively "unpacked" and differentiated out under conditions of activation by living contact with the objects, persons and processes of the external world that correspond to them and indeed may become, for the person involved, symbolic of them. As a result, these archetypal potentials take on something of the reality of flesh and blood, space and time. They can then be reintegrated into the whole once more, after which in due time further deintegrations and reintegrations can take place. Thus the self develops in complexity within and in realization without. Fordham's theory has proved to be a fruitful one and it has enabled Jungians both to contribute to and to benefit from a certain convergence of Freudian and Jungian viewpoints in theory and clinical practice which is beginning to emerge in some parts of the world.

This book reappraises and, with clinical examples, elaborates upon such themes in some detail. It demonstrates the way in which clinical activities, in the past more usually associated with psychoanalysis though in fact found in principle also with Jung, are being used by modern Jungians to facilitate, through repair or release, the psychological movement of patients into individuation. They include the analysis of resistance and counter-resistance and of transference and counter-transference. Furthermore reconstructive analysis together with the observation of vicissitudes in the formation of object-relationships and internal objects have become part of everyday clinical activity. In addition, the treatment of dreams and dreaming has gained sophistication in the analysis of personal life and its archetypal background.

Naturally, the dynamics behind such phenomena arise not only out of illusory or delusional or archetypal transference/counter-transference situations but also partly out of the relationship between patient and analyst as real persons. This book supports and elaborates upon Jung's insistence on the necessity for would-be analysts to undergo a rigorous analysis. This is not only to provide them with personal experience of their own inner psychological processes but also to enable the release within them of a wide range of their own potential as part of a movement towards integration and individuation. This can provide for them a certain amplitude of personality for patients to interact with, when in time they are ready to do so, and out of which analytic interpretation is likely to be effective. In addition the author holds that such a view gains plausibility by the fact that it is congruous in part with a medico–pastoral practice that is rooted and historically expressed in the Hippocratic Oath and the Pauline concept of agape.

Perhaps more than is usual in writings about individuation, the book attempts to demonstrate ways in which analysis and repair can be applied to damaged, distorted or blocked development in people as a priority and first step in releasing within them spontaneous processes of individuation. In such a context, an attempt to state a contemporary Jungian theory of individuation seems called for, and it is to this task that the last chapter addresses itself. It is followed by a glossary of some terms used in analytical psychology today.

Such themes are naturally the concern of psychiatrists, psychologists, analysts, psychotherapists, counsellors, social workers and ministers of religion. It is thought that in addition they may be relevant also to the interests of philosophers, sociologists and theologians—indeed to all those exercised by the problems of individuals in their personal and social relationships.

To

D.L., M.F., *and* F.F.

Chapter One

Individuation and the mutual influence of psychoanalysis and analytical psychology

I have written this book as one of the first trainees of the Society of Analytical Psychology, having become an Associate Professional Member in 1950. For me, membership of that society, together with participation for over thirty years in the general analytical scene in London, has provided sustained stimulus and support. In addition, I have enjoyed, from its beginning in 1964, membership of the Freud–Jung group, convened by Dr William Kraemer in London, where analytical psychologists and psychoanalysts meet regularly to discuss clinical problems. The whole period has been one in which considerable advances have been made towards finding ways of integrating the two main strands of analytical theory and practice, which had, earlier, during the second to fourth decades of this century, developed either in isolation from or very much in polar opposition to each other. The division into opposite camps afforded, in the earlier years, breathing space wherein each could grow and develop from within. Later on, however, what with the pressure of patients' needs on the one hand and natural curiosity on the other, analysts could be found peeping into each other's gardens—rather more obviously in the case of the London Jungians, rather more quietly, and more by private admission, on the part of the Freudians.

Such a splitting process, with the results just mentioned, has probably proved in the long run to be to the advantage of analytical theory and practice. In the shorter run, however, it was rather less of an advantage to analysts trained in the earlier days, not only in respect of their own analyses but also of those they offered to their patients at that time. That, of course, is a function of the problem of being born rather too early in the century—a matter of fate, certainly, but perhaps, after all, not entirely a bad thing provided analysts keep

1

themselves alive to new developments and participate regularly in clinical discussion and controversy.

It thus turns out that, as our understanding has increased, so more and more people have found it incorrect to consider the relationship between the two schools as inherently and permanently one of incompatibility, particularly to the extent of engendering mutually destructive hostility. Objectively speaking, the relationship at the present juncture is better described as one that is becoming complementary. Even the original personal clash between Freud and Jung, so often seen in the past in terms of temperamental or personality-type incompatibility, appears less strong today and more a matter of differences in background and family circumstance.

These can promote or evoke different conceptual patterns of what is psychiatric health or damage in a way that is much better understood now. The differences seem therefore today to occur over matters of emphasis, often generational in origin, rather than of total incompatibility of philosophy or temperament, though Jung emphasized typological differences between himself and Freud (Jung, 1963), while Winnicott much later, in his well-known review of *Memories, Dreams, Reflections,* felt that at that point in analytic history it would have been hardly possible for the two men to understand each other, so different were their personal problems (Winnicott, 1964).

In so far as theory and clinical practice are concerned, one way of demonstrating the complementariness in question to a contemporary mind is to use contrast. This can be done by columnizing some of the points traditionally conceived of as illustrating the fundamental incompatibility between the schools. I shall attempt to do this, and then describe shortly the ways in which the two schools have, historically, out of their inner logic and the pressure of clinical need, been able to surmount these apparent barriers and to draw closer to each other. My columnization, *which must not be misunderstood as referring to the contemporary situation*, runs as follows:

Some Attitudes of Classical Psychoanalysis and Analytical Psychology According to the Traditional models

Traditional psychoanalysis	*Traditional analytical psychology*
(1) The central interest was to analyse the psychopathology that can be related to early damage sustained by instinctual drive processes; to release normal development; and to strengthen the ego	(1) The central interest was individuation, integration and the realization of the self. Psychopathology was understood as arising out of important elements of the self remaining

Traditional psychoanalysis

for improved handling of super-ego and id.

(2) The analyst was largely a screen analyst and the transference largely a matter of the projection upon him of figures in the early childhood and the past of the patient in general.

(3) The analyst was, for a large part of his time, involved within the transference in reconstructing his patient's early history, in linking him with the emotions of his past and thereby releasing him from identifications with them.

(4) The analyst as part of his technique was relatively passive. He needed to have the ability to listen to the patient's mainly verbal communications. His own interventions too were mainly by verbal interpretation and strictly analytic in content and intention, at least in the long term, even when designed mainly to foster communication.

(5) The couch was used by the patient. Sessions were, if possible, daily and generally 50 minutes long. For periods in the analysis a high degree of dependence upon the analyst might develop in the patient.

(6) Dreams were considered in terms of the patient's defensive manoeuvres against acknowledgement of basic instinctuality. Arising spontaneously as

Traditional analytical psychology

unconscious 'in the shadow' and thus liable to function in distorted and inferior ways. Drive processes were considered to be structured and archetypal in nature.

(2) The analyst was another human being in a dialectical interaction with his patient. The transference was taken largely in terms of archetypal content, manifested in the here and now. There was a tendency to neglect the past, though *reductive* analysis was recognized and contrasted with *synthetic* analysis.

(3) The analyst was committed to the understanding of archetypal processes in his patient that appear in the here and now and prospectively both within the transference and outside it. For this he needed knowledge of archetypal material as found in religion, mythology, fairy tales etc. His interventions could be of many and various kinds.

(4) The analyst was a listening participator in a dialectical intercourse with his patient. Non-verbal methods of communication were taken account of as well as painting, modelling etc. Transactions were two-way and included for the patient confession, elucidation, education as well as transformation, a process in which the analyst might also change in various ways.

(5) The patient usually sat in a chair facing or a little oblique to the analyst. Sessions were not so frequent. The patient and the analyst were in some ways fellow students of the patient's material and indeed of archetypal material, conscious and unconscious, personal and collective.

(6) Dream content was interpreted much more simply as if the dreamer meant what he said but was using the pictorial symbolic language that is

Traditional psychoanalysis	*Traditional analytical psychology*
a mode of compromise or substitute satisfaction of id and superego pressures, they could be used through the rather devious imagery employed to obscure issues for defensive purposes.	typical of a side of the psyche known to poets and artists but often less developed, if not unconscious, in modern rational man. It was considered to be an important product of the unconscious matrix of personality. The interplay of archetypal images and various inner and outer figures and processes in the dreamer supplied the content and the meaning of the dream.
(7) Unconscious process was considered to be composed of repressed material and of damaged or unacceptable elements of the past—together with defences. Aspects of ego and superego were understood to be repressed as well as a great deal of the id, conceived of as unconscious, blind and undifferentiated will to survive and reproduce. Psychological maturity was to consist in strengthening the ego so that the individual's perception of external reality (the reality principle) could be freed from distortion by pressures from the id and superego. Thus the growth of the ego would give better expression to id and superego in a way that modified stress in the personality as a whole.	(7) Unconscious process was conceived of as (*a*) repressed personal experiences and so far unexperienced personal potential, and (*b*) more structured archetypal predispositions arising from the unconscious matrix of the personality, called collective because they constituted stereotypical forms shared by all people or large or small groups of people. The unconscious aim of the psyche might be discovered to be individuation, integration or the realization of the self in terms of flesh and blood, space and time. The essential service of ego-consciousness in all this was more and more emphasized by Jung as he entered old age (Jung, 1976, p.112).
(8) The analyst needed to be analysed in order to be able to preserve his boundaries; to be as free as possible from the projection of his own personal psychology, neurotic or psychotic, illusory or delusionary, on to that of his patients; and to be sufficiently aware of his own problems and defences not to miss or ignore elements similar to them in patients. Moreover, in cases where trainees had not already been propelled into analysis by personal need, their analyses were generally discovered by them to be essential for their emotional health, as well as for their ability to practise psychoanalysis.	(8) The analyst was to be analysed not only to preserve him from delusions, illusions and blindness about his patient, but also because his own individuation and integration, vital enough for him, were also considered vital for the therapy of his patient. Interpersonal interaction and induction processes were deeply involved. In other words the personality of the analyst was felt to be crucial and of an importance prior even to questions of technique.

Now it is clearly to be objected that a columnization like this not only misrepresents but also radically over-polarizes the Freudian and Jungian contributions to analysis and neglects historical development. It would, however, have been accurate enough, and certainly less of a distortion, fifty, forty even thirty years ago. It is a measure of the change that has taken place, often, perhaps, quietly and insensibly, that many analysts and patients of either school would find the account almost a caricature of their experience, beliefs and practice, and certainly outdated. They would be on the whole right. That this is so has not, however, arisen out of any attempt on the part of the two schools to organize themselves into some sort of synthesis or integration. The fact is that most members of each school have preferred to remain attached to their original professional associations, into which, by the nature of the analytical experiences provided by them, so much of personal involvement has been invested. As a result, they have mainly extended the range of their clinical observation and developed the inner logic of the foundational discoveries made by their own psychological family. Only later, by a slow process of ingestion, digestion and elimination, have they come to terms with the other stream, whether overtly or covertly, and sometimes as the results of pressures arising from within themselves or from their interaction with patients.

It would indeed take a large book to attempt to particularize the developments in psychoanalysis and analytical psychology that have rendered my columnization so out of date, and it is certainly not the purpose of this book to do so. However, as these developments represent part of the background behind the writing of this book, I propose to comment shortly on them from a Jungian angle under the eight headings already listed.

Developments in Psychoanalysis and Analytical Psychology and Modifications of the Traditional Models

1. *The Central Interest*

Psychoanalysts have begun to add to their central interest the notion of the self and to investigate the conditions that foster or damage its development at various stages in the early life of the individual. Jacobson, Winnicott, Kernberg, Kohut and Volkan are among the key figures here. At the same time Hartmann and the ego-psychologists have elaborated the nature and vicissitudes of ego-development. Indeed in all schools the precise link between ego and self is being explored.

Analytical psychologists have also continued their investigations into the self, particularly so in respect of the repair of damage sustained by it during its early development and in the analyst's care of the whole individuating and integrative process. It has become necessary to conceive of a psychopathology of the development of the self that cannot be ignored. This has been made more observable by the implications of Fordham's theory that, at the birth of the individual, the original self may be postulated to be an undifferentiated unity, with minimal consciousness, but carrying the potential for deintegration into archetypal drives when presented with, or when in collision with, the outer objects corresponding to them. (Fordham, 1957). We can now study, with the hope of repair: (1) damage to the process of deintegration as such (Fordham, 1976), and (2) damage to the deintegrates themselves. Further important studies of the self have been made by Redfearn, including his valuable paper (Redfearn, 1969) comparing Jung's concept of the self with that of Jacobson (1964). Alan Edwards (1976, 1978), Rushi Ledermann (1979) and Rosemary Gordon (1980) have also contributed to the study of the problems of early narcissistic damage in connection with the work of Kohut (1971, 1977), Kernberg (1974), and Volkan (1976). In Jungian circles, there has been debate on the question of whether it is useful to work with the notion of an ego–self axis, or whether ego-consciousness may be understood as the conscious aspect of the self, except where it has been organized rigidly in opposition to the personality as a whole. In extreme contrast, we have even witnessed an attack upon the ego as such as if it were really only a false "hero-ego" and a cramping or divisive factor opposed to spontaneity (Hillman 1975, pp. xiv and 21).

2. *The Function of the Analyst*

In respect of the function of the analyst, psychoanalysis has greatly modified the rigorous notion of the passive, almost impersonal, screen analyst and admitted the existence of a number of interactional processes in analysis. Rycroft (1968) writes of the formation within the analyst of a disposition towards his patient that influences his behaviour. Racker (1968) spells out some of the interactional dynamism activated by the analyst's mobilized predisposition to attend to his patient, by his concordant empathy, by his struggle to recognize within himself the operation of the *talion law* which blindly rewards the good done to him by his patient and punishes the evil, and by his ability to use the energy of the talionic emotion for the development of analytic insight. Winnicott describes the holding of his patient, over a long period of time when necessary, and his full acceptance of the patient's nihilistic resistances. Balint (1968) opens out the question of the special handling needed when dealing with a case where a "basic fault" is sensed to have developed at the heart of the infant self. Bion stresses the "full interpretation" regarded as an action taken by the analyst in loneliness and full responsibility. Schafer (1973) insists upon the essentially interpersonal processes of interaction in analysis whereby resistance is understood in terms of resistance to penetration by persecution or by engulfment, not only by the analyst himself but also by the paternal and maternal images or objects transferred on to his person by the patient. All these writers emphasize the personal and interactional function of analysts in relation to their patients, involving, as they do, more than the impersonal contrivance engineered by their acting as a screen.

Analytical psychology, however, especially in London, has begun to recognize much more fully the patient's dependency needs when in states of regression. This has been made possible as a result of the emergence of considerably increased understanding among Jungian analysts of early development, further implemented by the recently constituted training in child analysis which has begun to produce its first child analysts. It is now fully recognized that, in the adult, there can arise a need for his early childhood to be analysed both for the repair of damage, with a subsequent release of held-up development, and to enable the patient to link emotionally both with his childhood and, as a result, in more realistic ways, with the Divine Child archetype. Under these circumstances the patient discovers needs in himself to be dependent upon his analyst in an asymmetric way, which does not have to be thought of as an affront to dignity or equal human status in relation to the analyst. In this case the transference will be recognized to contain much early infancy and childhood material within which archetypal themes are discernible. The Jungian analyst, while understanding the advantages of acting as a screen, tends today to find a place for these advantages somewhat differently by taking a middle position and maintaining a low profile that meets his patients' relationship needs and transference needs by being appropriately contained within himself. He does not attempt either to act as a non-entity or blank screen nor to go out of his way to display his personality in an over-emotional or active manner. Of course he may sometimes find within himself strong pressures towards either of those extremes. In such cases, whether he expresses or contains such feelings, a contemporary analytical psychologist would certainly consider himself involved in a counter-transference process that calls for further analysis and self-exploration. On the other hand, in treatment of psychotic patients it is generally agreed that a certain modification of the low-keyed screen type stance and indeed a more active procedure may be needed.

3. *The Action of the Analyst*

In respect of the importance of reconstruction and the analysis of early childhood, considerable new developments have taken place in psychoanalysis. The establishment of an object-relations theory has been achieved by Winnicott (1941-1969), Fairbairn (1952), Guntrip (1961) and many others, while the notion of unconscious infantile phantasy has been generously elaborated by Klein. Their notion of internalized objects has greatly affected analytic practice. Internal objects and images containing unconscious infantile phantasies inhabit dreams and other material in the transference in a way that is near to the archetypal images familiar to Jungians. Some psychoanalysts have even tended to interpret the transference in terms of the here and now, and with little historical reconstruction (Blum, 1980).

On the other hand, analytical psychologists in London have realized afresh the importance and centrality of reconstruction within the transference and counter-transference. There is an increased understanding of the two-way interrelationship between the personal history of the individual and his archetypal development (Fordham, 1978; Lambert see pp. 106 ff.). Indeed, many cases suggest that the early events of the individual's life can noticeably activate certain groups of archetypal process at the expense of others. A reconstruction that can show how this happened in the patient's early history and how it operates in the transference and in other current situations can open the way to a much-needed understanding of the distortions involved and thus release synthetic processes in the future.

4. *Screen and Interaction*

On the question of the relative passivity of the analyst in the clinical situation, psychoanalysts such as Rycroft, Racker, Schafer and others recognize the extent to which analysts provide interactional messages and emotional experiences most of the time and indeed out of the whole of their personality. It follows that a careful analysis of what is actually happening between patient and analyst becomes doubly important. This shows that the problem is in fact much more complicated than was apparent in the earlier view that verbalized interpretations on the part of an outside, "objective", observing, listening and "scientific" analyst represented the essence of the analyst's function in the therapeutic procedure. That view seems to many people today to represent a distorted notion of "scientific objectivity" by its neglect of the importance of the personal involvement of the observer with the observed, i.e. of the analyst with his patient.

On the other hand, analytical psychologists have needed to reconsider some of the rather underdisciplined and technically too loose behaviour—appropriately spontaneous at its best, but blundering at its worst—that was frequent in the earlier decades of their therapeutical practice. Thus, elaborating upon the classical elements of confession, elucidation, education and transformation as described by Jung, many analytical psychologists today hold that their most effective tools are analytic abilities that function spontaneously out of the integration and individuation of a therapeutically gifted and suitably trained individual who participates regularly in a clinical group. I should like to amplify this by bringing in a modified and extended concept of agape (see pp.36 ff.) as a central element of the "being" or *"ontos"* of the therapist. All this represents the essentially personal equation needed as the basis of interpretations that are designed, for instance, to facilitate in the patient the repair of damaged capacities, to say nothing of their emergence for the first time. One example of this is the really reliable continuity and involvement needed to bring to birth and nurture basic trust within a patient of the sort that Plaut has convincingly argued to be a condition for the emergence of imaginative capabilities that are of a fruitful rather than a persecutory type (Plaut, 1966). In addition, considerable interest has focused upon the response of patients to their analyst's interventions in terms of their general psychopathology. Such responses may be understood not only as particular to the transference situation, but also as indicating the patient's response in the first place to the presence of other persons as such. Granted this last insight, however, analytical psychologists, like other analysts, then begin the process described by Meltzer (1967) as the "gathering of the transference".

5. Chair and Couch

As for the old problem of chair versus couch, considerable changes of practice have taken place. Both schools have modified the rigidity of their standard practices. Psychoanalysts find themselves employing the chair for psychotherapy cases where considerable regression and the need for the fostering of primary process thinking do not appear to be specially indicated. Questions of the relative merits of chair and couch have been reassessed and, for instance, a convincing rationale for the use of the couch has been worked out by Rubinfine (1967).

Many analytical psychologists in London use the couch a great deal—in contrast to their previous practice. This is in view of their renewed interest in psychopathology as a function of early damage and also the need on the part of many patients to regress and to experience themselves not only as dependent but also as rageful, as desperate, and as resistant as they really feel. This kind of patient discovers a need so urgent as to render arguments for the use of the chair, based upon the maintenance of the equality of the *I–Thou* relationship, though in principle irreproachable, yet for the time being both irrelevant and unreal. It becomes a matter of life or death for the patient to be enabled to relax into an asymmetrical alliance with the therapist so that the infant within, suffering as a result of privation or deprivation, may be met, related to, cared for and nursed into life in the symbolical way appropriate to adult existence. Many Jungian analysts find that a free and experimental use of the couch can, through the altered somatic states involved by a change of position, be conducive to a release of the feelings, emotions and imaginative processes of early life. This can be especially useful to patients who are highly organized in terms of logical propositional thinking and aim-directed activity. In such patients, their left hemispherical dominance needs modification from the right.

Finally and incidentally, it has been found useful also to interpret the unconscious processes of patients not only in the way they use the couch but also in their varying choices as to whether they use couch or chair.

6. Dreams and Dreaming

In the matter of attitudes towards patients' dreams, dreaming, and the reporting of dreams, there is considerable evidence that psychoanalysts have modified the early classical theory that dreaming represents in part a psychopathological activity on the part of the patient that contains defensive elements, however much, for early Freud, the understanding of dreams represented "the royal road to the knowledge of the unconscious activities of the mind". A shift has taken place amongst them away from interpreting dreams or dreaming as defensive manoeuvres on the part of the patient. Instead, they nowadays explore them more in terms of their content as representing the interplay between internal objects, figures and images of the inner world of patients (*vide* Altmann, 1975). Furthermore, unconscious infantile phantasies, represented in dreams, albeit often in obscure forms but interpreted within the context of the rest of the material, are very much part of the Kleinian world. That all this comes nearer to the approach adopted by Jung is obvious enough, while, recently, a step nearer still has been taken by Rycroft in his *The Innocence of Dreams* (Rycroft, 1979). As a Jungian I have profited from his writing and find much to agree with in it, but I think that he underestimates the extent to which both dream content, dream recall, together with variabilities in the timing and quantity of dreams recalled, argue for the possibility of a not so innocent use of them by the dreamer, at least when in a transferential relationship to an analyst (*vide* Chapter 8).

Analytical psychologists, on the other hand, have become much more aware of the influence of infantile archetypal phantasy and internal-object formation upon the content of dreams. Furthermore, in their clinical work they have become well aware that dreaming as such, apart from content, may be understood as *behaviour* on the part of the patient, often of transferential significance. It has become clearer, too, that the classical Freudian view of dreaming may be understood in similar terms as but one of many behavioural ploys (Fordham, 1978; see also this volume pp. 169 ff.).

In addition to the signs of *rapprochement* so far described, it is evident that both schools are likely to be influenced in parallel ways by the work of the sleep laboratories and by that of the neurophysiologists of the brain, much of which may be seen to lend support to Jung's original views about dreams (*vide* J. P. Henry, 1977). A further elaboration of this theme will be found in Chapter 8.

7. Ego and Self

Over the question of the relative importance of ego and self, we may sense in psychoanalysis a subtle shift of emphasis from the early notion that an ego, needing to become more conscious both of itself and of the reality principle, the id and the superego, can thereby become capable of functioning in a rather "royal" directive and mediating manner in respect of those factors and their interrelationship. The notion of the self is being attended to, particularly, by writers like Jacobsen (1964) and Kohut (1971). Implied in Winnicott's and Guntrip's therapeutic care of the "true" self is the same notion of a central core of the personality and its need for ego-consciousness to aid it into healthy "being" and "becoming". Furthermore Kohut (1971), Kernberg (1974) and Volkan (1976) in the U.S.A., as well as Winnicott and his followers in England, though with a different slant, have all explored early damage to the development of the self, particularly when an inflation of narcissistic self-love develops in the individual as a substitute for the early care and love he needed from his parents but which for some reason, subjective or objective, he had not have sufficiently experienced. These shifts of emphasis in psychoanalysis represent a movement in the direction of the understanding of the self according to analytical psychology.

On the other hand, analytical psychology has elaborated its description of the self, as distinct from self-representations, particularly in respect of the dynamic processes whereby the original undifferentiated self at birth proceeds under favourable circumstances to deintegrate and reintegrate as inner development and growth proceed so that the individual becomes ever more ready to meet both inner and outer reality through each stage in life (Fordham, 1957). The *deintegration* involved, and any distortions arising in its functioning, need to be distinguished from *disintegration*, which can be the result of shattering rage arising in infancy due to environmental failure. Disintegrative processes can sometimes be so severe that a state can arise whereby the individual involved is almost wholly taken up by what Fordham has called ''defences of the self''. These can bring about an extremely negative expression of ''do-it-yourself'' psychology requiring endless patience, skill and belief from the analyst attempting its treatment (Fordham, 1974). In this way, analytical psychology has, with the assistance of psychoanalysis, added to the far-reaching and subtle descriptions of the self by Jung a study of the early developmental processes leading to the adult states he describes, together with some understanding of the hazards and vicissitudes involved.

8. The Analysis of Trainees

With regard to different attitudes towards the analysis of the trainee-analyst as between psychoanalysis and analytical psychology, we are also finding modifications in each other's direction. Thus, Rycroft (1968), Racker (1968) and, in a special way, Bion (1962) have demonstrated that the demands upon an analyst extend a good way beyond technical competence or analytic insight. They include integrity, the capacity for sustained involvement, reliability, conscious containment of the workings of the talion law, the sacrifice of knowingness, and a tolerance of the anxiety that accompanies phases, during an analysis, of feeling lost and unable to see any light.

When it comes to analytical psychology, people have become more conscious that any temptation to rely upon his ''integration'', ''individuation'' or the ''self'', when the analysis of his childhood and infancy has been neglected, lands the analyst into an unconcious cover up of early distortions that warp his perceptions and leave him at the mercy of destructive impulses towards his patients and blindness to their deepest problems. This whole development has no doubt placed a heavier and even more demanding burden upon analysts and, of course, trainees. There is some consolation in the thought that the availability of improved analyses is increasing all the time.

The Scope of the Book

It is against this general background that some papers I have written during the past ten years have been brought together into this book—considerably altered or expanded in view of my developing thoughts and experience. They have all been written from the point of view of an analytical psychologist attempting to integrate into his original Jungian background both psychoanalytic developments and the changing emphases of analytical psychology. I consider myself to have benefited from these efforts and I think that this has also been the case with a number of my patients. In other words I hold that, though my original Jungian upbringing has been modified, it has been enriched and certainly not abandoned. Even when two lines of development in a field like dynamic psychology are found in the course of time to be complementary in more ways than had been thought, it remains likely that in most cases the originally chosen line still suits the individual brought up in it, provided that contributions from the complementary line are integrated enough and according to need.

I have accordingly included chapters on some fundamental clinical themes: the personality of the analyst; resistance and counter-resistance; object-relations and archetypes; reconstruction within the transference and counter-transference; interpersonal factors in the transference and the counter-transference; the clinical use of dreams and dreaming phenomena. In each case, however, I have described in historical terms how theory and practice have developed in both psychoanalysis and analytical psychology in ways that are often parallel, sometimes mutually interactive, and occasionally divergent. In each case, too, I have made links between clinical practice and the way in which it can release and foster the individuation process.

I hope therefore that it will become evident that the title of the book, *Analysis, Repair and Individuation*, is intended to point to the fact that individuation, as a specifically Jungian notion, is, in many cases, intimately linked, when it comes to its realization, with the analysis into its elements of unsatisfactory end-product complexity. The aim is to bring about repair in the patient's personality in the case of psychopathology and thus to make possible a fresh start. This inaugurates a spontaneous (not contrived) growth of integration and individuation, much of which is expressed by a released, renewed and expanded capacity for imagination on the patient's part and implemented by the improved object-relations brought about by the analysis of the transference.

The previous chapters of this book required to be put into perspective by a final chapter on the *individuation process* as such, both in the thought of Jung and that of later analytical psychologists, and this I hope will make the links clear enough. A further aid to clarity is, I hope, provided by the Glossary of terms used in the book in cases where obscurity and confusion of an undesirable sort can creep in.

Chapter Two

Personal psychology and the choice of analytic school

My reference to imagination has made me think that, in view of the very personal and individual aspects of analytical psychology, I should acknowledge the personal aspect of my interest, first, in analytical psychology and then, later, in the marriage of Jungian analysis with the disciplines arising out of psychoanalysis. It is traditionally thought that the language of imagination, phantasy and imagery was particularly meaningful to the early analytical psychologists by contrast with the more intellectualistic if not rationalistic style of the early psychoanalysts. I think this probably appealed to me when I was young. Being Anglo-Irish I was torn unknowingly by some such dichotomy both from within and, to an extent, from the environment. The latter was an English one, in which I was exposed to a fairly traditional mode of education, attitude and manners.

That attitude has sometimes been designated as dominated by extraverted sensation-thinking and not very imaginative. It has been, probably wrongly, used by some critics to explain the special slants of the Society of Analytical Psychology in England. Of course, such issues are always open to generalization and to becoming stereotyped. I well remember an interesting example of it when, in 1950, I was able, as a nervous young man, to spend some hours in conversation with Jung, who incidentally used a good deal of imaginative imagery in his conversation. He asked me my nationality. I replied that I was Anglo-Irish. He seized on the Irish side and exclaimed "Ah! Irish. That is good. The Irish, they have the imagination. You will make an analyst!" I hardly knew my reactions at that time. I was respectful. I naturally half liked what he said and yet felt slightly guilty and affronted. However, it was in fact true that I had always felt, both throughout my education in England and in the company of my well-liked English relations, slightly in collision with what I probably wrongly understood as their practical common-sense approach to life, the correctness of their behaviour and perhaps, above all, as it so happened, their somewhat puritan and evangelical views. The puritanism was felt by me, at that time, to impose a cramp upon imaginative religious and moral experiences, while the common sense, with its successful aim-directed activity, recommended to me as it was in my education, was something I to some extent admired and yet could not quite emulate. Those positive virtues seemed to me, wrongly as I now think, to have become unconsciously entangled with fear and distrust of spontaneity, imagination and humour, for which latter capacity I managed to get into trouble at school sufficiently often to end up quite inhibited. I now think that my Irish mother suffered in the same way, through not quite understanding the English people she lived with.

Today, of course, I know much more of the great English tradition of imagination, spontaneity and humour. Some of this is expressed in poetry, literature, music and the arts and humanities in general. Much of it is found in inventiveness in practical affairs and organization, to say nothing of the sciences. It has nevertheless to be admitted that its presence in people is often deeply contained and hidden, if not unrealized. Furthermore it has to be admitted that imagination can be distinctly hamstrung on the Irish side as well—witness the amusing dialogues of the comic littérateur, Myles naGopaleen, with his creation called ''The plain people of Ireland'' (Gopaleen, 1968). There are some, too, who would feel that the bourgeois society of Dublin has not quite lived up to W. B. Yeats's famous line ''A terrible beauty is born'' as applied to the revolution. The fact is that the problematic notion of national psycho-cultural characteristics was something more plausible to me when I was young than it is today. Apart from the notion that cultures support the emergence and development of some aspects of the archetypal potential of the individual rather than others, I am now much more aware of psychopathology in the individual. It seems to me today, for instance, that imagination, though no doubt an inborn gift, can be used in distorted ways as part of a manic defence against feelings of depression. It can also be temporarily destroyed in the inner emptiness and isolation arising out of destructive rage activated by neglect of many sorts in infancy. Here we are dealing with individual history. In this area, of course, a psycho-cultural reference would arise only if certain standard methods of infant care and child education were found to be very widely accepted and supported in any particular society.

For all this, however, it remains true that, at the time of my life when

I first came across analytical psychology through Kathleen Kitchin and, later, Gerhard Adler, I experienced a release from emotional cramp over imaginative process issuing in, among other things, a new experience of becoming aware of dreaming and of dream content in quite rich detail. This experience made sense of an abiding adolescent memory of the half-embarrassed and half-grudgingly proud feeling that arose in me when out of the blue a letter came from an Irish uncle deeply involved intellectually and imaginatively in the Irish renaissance of the early nineteen twenties. He would have me understand that I came from a line of Irish "poets, scholars and mystics" which I must not neglect and that even my mother who had married an Englishman had something of this in her as well! When naively I showed this letter to my English father and relatives, their response was hardly cordial. My mother kept silent. Of course the letter contained a slight and I was too young to perceive its shadow aspect. The release experienced through analytical psychology linked up with this memory, but the English side was still to have its influence as a complementary movement arising from personal aspects of my as yet unanalysed childhood. This analysis was later undertaken by Michael Fordham, who helped me to understand in a new way distortions in my development and the way in which certain archetypes rather than others became dominant in the world I had "created" for myself to live in. It was along these lines that the two sides of my nature, which in some ways I could see reflected in the two main streams in psychodynamics, were now to find something of a *rapprochement* within the tentative syntheses being worked out in the London school.

The Language of Imagination and Intellect

These experiences began to help me to understand better the two sorts of language, the use of which seemed to be divided between psychoanalysis and analytical psychology. I close this chapter with two examples of how the different languages, dealing with practically the same content, operate.

The first is about the condition described by contemporary psychoanalysts who are working upon early narcissistic damage that occurs in a baby deprived, for whatever reason, of the experience of parental care, involvement and facilitation, particularly in the realm of early relationship. If we summarize this briefly, to the point of caricature, we could say that the personality that emerges can be so intensely overwhelmed by rage that feelings of hollowness, defiance and despair are the order of the day. A protective image of the "grandiose self" is activated—sometimes projected upon seemingly suitable people, but really covering over an intense distrust of any person's goodwill, helpfulness or skill and, in particular, that of the analyst. Interestingly enough, elaborations of this have been worked out by Rushi Ledermann, a Jungian, who emphasizes the presence in such personalities of a markedly premature development of anality that empowers and energizes a "do-it-yourself psychology" seeking to provide self-nourishment together with a sadistic super-ego-originated self-control (Ledermann, 1979). Aspects of the same phenomena have also been described by Michael Fordham in *Defences of the Self* (1974).

Now it cannot be denied that such a mode of description is extremely valuable and can go into considerable detail to the benefit of all. However, readers of some of the hero stories assembled by Jung and Kerenyi (Kerenyi and Jung, 1949), and indeed in the literature generally, will find in imaginative form many of the features described in the more abstract language used above. Out of the many variations, certain features in hero stories often emerge, and they could be summarized thematically as follows. The hero experiences his parents as neither good nor his real ones. They may, indeed, be foster parents, sometimes kind but often cruel and depriving. Showing all the marks of defiance, anger and rage, he sets off *alone* to seek adventure. He is a sort of sleepwalker, a *Steppenwolf* (Hesse, 1979), isolated, alienated from the world and ruthlessly exploiting both it and the helpful figures of animals and old men and women who provide magical help and directions. He finds money in underground places. He exercises power and control. He overcomes the dragon of rage and violence by courage and sleight of hand. When he wins the king's daughter and eventually rules as king in full power, he remains by virtue of his position still isolated and alone.

A second example may be taken from Jung's *Answer to Job* (1954). Jung paints a vivid picture of the dynamism and conflicts in Jahweh's family as depicted in his reading of the literature. The *dramatis personae* are Jahweh, his temporarily alienated wife Sophia, the good son Jesus, who will become incarnate, the dark evil son Satan who remains a spirit, the good daughter Mary and the babies to be born, i.e. humanity. This pictorial description contains beings in interaction. On the other hand, in the language of psychoanalysis and Kleinian psychology, Meltzer (1973) describes the outcome of his researches into "primal scene" phantasies in patients. Precisely the same six elements are described by him, and the equivalent to Satan is the critical element waiting to pounce upon and destroy or bring about change if the family matrix shows signs of imperfection in any way (Lambert, 1977). It should perhaps be added that we have recently had our attention directed afresh by Maria Teresa Colonna to the archaic figure of Lilith who in Hebrew mythology was Adam's first wife. As the result of a dispute with Adam over their sexual relationship, she went into the wilderness on the shores of the Red Sea and became destructive, besporting herself with demons and bringing to birth a hundred new demons a day, and so on (Colonna, 1981). Colonna's view is that Lilith needs re-inclusion in our contemporary culture and that she stands, in contrast with but complementary to Eve, for a kind of feminine counterpolar eroticism of enormous value and significance in Hebrew Christian culture. Lilith has existed uneasily in a somewhat negative form as the result of her partial self-exclusion from it. It seems to me that she has a part to play in the family matrix in a way parallel to that of Satan.

In considering these two examples a few points emerge that might carry illumination:

(1) One way of expanding upon the difference of language expression could be to explain the traditional Jungian more pictorial mode of expression as influenced by its focus upon the archetypes postulated to be present behind or within the concreteness of the two situations just described. Sometimes well-known patterns may be observed expressed in visual (or auditory) thematic imagery and in connection with which the concept of the archetype as such was formulated by Jung, and later designated by Stein as an example of a theoretical entity (Stein, 1958). It is a potential, a predisposition in a child, for instance, to experience his situation for better or for worse according to patterns of expectation imaged as the "good parents" when his life is happy enough and as the "bad parents" when he is coping with gross deficiencies in early care or worrying about the internal dynamics of the family of which he is a part. We may note the ambiguities and dubious aspects of such archetypally saturated experiences and in addition the image-laden pictorial mode of grasping the situation as a whole, which is such a marked feature of right cerebral hemisphere based holistic perception, though often unconscious to the individual in whom it takes place. Unconsciousness of that sort carries danger because it lacks awareness of the stereotypifying and distorting influence of the archetype that is operating, so to speak, "behind the scenes".

(2) Once the pictorial holistic image has been established, however, it then remains for the rational and concept-forming side of the psyche to work upon it in a discriminating way and to attempt to make a suitable relation to it in the furtherance of individuation. For Jung, no doubt, this whole transaction would be expressed in terms of content

emerging from the unconscious matrix of the personality and then becoming subject to the critical and refining work of ego-consciousness. The latter, however, is also an emergent from the same source and highly esteemed by Jung. The whole operation is thought of as an example of *natura contra naturam*.

(3) In this type of formulation we may be dealing with temperamental variations, not unconnected, perhaps, with the early history of the individual, and phantasies arising within him about the balance of significance and meaning as between mother and father in the primal scene experience, to say nothing as to which mode of experience, "artistic" or "scientific", prevailed in the original family matrix. For some, Jung's approach rings true; for others, it feels safer to speak of the primacy of the aim-directed ego in the transaction. Others may find themselves more at home with Jung's vision provided that the notion of complementariness between the old ego-consciousness and the newly emergent content is given full value. I find myself in sympathy with this last point of view, and it is with this in the background that much of this book has come into being.

Chapter Three

Individuation and the personality of the analyst

Analysis and Interaction

A study of the process of analysis, repair and individuation will almost
inevitably focus, as a matter of prime importance, upon a
consideration of the quality and function of the analyst's personality.
In history, his forebears are the doctor and the priest, whose actions
and personality-functions are defined, for instance, in two classical
documents respectively: the Hippocratic Oath and St Paul's concept of
agape. For centuries, this kind of work has been understood to depend
upon a certain specificity of personal relationship entered into by the
doctor with his patient and the priest with those under his care. That
the work is full of possible pitfalls and draws upon profound levels of
emotion, being (*ontos*), and outlook is illustrated by the stringency of
requirement and the severity of prohibition imposed by the documents
in question. Indeed, any disregard or flouting of them is said to render
the work worthless and nugatory, whatever the skill or knowledge
involved. Furthermore, the naive public shock aroused by the possible
misuse of medical or pastoral power suggests deeply rooted attitudes
based upon long-term, and often repeated, experiences of what works
best in this field.

Despite this early background, however, when it came to the
emergence of analysis, and particularly early psychoanalysis, we find
that its practice was at first much influenced by late nineteenth century
scientific preconceptions involving, among others, the idea of the
neutral uninvolved external observer with an object under
observation—almost in isolation—and with a low level of interaction
between observer and observed. This idea seems strange today when
we consider both Freud's lively interaction with his patients as
described in some of his classical case histories, and also Bakan's
account of Freud's interest in Jewish mysticism (Bakan, 1975). For all

20

that, early psychoanalysis seems to have taken the position just described and to have implied that the skill and knowledge of the analyst was, if anything, of greater importance than his personal integrity, once minimal requirements in this respect had been met. Jung's view of the analyst's function, on the other hand, while influenced by psychoanalysis, seems more deeply rooted in medical and pastoral tradition, so that he came to rank the personal integration and individuation of an analyst in personal interaction with his patient as foremost in importance in the therapeutic relationship. It must, however, be said that, by today, it is possible to understand that the gap between the emphases of psychoanalysis and analytical psychology in this matter is not nearly as wide as might have been thought. Freud's emphasis on objectivity remains valuable provided it is recognized that objectivity does not come out of the stance of a non-involved external observer, but rather from the ability to stand a hair-breadth's distance outside a nevertheless real involvement in the patient–analyst bonding process. This enables an analysis of the nature of the relationship to take place with some hope of objectivity. Jung's emphasis upon the integration of the analyst and the effect of his involvement upon the patient remains valid provided that it is continuously subjected to an analytic critique in the analyst's mind and provided that the nature of the interrelationship in the process of constellation is conveyed through interpretation to the patient.

Some Accounts of Analytic Practice

It seems fairly clear that both Freud and Jung, as the founders practically *ab novo* of analytic therapy, had to start as empirically as possible—devoid as they were of mentors in the field. Nor is it likely that they could be fully conscious of the effects of the *Zeitgeist* upon their presuppositions. Later analytical psychologists and psychoanalysts, however, by virtue of their training, start from a more privileged position, so that in the writings that emerge from the empiricism and struggle of the clinical situation today we can glimpse something of their view of their analytic functions. I shall therefore consider the following sources of evidence:

(1) Some papers published in 1970 – 72 in the *Journal of Analytical Psychology* based partly on discussions in clinical meetings in London;

(2) Some statements of two well-known psychotherapists with no particular psycho-dynamic affiliation;

(3) Some descriptions by contemporary psychoanalysts, like Rycroft, Racker, Winnicott and Shafer, of non-analytic personal and emotional involvements and interactions that take place between analyst and patient.

(4) For the sake of comparison, some statements made by Jung in his model of the four main elements in analytical therapy, after a number of years of practice, and published in *Problems of Modern Psychotherapy*, written in 1929 (Jung, 1931).

I shall then point to a common factor behind these statements, which, though strictly non-analytical is essential, and could be designated by a revived and modified use of the Greek word agape. This leads to an investigation into the special meaning of the word as shaped by St Paul for delimited application to the pastoral function.* This will be compared with the early use of the word in classical Greek and in the Septuagint and with its later use in early and modern Christianity. Finally it will be argued that the word has a history with implications and undertones that could be applied to the central attitude behind the analytical function in a way that is comparable to that behind the medical function as expressed in the Hippocratic Oath.

The Personal Factor in Contemporary Analytical Psychologists

It is now time to return to the evidence of contemporary analytical psychologists. First, a paper was given by Michael Fordham on "Failure in analysis" (Fordham, 1971). Two issues emerged: the failure of an analysis which could be described exactly, and the failure of therapy, which is less easily assessed. The analytic failure was to enable the patient to understand or benefit from the analysis of a projective identification that had always influenced her personal relationships and was deeply built into the transference. Her block after many years' work was judged to be unshiftable so that the treatment, after good notice and much heart-searching, was terminated by the analyst. In other respects the patient's fulfilment in her life had improved considerably—as well as her general capabilities and success in her profession. This, however, could not with certainty be attributed to the *analytical* treatment, although to the onlooker it appeared as if successful *psychotherapy* had taken place. In addition to

---

*The word *pastoral* is used in preference to the word *priestly* because the context suggests a wider range of function over and beyond that of the priest.

this paper, we may note that a discussion took place the same year in London, to which Fordham, Strauss and Bosanquet made contributions on the question of whether the term analysis should be confined to the process of the reduction of complex structures to their simple elements or whether it should be applied to the whole process of psychotherapy including its synthetic aspects, in which also the action of the therapist as a person transcends his reductive function.

Other papers seemed to centre on basic personal attitudes on the part of the analyst. For instance, Judith Hubback, in a paper on envy and the shadow, shows the extent to which a test of the analyst's integration is involved if he is to deal satisfactorily with the often overwhelming envy exhibited towards him by his patient (Hubback, 1972). Plaut (1972) also demonstrates the analytic attitude employed by Bion (1970), whereby, in pursuit of 0 (nullity) the analyst deals with each session without desire, without memory and without understanding—the way of negative capability—a way designed to enable his patient to develop in his own way and in his own time. In this process, the analyst intervenes either to foster this development as it unfolds or to interpret at a point where a decisive change is perceived as imminent. This indicates the degree of patience, humility and freedom from the temptation to prejudge that is required of the analyst and the vigilance needed from him lest he operate in a preconceived controlling way.

A further development may be seen in the January 1972 number of *The Journal of Analytical Psychology*. Here Hillman (1972) writes about failure in terms of failure in analysis, of analysis and as analysis. This is no doubt intended to startle, though analysis turns out to be both a success and a failure. Analysis as "failure" does not amount to much more than that a good deal of analysis should be helping patients into an experience of their depression, diminishment, despairs, etc. We may agree that analysts should avoid irritating depressed patients beyond limits by emphasizing the virtues of progressiveness. Success, creativity—even individuation and integration—can be misused into being treated as virtues, or (an even greater distortion) as something to be aimed at. Equally so, however, there can be a danger of analysts treating depression, diminishment and despairs as virtues to be aimed at. What seems to be required of an analyst, in this context, is that he is no more identified with ideas of progressiveness and success than he is with those of depression, diminishment and failure.

Next, Mary Williams (1972) deals with the plight of the patient overwhelmed by primary envy towards his analyst and a compulsion to destroy his efforts to help. In this paper the special qualities of response demanded of the analyst if he would succeed therapeutically are emphasized. Another paper, by myself, shows the therapeutic effect of the mastery by the analyst of the operation of the talion law that is activated within him out of his complementary counter-transference. Through such mastery and the insight thus gained, he may renew his concordant counter-transference and, as a result, become able to make interpretations that can be assimilated by his patient not only because of their truth but also out of positive feelings activated by gratitude, often only after years of waiting.

Yet another paper, by Norah Moore, demonstrates the therapeutic effect upon a patient of the analyst's work upon herself in connection with a patient who felt impinged upon by environmental changes in the analyst's new consulting room. What was important was the experiencing of a sequence of anxiety, defensive denial and repression, assimilation, fear, resentment and ambivalence prior to the repair and a return to a quiet state. This sequence took place quickly in the analyst, but lasted over several sessions in the patient, for whom the analyst-mother could wait not too impatiently, and without unduly hurrying the patient's participation in the process (Moore, 1972).

A glance at this considerable variety of therapeutic attitudes should demonstrate that though analytic interpretations, within the transference/counter-transference situation, have a fundamental function to perform, they do not cover the whole range of therapy. Behind all these transactions and the skills involved in them, another therapeutic factor seems to be implied. It may be judged to be an ability, on the analyst's part, both to undergo an inner process within himself and to have at his disposal a certain quality of personality ready to be mobilized on his patient's behalf. This quality of personality seems to be connected with concern, patience and a capacity to remain-in-being for his patient. It is a combination of eros, humane feeling and respect, together with a freedom from god-almightiness. It implies cognizance of his shadow, an ability to use it, and a willingness to accept a limitation of aim and scope—enough to meet the need of a few patients. This attitudinal substratum underlies the transference/counter-transference and the analyst's skill, knowledge, or his personality type or function. A possible name for it could be the agape-factor (to be defined later in this chapter), and it may be understood as a function of the self. This consideration represents an attempt to recognize that even though analysis is the most fundamental of all the therapeutic elements in work with patients, nevertheless success is dependent on other factors which may be regarded as enabling analytical work to be accepted, rejected, modified or elaborated upon by the patient in ways that really meet his needs.

The Personal Factor and Contemporary Psychotherapists

Among recent work done on this last subject by psychotherapists we might mention the well-known researches of Truax and Carkhuff into the nature of the basic personal gifts out of which the therapist may apply his techniques and specialized knowledge and without which he is likely to fail. It was found that three qualities—genuineness, non-possessive warmth, and accurate empathy—seemed to be essential to the successful therapist. Incidentally it was also found that patients most likely to benefit were those in whom, first, a high degree of inner or "felt" disturbance was combined with a low level of behavioural or overt disturbance; secondly, a high degree of readiness and positive expectancy supported hope for personal improvement; and thirdly, deep and extensive self-exploration was desired (Truax and Carkhuff, 1967).

In principle, Truax and Carkhuff in their emphasis upon the therapist's personality seem to be making a valid point, although their statements suggest a greater idealization of the "good" therapist than most analysts would find acceptable. Perhaps the most significant point for those engaged in the training of analysts is the belief of these writers that they have demonstrated that the qualities of genuineness, non-possessive warmth and accurate empathy can be improved by training. This may well be so, though Jungians will be inclined to think that they are more likely to be the result of an analysis of the *shadow* in would-be therapists.

Incidentally, these authors considered their findings to be valid for all types of contemporary psychotherapy, which comprise a broad spectrum indeed. At one end will be found the procedure of pure classical psychoanalysis. In the middle will be found the procedures of a large number of both Freudian and Jungian analysts and analytical psychotherapists. The nearer to the analytic end these therapists are, the more likely they are to judge every transaction in their therapy by the extent to which it serves the process of analysis. At the other end are methods that are mainly concerned with securing for the patient "cathartic" emotional experiences, though often these are better understood as types of discharge, together with methods that resemble acting out in non-analytical group therapy. Included at this end as well are methods of behaviour therapy with minimal interpretation or verbalization. Interestingly enough, however, we can discern signs of the extremes meeting. Thus, in behaviour therapy, analytic attitudes like transference and resistance have been explicitly recognized by

Rhodes and Feather (1972), though in elementary and over-simplified forms. Furthermore, in all these "cathartic", behavioural and "acting-out" therapies, it is clear that there is a considerable emphasis upon the therapist as "agent".

The Personal Factor and Contemporary Psychoanalysts

The second group of evidences come from those contemporary psychoanalysts who recognize non-analytical and interactional elements in their work. Among these we may consider shortly the work of Rycroft, Racker, Winnicott and Shafer. Thus Rycroft (1968) has pointed out that there is much more content and implication even in the pure analytical work of the psychoanalyst than simply verbal analytical interpretations on a symbolic level. There are also the following factors which can carry considerable significance for both patient and analyst:

(1) There is a room which has a door closed against interruptions and which is quiet enough. There is a couch.

(2) There is an analyst present who is a person responding to the patient.

(3) This analyst has an attitude. It is ideally not neutral, not purely intellectual, not a feeling, but something that Rycroft, following MacDougal, calls a "sentiment". This is an organized enduring disposition of emotional tendencies maintained more or less consistently even though it may suffer passing disturbances due to fatigue, preoccupation, etc. Most importantly of all, perhaps, this "sentiment" arises from the analyst's prior experience of himself as a patient who has been the object of similar steady concern on the part of another, his own analyst. This seems to be the basis for interest in, concern for and empathy with the patient—a natural activity, spontaneous, I would emphasize, rather than contrived, over-compensatory or part of an idealized system of good actions and attitudes.

(4) This analyst makes interpretations designed to promote analytic understanding in the patient, and the making of them is a sign that the analyst is interested enough to be present and alert, to listen, to understand, and to remember. Furthermore, the analyst, by interpreting, shows that the patient's feelings and attitudes are known and shared by others. They are not so freakish, unique or incomprehensible as to induce in the analyst an undue sense of shock, nor does he experience a strong need to make the patient conform to his preconception.

(5) The steady consistent and sustained maintenance of the analyst's professional life and therapeutic disposition is based largely upon his experience of those qualities in his own analyst and, I would add, through the latter forming part of an internal analyst-object in the trainee. It is helped, however, by the analytic setting which can be framed to meet his needs as well as those of his patients, to protect from distraction, and to set limits and boundaries to the contact with his patients. Furthermore some pressure is exerted by the fact of his recognition that a number of patients are, in fact, dependent upon him. Finally he needs to have developed in such a way as to enable him to enter into an imaginative involvement with each one of them.

The considerations adduced by Rycroft appear to be of equal importance to Jungians, though we may wonder whether Rycroft is not dealing with the analyst's "sentiment" in somewhat static terms, almost as if it arises solely out of himself. More usually, it seems to me, it grows out of an interplay that gradually develops between patient and analyst, as they begin to form a relationship between each other as real people. I suspect that he is writing with the situation in mind where interaction is blocked and the patient behaves for long periods in a hating way, resisting every one of his analyst's responses and approaches, despite the most careful analysis of his negative behaviour. It is the painful situation where the patient feels utterly destroyed, devoured or sadistically penetrated by the very sentiment of concern that Rycroft speaks of. In such a situation, of course, most of the "sentiment" has to be generated out of the analyst alone.

The analyst, in these circumstances, may indeed be able to turn his complementary counter-transference feelings of hate into concordance and empathy and be able to respond to the whole matter as a challenge. But he will not be able to rely upon any help afforded him by the patient and he will need all the inner and outer assistance described by Rycroft. Even then, as we all know, there remains the possibility of partial or complete failure as described by Fordham (1971) and Hillman (1972). This seems also true of Bion's unshakeably envious patients with their totally negative therapeutic reaction described by him as the − K factor.

Racker (1968), however, describes in more dynamic terms the process that arises out of the patient's application for help when it is matched by the analyst's predisposition to mobilize his feelings and skills to be the analyst of this particular patient in a concordant way. A response and counter-response situation may then get activated in the following way. The analyst's predisposed concordance may be met with the patient's beginnings of a positive transference, with a resultant deepening of the analyst's positive counter-transference.

A safe enough situation is thus provided for the patient tentatively to bring out some negative transference. Then, through the operation of the talion law, complementary negative counter-transference in the analyst becomes activated. The critical point then is whether the analyst can master his own revengeful talionic feelings enough to become able to interpret, in a concordant way, the patient's inner drama into which he, as the analyst, has been drawn. At that point gratitude for such a non-talionic response may promote further positive transference in the patient, to allow him to benefit from further analytic interpretations.

It would seem therefore, that Racker adds to Rycroft's rather static-sounding concept of the analyst's "sentiment" the understanding that an appropriate therapeutic attitude in the analyst may sometimes arise rather spontaneously out of the dynamic interplay between himself and his patient. His own experience of gratitude, felt in the dynamic interplay between himself and his own analyst, supervisors, colleagues, etc., provides some of the motivation for the practice of therapy. That also enables him to develop the skill to use, for concordant and therapeutic purposes, both his real involvement with his patient and his actual experience of the reverberation within his own psyche-soma, caused by the patient's disordered or primitive love and violence. The connection of this with Jung's notion of induction and transformation may be understood in terms of its being a description of some of the underlying mechanisms involved.

Similar implications may be seen in the work of Winnicott (1956) and Schafer (1973). The former elaborates on the subject of the *holding* work of the analyst and his function in permitting the patient to go through, in suitable symbolic ways, the work of forming a relationship with him as an object in Winnicott's sense of the word and in establishing object usage with him, leading on, of course, to the possibility of internalizing him as an internal "analyst-object". This requires more than passive impersonal screening, as is also the case with Schafer and his insistence upon the maintenance of interpersonal relations, so that the analyst's response is understood and meant by him to be personal in origin and intention.

The Personal Factor and Jung

We can conclude this short survey of the views of some contemporary analytical psychologists, psychotherapists and psychoanalysts on the nature of their personal involvement as analysts or psychotherapists by comparing them with Jung's contribution made as long ago as 1929 in *Problems of Modern Psychotherapy* (1931). Here, as is well known, he considers the work of psychotherapy under the heading of four stages: confession, elucidation, education, and transformation. Today, most of us would not think in terms of stages, but rather of certain ingredients intermingled and interrelated in many directions, and certainly not developing in a straight line from confession to transformation. All four processes may even be observed to be taking place concurrently in the same session. Thus confessions of the patient may have to await the transformation of the analyst and may depend upon elucidation and education, as enabling events, just as much as the other way round.

It is, however, the content distilled from these processes by Jung that it can be rewarding to re-examine.

Confession

For Jung, confession is the cure for psychic isolation—both from oneself and others. Repression and psychic concealment represent greater "sin" than that which is concealed. In large doses, absolute secrets are poison, though in smaller doses they can be medicament and the basis of individuation. Unconscious secrets are more injurious than conscious ones. Purely private secrets can be destructive, whereas secrets shared with one or several persons can be beneficial. Complexes are composed of non-shared secrets and develop a malign life of their own. Without benefit of cathartic confession "an impenetrable wall shuts a man off from the vital feeling that he is a man among other men" (1931). However familiar, what Jung says is, in reality, strong meat, so that a therapist, who puts himself at the disposal of another human being for this purpose, is involved in providing one of the most fundamental services of all. It is so fundamental, and the relief experienced by the patient so dramatic, that quite a number of patients feel that this is basically the whole story.

I can think of a patient for whom cathartic confession, as a long-term often repeated process in session after session, seemed to be the essence of his treatment. Interpretative elucidation came very much as a runner up in his estimation of the worth of his treatment. Yet he needed elucidation on the subject of what it was he was feeling so guilty about and also reconstructive interpretation of how he lived his past in the present in the transference/counter-transference situation and in the outside world. This work was, in fact, systematically done by me. Certainly transformation and change very slowly took place, but it also remained true that he leaned very much on the side of catharsis, together with a need for validation, by which I mean that he needed from me some implied or explicit confirmation that his feelings, emotions and passions, although greedy and anal, were not uniquely bad or alarmingly different from those of the rest of humanity. His link with humanity was thus renewed and a cleansing through discharge effected, though it needs to be remembered that this kind of discharge catharsis differs in some ways from catharsis in classical drama. In the latter, the contemplation of the profoundly fateful human processes, quandaries, loves, envyings, jealousies and murders that are being acted on the stage can alleviate the human burden by purging or at least modifying similar tendencies within the members of the audience through pity and terror.

Jung pointed out that a problem arises in connection with this kind of psychotherapy owing to the fact that the release of suppressed emotion, recognized with the head and confirmed by the heart, is sometimes felt to be all that is needed. People who have had a vivid experience of that kind can feel that the process has an air of finality. Sometimes this may be the case, but, Jung added, the cathartic confessional process does not work in those cases where a resistance to uncovering any unconscious guilt or emotion is so great that the patient sticks absolutely to his conscious version of his trouble or secret. It also fails if the patient remains bound to his doctor or, on the other hand, remains out of real touch with the doctor and glued to an endless repetition of catharsis by discharge without reference to his doctor's insights and at the expense of a sound adaptation to life.

My patient was in danger on all three counts. There was a great resistance to becoming more deeply conscious of any aspect of the problems he posed. He tended to remain attached to me, and yet tended to repeat his statements of his problem continuously with very little reference to me as a person. It was as if I was to be cast for the archetypal role of the priest in the confessional. I was viewed impersonally—enough to suggest a reaction formation against his secret, intense, but split-off interest in me as a person with an arse to be sniffed. Such a patient experiences real difficulty over analytic interpretations, for they often appear to be either insulting, persecutory or useless. Hence the analyst must be patient and in no hurry if he is to succeed. In the end, this isolated man gradually became able to participate soundly enough in the domestic and business world in a way that may be regarded as sufficiently constructive and co-operative—and indeed creative enough.

Elucidation

It is clear enough that my patient belonged to those that are covered by Jung's assertion that when catharsis is insufficient, the psychotherapist is bound to go on to elucidation, compared by him with Freud's "interpretative method". Jung's idea, it is worth recalling, was that those who cannot give themselves to catharsis stand in an identity relationship to parents and hence prematurely usurp the parents' authority, power, independence, etc., presumably, though he does not say so, whether they are conformists or rebels. Hence, he held, the transference has to be interpreted somewhat minutely in accordance with Freud's method, so that the "shadow" side comes out. While very critical of Freud for "reductionism", Jung nevertheless described the results of elucidation through the method of interpretation in the following terms. They resulted first in a greater modesty on the part of patients through recognition of their inept childish self-indulgence, and secondly in an ability to replace that childish self-indulgence by a sense of responsibility. The man with this insight will turn his retrogressive longings for a child's paradise into the service of progressive work. He will then be able to enrich his normal adaptation to life by developing forbearance with his shortcomings and freedom from sentimentality and illusion.

This somewhat severe statement seems to miss the positive and lively aspects of the child-like qualities of the human being and to concentrate on negative aspects like "inept childish self-indulgence" and "retrogressive longings for a child's paradise". Indeed we are bound to admit that Jung rather underplayed the fact that elucidation or analysis can release the creative forward movement that is also part of a healthy child's development as well as part of the positive growing child-like qualities found in the adult. Sometimes, indeed, the childishness that is criticized is a function of unlived childhood, needing some symbolic recognition and satisfaction in the analysis.

Education

Whether that is so or not, Jung moves on to the question of what he calls education. He feels that though elucidation helps people with imagination and enterprise, it does not help those with little moral imagination, who cannot tolerate deflation, who can only doubt their new self-knowledge, and who hence are left as intelligent but still incapable children helplessly striving to gain the power to become successful beings. Such patients, as we know, he felt could be helped by Adler, the great educator—beloved, as he says, by clergymen and teachers in contradistinction to doctors and intellectuals, who fancy Freud and "who are one and all bad nurses and educators". It is by this third aspect of psychotherapy, called education, that Jung reckons the psychotherapist may manage to bring his patient into normal adaptation to everyday reality.

Transformation

Catharsis, elucidation and education then are linked as three processes that seem to be assigned by Jung to one side of a divide. On the other side, a fourth process, which he obviously especially values, he calls the stage of transformation. Under it a number of ideas are subsumed. They might be distinguished as follows:

(1) To be "normal" or "adapted", though a necessary aim for the unsuccessful and unadapted, involves, for exceptionally able people, the danger of neurosis as a result of feeling cramped in a Procrustean bed of standard collective living.

(2) The personalities of the doctor and patient are "infinitely more important for the outcome of the treatment than what the doctor says and thinks".

(3) For "two personalities to meet is like mixing two different chemical substances". Hence, if the doctor shields himself, he "denies himself the use of a highly important organ of information" and here counter-transference, as an aspect of this, is already in 1929 being recognized by Jung.

(4) An ethical demand is made of the doctor, namely, that he must "be the man through whom you wish to influence others" (Jung, 1931, p.73). In other words, "the fact of being convinced and not the thing we are convinced of—that is what has always and at all times worked" (ibid., p.73). Or again "what happened to the patient must now happen to the doctor". "The doctor can no longer evade his own difficulty by treating the difficulties of others" (ibid., p.74). These, it must be said, are daunting demands, but it should be remembered that Jung was writing as one who had had only a self-analysis and so was learning all the time as he went along. Today the new analyst has been through a relatively long and demanding analysis.

(5) In a treatment involving transformation, there is a kind of interaction between patient and doctor whereby a process called "subduing the demon of the disease" may take place in the doctor—if he is the stronger and more stable personality. Otherwise the patient's illness may overcome the doctor to the traumatic disadvantage of both. The doctor is in the analysis, so that self-criticism and self-examination become essential as he needs to be able to be transformed himself.

These five points show plainly that Jung's concept of transformation refers to a rich experiential content which may be stated in the following two sentences:

A therapist, working upon his own development in a self-critical and transformative way, may be able, through the admixture of his own personality with that of his patient, to bring about a subduing of the demon of the patient's disease so that the patient is transformed. Transformation refers to a radical personality change—to be contrasted with a less radical movement into normality or social adaptation.

Now, when we look at this statement from our present vantage point we can see plenty to criticize:

(1) There is no mention of the therapist's own experience of analytic psychotherapy, owing to the fact that the pioneers had to hazard a self-analysis.

(2) There is an absence of any description of processes of projection and introjection in the analyst–patient relationship whereby, for instance, the analyst introjects something of the patient, compares it with his own experience, and with reasonable good fortune can give it back to the patient in an assimilable form in an interpretation. This lack makes the transformation process in Jung's essay seem cut off from and devoid of the elucidatory or educative processes already mentioned.

(3) The distinction between normality and transformation is so sharply made as to suggest that normality equals false conformity.

(4) It leaves out the fact that in early development we can in fact find individuation, genuine growth and integration. In other words the statement seems to be that of someone without an analyst and with memories of having to relate to a dubiously sound early environment, in both of which areas we now know Jung to have suffered deprivation.

(5) The final criticism of the essay as it stands is that, although it implies the concepts of the self, individuation and integration, these ideas are not mentioned. Yet it seems as if the importance he places upon the personality of the analyst involves the latter in some realization of the processes in question.

Nevertheless, if we consider this essay of Jung in terms of its essential content and disregard any suggestion that these four features represent well-defined stages of therapeutic development, we have surely a useful seed-plot essay on analytic psychotherapy. What we know and practise today represents a development, refinement and elaboration of the essential points raised by Jung, and we find confession, elucidation, education and transformation all working together, often at the same time within one session or over one phase of treatment. Furthermore, we may say that the whole spectrum of psychotherapy could be surveyed in terms of the relative significance and meaning given by therapists to the four ingredients named by Jung. Thus this early work of Jung retains its importance, even in the light of his later studies of alchemical symbolism interpreted in terms of the patient–analyst relationship in *The Psychology of the Transference*, published seventeen years later in 1946.

Agape, the Hippocratic Oath and Effective Therapy

Our brief survey then of the evidence produced by contemporary psychoanalysis, when set out alongside of Jung's 1929 essay, suggests a development within it of attitudes towards the importance of the analyst's personality in therapy that are both concordant with and amplificatory of Jung's position. His dual emphasis upon the interpersonal interaction between doctor and patient and upon the personal development, the integration, and the capacity for growth and change in the therapist involves the possibility of two kinds of change. The first is change in the therapist's knowledge of and experience of psychotherapy. Jung's statement that "Therapy is different in every case" (Jung, 1963) sounds somewhat extreme but must be understood partly in the context of the newness of the psychotherapy in those days. His idea is not, however, so frightening for a trainee-analyst of today, for unlike Jung he has access to patterns of possibility that have been mooted during the last fifty years. This is not to deny the elements of uniqueness and newness that he finds in every patient he takes on. The second kind of change involves the idea that an analyst may need to be able to tolerate changes in his own personality if he is to meet the needs of certain patients. While this idea may arouse fear in the heart of the neophyte and seem impracticable and far fetched to the hard-headed psychiatrist, it must be remembered that not every patient–therapist interaction touches such depths. By and large it remains that the treatment of many cases does make heavy demands, as envisaged by Jung, upon the agapaic capabilities of the analyst—a view that certainly has its roots in history.

Accordingly, I turn now to examine two famous statements about the therapeutic function in classical times: the Hippocratic Oath dedicated to the deities, Apollo, Aesculapius and Hygea, and dated about 430 BC; and the concept of agape formulated in I Corinthians 13:4-8 by St Paul, dedicated to Christ and dated about 57 AD. The two texts in English translation are as follows.

The Oath of Hippocrates

I swear to Apollo the Physician and to Aesculapius and to Hygeia and to all the gods and goddesses whom I name my witnesses, that I shall fulfil, to the best of my ability and judgement, this Oath and covenant.

My teacher, who instructed me in this art, to hold equal to my parents, and his male descendants to hold as my brothers, to teach them this art and all the medical knowledge, should they ask me to, without any reward or covenant, and to do so too, to all those who have taken the medical oath and to none other.

According to my power and judgement to use the medical knowledge for the benefit of those who suffer, as judged by myself to be fair, and to avoid doing any harm or injustice.

Not to give to anyone any lethal drug, even if he asks it of me, and neither to suggest such. Also not to supply any woman with the means of abortion.

To preserve pure and immaculate my life and my art. Not to render eunuch even those that may ask me but to leave this to the manual labourers [!].

To any homes I enter, to do so for the good and benefit of those that suffer and to abstain from any premeditated injustice or harm of any sexual acts upon the bodies of women or men, be they free citizens or slaves.

And anything that I may hear or see during the course of treatment, even outside the space where such treatment is being constructed, even during the course of the daily life of man, I cannot invoke, but on the contrary, to conceal and keep forever secret.

This Oath of mine, keeping it and without ever violating it, may I have as assistant throughout my life and in the conduct of my art as well, so that I may have the respect of all men. But should I ever transgress it and commit perjury, that I may be punished with the opposite''.

Agape in I Corinthians 13:4-8

The famous Authorized Version translation runs as follows:

Charity suffereth long and is kind, charity envieth not; charity vaunteth not itself, is not puffed up. Doth not behave itself unseemly, seeketh not her own, is not easily provoked, thinketh no evil; Beareth all things, believeth all things, hopeth all things, endureth all things. Charity never faileth.

The argument behind this statement is well known, though the context is not always appreciated. St Paul is addressing persons involved in ministering to others in the church within a wide spectrum of function. The reference is to *particular functions* and not so much to *universal behaviour*. Speaking with tongues, the gift of prophecy, the understanding of mysteries—also knowledge, faith, and giving away of goods to feed the poor, even self-sacrifice—these pastoral capabilities are deemed worthless without charity or agape. These activities will pass away, because they are partial, but agape never fails.

This is clearly a reification of a complicated psychological state of mind or attitude. Furthermore the translation of the Authorized Version of this as *charity*, and indeed the rest of the passage, suggest a poetic idealization of a human capability with the suggestion that it should be universalized. It sounds, however, rather different in content when a more literal translation is given. It would run as follows:

"Agape defers anger, is long-suffering or long-tempered (μακροΘυμεῖ), and is kind in demeanour or plays the part of a kind person (χρηστεύεται); agape does not envy (ου ζηλοῖ); agape does not play the braggart (περπερεύται); is not inflated with pride, is not vain (φυσιοῦται); does not have unmannerly or unseemly (a-schematically; ἀσχημονει); does not seek its own advantage (οὐ ζητεῖ τὰ ἑαντῆς); does not fly into a rage quickly (παροξύνεται), does not keep an account of evils suffered (λογίζεται); is not glad (χαίρει) over injustice or wrong, but sympathizes (συγχαίρει) with the advancement of truth; roofs over or keeps out the weather (or endures; στέγει); believes all things (πιστεύει); hopes for all things (ἐλπίζει) and stands ground in all things (ὑπομένει). Agape does not fail or fall down (πίπτει). It will be apparent that this sort of attitude, to the extent that the shadow elements are sufficiently integrated to embrace both love and hate for the patient, facilitates the work of therapy. It is practicable in principle provided that the number of patients taken by the analyst is limited and within his capacity. One element that smacks of idealization is the statement that envy and the agapaic element are incompatible. Inevitably the analyst may envy his patient. What matters however, is the therapist's ability to master his envy, so that it ceases to be destructive and becomes a stimulus to constructive work. It is the same with his anger, hatred and wishes to frustrate or punish his patient.

If, therefore, with the hindsight of analytic knowledge, we compare the contents of the Hippocratic Oath with the implications of agape, we shall find a greater similarity between them than might have been imagined. Thus:

(1) Both documents involve an invocation of or dedication to the deities appropriate to the work. These may be regarded as personified images of archetypal potential that could be regarded as specialized for or dominant in doctors or pastors and analysts.

(2) Both imply membership of a therapeutic or "caring" group, functioning within a larger group, i.e. community or church, and refer to a professional or functional ethos.

(3) Both assume the making available of knowledge to fellow members and its usefulness to those they serve.

(4) Both make central the care and therapy of persons.

(5) Both describe the nature of the relationship with those that are

being helped. In the case of the medical oath this is envisaged largely in terms of action; in the case of agape more in psychological terms:

On the one hand *the Hippocratic Oath* promises the use of medical knowledge fairly and harmlessly for the benefit of sufferers of all classes. It foreswears the breaking of confidence, the destruction of life, the castration or sexual abuse of patients (made possible by the power of the doctor). The latter promises to preserve the integrity of his life and to use the oath as a help to do so. So the theme is the centrality of the personality of the therapist in his use of medical knowledge and power. Most striking is the emphasis that whatever his knowledge, the doctor who breaks the oath loses the respect of all men. In modern times, of course, a problem remains as to how the spirit of the oath, as against the letter, is to be respected and implemented at deep levels, whether in medical or pastoral work, or analytical psychotherapy, but the inner content retains its validity.

On the other hand *St Paul's description of agape* is centred round the psychology of the pastor in a way that is congruous with analytical attitudes. It may be considered in this way under three headings: (i) the health or maturity of the pastor; (ii) two ethical injunctions; (iii) two persona considerations.

(1) Under the notion of maturity or health, we can group (i) sympathy with the advancement of the truth, i.e. the scientific aspect of analysis; (ii) the ability to remain constant and reliable, translated "believes all things, hopes all things and stands ground in all things"; (iii) an ability to manage the effects of what we may call psychopathology in the pastor. This includes envying ($\zeta\eta\lambda o\hat{\iota}$) ; playing the braggart or being inflated with pride and vanity ($\pi\epsilon\rho\pi\epsilon\rho\epsilon\acute{\upsilon}\tau\alpha\iota$), or identifying with the working of the talion law and piling up grudges ($\lambda o\gamma\acute{\iota}\zeta\epsilon\tau\alpha\iota$) against obstreperous church members. The Authorized Version translation here is "thinketh no evil", but the correct translation is "not setting down evil as a matter of account" with the implication of paying off old scores. The final problem is deep down being glad about or rejoicing ($\chi\alpha\acute{\iota}\rho\epsilon\iota$) in injustice or wrong. Today, of course, we would hope that the analyst's own analysis would have dealt in depth with the psychopathology of envy, of the depressed impotence defended against by playing the braggart, of primitive identification with talionic processes implemented by grudging calculation, and of nihilistic sado-masochistic excitement over evil or injustice wrought in the patient's life or family. We would hope that his analysis might have sufficiently assisted the analyst to understand and control such tendencies in himself and also to have established sufficient boundaries to enable him to distinguish his psychopathology from that of his

patient's, sensed by him as such by means of his introjective or projective identifications in the counter-transference. It seems clear that vigilance in these matters is one of the agapaic requirements of the analytic function.

(2) The two ethical injunctions involved, are, translated literally, that agape, first, (οὐ ζητεῖ τὰ ἑαυτῆς) does not seek its own advantage and, secondly, does not behave unmannerly, unseemly or, more literally, unschematically (ἀσχηνονεῖ). The first stresses how persons in one's care should not be used for exploitation purposes. The second stresses the need to be able to keep to the agreed function, i.e. the schema. In the case of the analyst, this means keeping as the central aim the analysis of the patient or the enabling of it. In both the aspect of ego-functioning is required for the definition of aims, ways and means, etc.

(3) Finally, we are presented with two functions that are to a degree part of the persona, not least in the case of the analyst. The first is about containing rage and anger. Μακροθυμεῖ refers to control of anger and translates in terms of "deferring anger or being long-tempered". Παροξύνεται refers to rage and translates in terms of "not flying into a rage quickly". The interdiction is not so much against anger or rage as such but more against the hasty, unconsidered and untimely expression of such emotions. Furthermore, in analytical therapy, it is necessary to clarify the issue as to whom the anger or rage belong, i.e. patient or analyst.

The other persona position, for which the word χρηστεύεται is used, translates in terms of "kindness in demeanour or playing the part of a kind person". Kindness, of course, refers to the recognition of kinship—in this case with persons in trouble or psychological distress. Owing to the fact that feelings about, as distinct from the fact of, kinship vary from day to day, from person to person, and in connection with general health, the recognition of kinship in analytic practice may have to be maintained *to some degree* in persona terms, particularly when the repair of patients in need of steady and reliable response from their analysts is undertaken.

I think that this short investigation into agape as used by St Paul should demonstrate that the word is being used with a down-to-earth content and is to a degree, able to stand up to analytic investigation, particularly in respect of the idealizing and universalizing features suggested by the translation in the Authorized Version of the New Testament. His recognition of the difficulties and pressures of the therapeutic situation is parallel to the content of the Hippocratic Oath, though on a more psychological level—a consideration that fits in well with Jung's view that the religions often express early psychotherapeutical principles. Analysts, of course, are bound to wonder whether the word is being applied to a situation where the shadow has been denied—or whether it has been integrated. The context of St Paul's writing seems to suggest that the people he was addressing understood only too well the problems of the pastoral profession in respect of envy, pride, self-seeking, angry response, the enjoyment of evil in others, a subtle need to undermine or castrate, the lack of patience and endurance and the tendency to obscure the truth. It remains unclear whether he felt that the value of these shadow factors was to be understood in any other terms than that of an "awful warning" that causes us by contrast really to appreciate agape—or whether in addition something constructive can be distilled from these phenomena in their own right.

In classical Greek there was no noun agape, but the verb *agapao* tended to be used indiscriminately with two other verbs *erao* and *phileo*. Both words referred to love, though sexual passion was more associated with *erao* (eros) while warm domestic affection, the ties between master and servant and, in Homer, between gods and men were more associated with *phileo*. *Agapao* was used in a way similar to *phileo* but contained in addition the notion of esteem. This all suggests that the words for love were not yet at that time used in a compartmentalized way.

In the Hebrew-Christian tradition, the word agape came to be widely used in the Septuagint—in fact 268 times as compared with 12 times for phileo. It covered such a wide range of meanings as to include family love, the love of Samson and Delilah, the love of Hosea for his adulterous wife—right on to the love of god for man and vice versa—not excluding severity, anger and hate (Sanday and Headlam, 1908). Agape seems to have referred to "bonding" in general—including that between gods and men. In the New Testament, however, apart from St Paul's usage, agape appears in the Fourth Gospel and the Epistles of St John etc. in a very idealized, one-sided seeming form, although there, and in the Apocalypse especially, this ideal love was fostered mainly inside the Christian thought, while in relation to the pagan persecutors outside, hatred and revengeful feelings were entertained and nourished, as pointed out by Jung in *Answer to Job* (1954). As time went on, and more recently in some Christian thought, an ever wider distinction has tended to be made between eros and agape by refining the latter to a spiritualized non-erotic care for the eternal destiny of others arising from the action of God upon the soul, rather than from the feelings, emotions, and sexual bodily basis of human beings. It seems clear that this highly specialized meaning is far removed from the undifferentiated togetherness of agape, eros and philia.

It is, in view of the noticeable variations in the meaning of agape in history, arguable that the meaning of the word could be stretched to include experiencing and coming to terms with primitive or infantile impulses of hatred, anger, murderousness etc. towards the object as well as deploying the generous impulses usually associated with the word.

Naturally, everything depends upon what is done with the emotions thus entertained. Hillman in his lecture "Schism as differing visions" (Hillman, 1971) refers to the tendency for animosity to develop in states of schism and adds, "We may after all stay together in hatred, just as we may separate in love. Psychology usually puts hatred with parting, love with union, but is this not too easy? It is easy to leave you in hatred, and easy to stay with you in love. But the reverse of these pairings is that psychological art we call "consciousness"!

I think that this is a way of stating something important for the quality of an analyst's agape—even if it still contains an element of idealization. What is required is an attitude that is benign enough because the malignant elements have been made conscious and partly overcome. Some work gets done for a few people who come the analyst's way and who can benefit deeply from this special attitude. In addition, it could be argued that the later, rather over-spiritualized Christian view of agape already mentioned does nevertheless foreshadow something central for the therapist as well. This view is closely connected with the idea of love of fellow man (or fellow Christian) as child or creature of god. It is possible to translate the essence of this into the Jungian analyst's respect of his patient's potential self, containing yet transcending good and evil, cf. Jung's work in *Answer to Job* (1954) on the two sides of God and their incarnation in the two sides of the psyche of man, who is his creature and made in his image.

Having stated this, we may take soundings from the few papers of analytical psychotherapists that we have mentioned already. If we do so, aspects of agape, as I have described it, seem to be involved. In Fordham's case of failure, for instance, he maintained a long-sustained effort, plainly costly to himself, for the case exercised him enough to present aspects of it to the Society of Analytical Psychology on several occasions. In the cases of Judith Hubback (1972) and Mary Williams (1972), as well as in Bion's case (1970), the response demanded of the analysts by their intensely destructive envious patients requires patience, control of anger, and subtlety to a very high degree.

Hillman's paper requires of the analyst the willingness to go along with tendencies to depression, diminishment and self-destructive feelings on the part of the patient, however painful to the analyst they may be, and however tempted he may be as a result to promote premature positiveness and growth (Hillman, 1972). In Plaut's paper, the attitude of 0, (or unknowingness resulting from an emptying of the mind of presuppositions), requires a considerable quality of non-godalmightiness, respect for the unknown future development of the patient and a restraint of other aims for the sake of that development. As Plaut (1972) pointed out, following Bion (1970), if the main vertex* of the analyst's aims is elsewhere, say, the aim to make money, then the patient will not reach his real development. In Norah Moore's paper (1972), the analyst not only had to solve the problem in herself of the emotions brought about by the change in the environment, but also to restrain herself and wait for the patient's working of it out herself at her much slower pace. In my paper on transference/counter-transference (Lambert, 1972) the analyst has to struggle with the activation of talion law responses within himself producing angry feelings that tempt him into inappropriate action. This impulse must be translated into analytic understanding in order to serve the development of the patient in a concordant way. Finally, in Jung's papers, the analyst must risk change in his own personality for the sake of his patient.

All these papers can be seen to contain something of the agape factor involved in the therapist's work. However, the vertices involved, as mentioned by Plaut, are not maintained by the analyst out of saintly or masochistic motivations, but rather for scientific reasons which may also be understood as an expression of agape. It may be added that the scientific attitude in question, which in the case of analytical psychology embraces elements that are not only cognitive but also, at the same time, therapeutic, demands from the analyst the capacity to *listen*. This skill is not necessarily exercised through techniques like screening, keeping silent, etc. It may operate within dialogue just as well. It involves the ability to pick out the essential communication of the patient, whether it turns out to be a clear central theme illustrated by a wealth of material, or on the contrary some quite small thing on the periphery of a long wordy communication that looks more pertinent than it really is. In this connection two important points stand out about the analyst's ability to listen. The first is that it is based upon a capacity on his part to form object-relations, that is to say,

*Vertex is Bion's term, which he uses in preference to "point of view". See *Transformations*, London, Heinemann (1965), pp.65, 91.

relationships to others as real people rather than as images arising mainly from phantasy and projection. That in turn depends upon whether his parents could establish such with him—or, if not his parents, then his analyst. The second is that the analyst's capacity to listen depends upon his own experience of being listened to either by his parents or sometimes his intimates, or by his analyst. It is experiences of this sort that lie behind the agapaic function of listening, as much as is possible, to what the patient, as a real person rather than as a phantasy one, is trying to communicate to his analyst. Finally, lest agape be considered mainly as hard work and highly disciplined achievement, it should be emphasized that it is a source of the solid gratification that is experienced by an analyst who has done a successful job in genuinely promoting the true self of his patient. An amplification of that last point would be to consider quite another aspect of agape. It was the name given to a feast. The Jews, the early Christians and many others at the beginning of our era held community meals and feasts, and the name given to them by the Christians was the agape, which no doubt had links with the Eucharist. In contemporary terms, the image of the feast often appears in patients' dreams with its oral and other instinctual associations. These sometimes point to experiences of feeding, growth and integration within the analytical relationship that may be enjoyed by patient and therapist in accordance with whatever level of development each has reached.

Facilitating Conditions in the Therapeutic Set-up

There is, however, a growing body of experience to suggest that, apart from the knowledge, the skill, the personal motivation and the agape factor of the analyst, the therapeutic set-up, in order to be a facilitating one, demands certain other conditions. These may be established by mutual agreement between the analyst and the patient and are helpful in enabling the patient to use interpretations to his benefit. They bring certain reality factors into the treatment and may be termed limitation, reliability, continuity and ritual. Their importance is based upon the fact that the analytical situation activates the feeling sensitivities of early infancy—in the patient certainly and sometimes in the analyst.

Limitation

It can hardly be denied that a certain delimitation of the agape factor of the analyst is important. The mobilization of a therapeutic disposition to be concerned with and open to the needs of his patient forms the subjective aspect of his specific sentiment towards him, and is bounded by the actualities of his psycho-somatic constitution scope and capability. He can do this for fewer or more people at any particular point in his life, but if he stretches himself too far or dissipates such capacities for agape as he possesses, his sensitivity to his patients and their capacity to benefit from treatment can diminish. If this happens, a certain reality element enters into the situation, so that the patient becomes hostile and resistant to interpretations for reality reasons rather than transference reasons. Other reality limitations to the analyst's agape factor are connected with the individual analyst's needs, which vary widely; these limitations are connected with fees, optimal hours and suitable conditions of work, enough satisfaction of scientific curiousity, and a due respect given to the claims of his private life.

Reliability

The analyst must be capable of mobilizing such capabilities for reliability as he may possess, if the need arises, for the patient to be able to feel safe enough to regress and depend upon him. The patient must be able to trust that his therapist will be there at the agreed time to receive him and attend to him. Otherwise, destructive rage activated by reality factors, though originating in early privation or deprivation, will bring about a shattering of the interpretations in the mind of the patient and in his capacity to make use of them.

Continuity

A further important piece of reality background to treatment is continuity—"a keeping up of steam", a steady continuous working with the patient that is as little interrupted as possible. This involves the well-known point that the patient's holidays should coincide with those of the therapist as much as possible, and the point about securing that number of sessions that is optimal for the work of both analyst and patient. This last point is often argued in terms of estimating how much in the way of gaps a regressed patient can tolerate without spontaneously developing defences that become progressively more difficult to analyse. I personally feel this consideration to be true and vital for the patient's well-being. When we consider the needs of the analyst as well, we may remind ourselves of Plaut's observation that frequent sessions assist the analyst to maintain the state of mind necessary for the open-minded pursuit of Bion's 0. There is also another sense in which it is helpful for the analyst as well as the patient. The point has been made by Meltzer (1967) in his paper "Psychoanalysis as a human activity". He describes psychoanalysis as an act of virtuosity, a combination of artistic and athletic activity—with strenuosity, pace and a keeping up to form—a sustained effort depending upon regularity of analytic activities, not only with individual patients but also in terms of the organization of his practice. He reports the figure of the analyst, thus stretched, at certain phases of the analysis, as appearing in the dreams of his patients as "the long-distance runner" or a "mountain-climber" (1967). Sudden interruptions to this continuity, apart from holidays, whether inaugurated by patient or analyst, can temporarily knock the analyst off form, injure his sensitivity, and render his interpretations off-centre.

Ritual

My last point is concerned with certain aspects of "ritual" that are discernible in the analytical process. I remember our attention being drawn to this by Plaut some years ago and my not taking too kindly to it as, at the time, I rather undervalued ritual as such. Recently Home (1972), a psychoanalyst, has also raised the question in a discussion of whether enough has been made of the ritual aspect of analysis and whether the analyst may not suitably be thought of as in a way analogous to a priest presiding over a ritual, within which the patient and the analyst may feel safely contained and sustained, so that analysis, experimentation and synthesis may be set free. I find this suggestion to be close to my experience and a meaningful analogy that has the advantage of being rooted in the past. The constantly repeated ritual includes the frequent regular sessions, the normal length of the sessions, the familiarity of the waiting room and the regular progression from it to the consulting room and the furniture of the consulting room, the relative positions of the couch and chair. Within that containing ritual, freedom of speech and feeling and movement on the couch are possible. Regression, change and growth suffer minimal disturbance and all are allowed maximal dynamism against a steady background. The patient can "cut and come again", repeat, relive and repair within the familiar round of sessions, with time enough and minimal pressure from external sources. Furthermore, the relative security provided by the analyst has a basis in his analysis and training by a professional analytic society with a developing life of its own, and his strength and effectiveness depend upon whatever validity of personal experience and whatever ability to stand by it is fostered by that society.

The obviously comparable activity is that of the priest, authorized by the church and believing in the ritual process over which he presides. Within the ritual, changes take place according to the calendar and some spontaneity is allowed in the sermon. The difference is that a greater degree of spontaneity is appropriate within analytical psychotherapy whose ritual is less rigid and closer to that of the kind of family life within which certain orders and patterns emerge spontaneously and can be maintained flexibly.

The Nature of Interpretation

We have so far considered the agapaic function of the analyst and some conditions that facilitate its exercise. We must now examine how the main elements of the process of *interpretation* have emerged in the history of analysis and have come to be regarded as the main agents of the analyst's therapeutic activity.

Derivations

Partridge in *Origins* (1958) demonstrates the derivation of the word "interpretation" from the Latin *pretium* meaning "price", with parallels in praise, precious, appreciate and depreciate. An interpretation refers to the work of a negotiator, intermediary, commission agent or a go-between. Presumably analysts are each of these to some extent. They describe and negotiate between various parts of the patient's personality and, in discussion with the patient, assign them weight or value as between, for instance, his complexities and his simplicities, his ego and the unconscious matrix of his personality. This also applies to the patient's transference and other interpersonal relationships.

Definitions

There have, of course, been many definitions of interpretation in analytical psychotherapy, and investigation shows that the subject is not quite simple. We may take a few samples. Bion (1970) describes interpretations as transformations that display the invariants when an experience felt and described in one way is described in another. As a painter's experience is transformed into a painting, so a psychoanalytical experience is transformed into a psychoanalytical description. Rycroft defines interpretation as "The process of elucidating and expounding the meaning of something abstruse, obscure, etc.'' and psychoanalytic interpretations as ''statements made by the analyst to the patient in which he attributes to a dream, a symptom, or a chain of free associations [surely we would add behaviour, phantasy, visions, painting, models, etc.] some meaning, over and above (under and below) that given to it by the patient'' (Rycroft, 1968). Fordham (1971), in relation to work with children, gives a simple definition; ''interpretation is one means of communication with a child with a view to bringing unconscious contents into consciousness and to explain the origin of his affects''. There is, indeed, something in common in all three definitions, namely, the making of a content easier to understand through its translation into different linguistic terms. Nevertheless, it is worth while looking into something of the history of the idea of interpretations, helped as we are now by the work done on the subject by Sandler *et al.* (1973).

According to these authors, the early Freud (1893–5) held in the mid-1890s that verbal interventions (not, by the way called interpretations by him) were to be used only to facilitate the stream of associations and material. The idea was to release dammed-up affect relating to important traumatic events in the patient's past. That was all.

At the turn of the century, the word interpretation became used for the analyst's understanding of the latent content of dreams, namely their hidden sources and meaning. At that time it was considered that the analyst should didactically communicate their meaning to the patient (Freud, 1900).

From 1910 through into the 1920s Freud's attention shifted to the timing of the communication of interpretations to the patient. Now the analyst was to withhold his interpretation until the right moment, sometimes thought of as the point when resistances appeared (Freud, 1926). In 1937 Freud began to differentiate between ''interpretations'' and ''constructions'' in analysis – reconstruction as we call it today (Freud, 1937). Construction was to lay before the patient a piece of early history—a preliminary labour designed to facilitate the emergence of memories of the past and their reflection in the present. Interpretations were to deal with particular and single elements. In general, during this time, debates centred round issues like those of the *when*, the *what* and the *form* of interpretations. Behind this, shifts in orientation from *topographical* to *structural* theory were accompanied by a concern as to the effect of the analyst's interventions upon the patient's response on many and different levels. Indeed, by 1945 we find Fenichel so aiming to diminish all possibility of clash between his interpretations and the patient's response and so emphasizing the timing element that he can assign to interpretations the task of "helping something unconscious to become conscious by naming it at the moment it is striving to break through" (Fenichel, 1945).

Since then, ever greater elaboration and expansion of the subject has taken place, and a good deal of differentiation has been worked out between interpretations proper and a wide range of other verbal interventions which included instructions given for setting up the analytic situation, reconstructions, preparations for interpretation, questions or comments aimed at eliciting and elucidating material, confrontations, and clarifications. Later there arose a general agreement to use the word interpretation for all interventions having the aim of making the patient aware of some aspect of his psychological functioning of which he had previously been unaware.

Under this heading, we find the following types of interpretation:

(1) Content interpretation, comprising:
    (a) the relating of manifest surface material to childhood wishes and phantasies;
    (b) the translation of symbolic meaning in dreams and phantasies.

(2) Defence interpretations.

(3) Transference interpretations.

(4) Direct interpretations, i.e. those made "as an immediate response to the patient's material without waiting for further associations or clarifications" (Sandler *et al.*, 1971).

(5) "Mutative" interpretations. These were described first by James Strachey (1934), who thought that crucial change could only be brought about in a patient by interpretations made in direct connection with the here and now transference situation. Strachey gave great prestige to the mutative value of transference interpretations, and this has been felt strongly in the Society of Analytical Psychology as well.

A further development in discriminatory work upon interpretation has been elaborated by Bion (1962) with his differentiation of the analyst's interventions into six types of event. The first is a "definitory hypothesis" which is conveyed to the patient by a sentence such as "I think that you are showing the signs of suffering from an underlying depression" or by something more direct. The second is "notation", where the material is compared with similar material brought up in past sessions. The third is "attention", when out of a kind of reverie the analyst finds the central point that gives coherence to a mass of chaotic material conveyed in a session. The fourth is "enquiry" in which the analyst makes a "probing" intervention in order to release further material.

So far these four events are all interventions that can be seen as enabling or conducive to interpretation. The other two interventions are expressive of something central to the personality of the analyst. One, understandable as potentially benign, is actually called "action" by Bion, and like Strachey's "mutative" interpretation is designed to operate upon the patient's problems of development in some decisive way. Here, out of his transference/counter-transference involvement, the analyst decides on his own responsibility to make an interpretation intended to be a meaningful and decisive communication from one person to another. The other intervention must be regarded as arising from a more or less malign happening in the analyst. Bion calls it a "psi" phenomenon, and it represents an intervention by the analyst designed to relieve anxiety in himself based, as is now known, upon unanalysed neurotic counter-transference, or upon feeling lost or bewildered about the progress of the patient, or upon some desire for the "success" of the treatment. Unless corrected and repaired, it is likely that "psi" responses by the analyst may, through serious omission or distortion, operate destructively upon the patient's developing psyche, for "psi" interventions are really evacuants rather than meaningful communications.

These two interventions, as described by Bion, are decisive impacts made by the analyst's personality upon the patient. In the first case, the analyst is in a position to operate meaningfully out of his agape-originated involvement for the benefit of his patient. In the other case, the analyst's agape has failed in so far as his concern is not for his patient but rather for the relief of his own anxiety and the promotion of his own peace of mind.

Part-object Psychology in Interpretation

That the personality of the analyst is involved in his interpretations raises the whole question of part-object psychology. This well-known concept of Klein's has led us to understand how, for the infant, the breast, the breast–penis, the penis and, later, other parts of the body represent, in a central way, the mother and, later, the father in his perception and experience of them. Transactions between the infant and the mother/father are readily understandable when they are seen as varying ways of relating to these part-objects prior to the infant's becoming able to perceive mother and father as whole persons. Many patients relate to themselves and to others as if to the part-objects of their infancy, and this comes out when they deal with their analysts' interpretations as if they were part-objects. Racker (1968), as well as other workers, has demonstrated that violent attacks, rejections, loving regard, sucking, biting, pulling, devouring—all these may be understood and felt by the analyst as directed upon his interpretations as if they represented a breast or penis or breast–penis. The patient's response is not understandable as a response to the meaning conveyed by the interpretation, for the latter has become for him something else. This point has also been made by Fordham in his description of ways in which patients deal with interpretations: "For instance, the analyst's interventions can be ignored, spoiled and distorted, their meaning twisted and made unreal; they can be muddled up, chewed, hollowed out to become empty, spat out, pushed back into him and made into persecutors. On the other hand they can be admired, loved, tasted, savoured and ingested to be built into the patient's self with profit and concretely paid for with gratitude. None of these consequences need have bearing on the accuracy or relevance of interventions themselves, though they often have much to do with how they are expressed" (Fordham, 1962). Again, we see the interpretation being treated as essentially one part of the analyst by the patient, though in time the patient may in favourable circumstances become able to treat the interpretation not only as a part-object but also, even more, as an interpersonal meaningful communication between two whole persons.

On the analyst's side, the agapaic requirement is to become able to tolerate his feeling response to such subtle violations of his interpretative efforts, originating, as they do, from primitive and infantile wishes to "attack" parts of himself. However, the holding in check of immediate talion response gives him time or, at least, the opportunity to profit from the satisfactions to be obtained from understanding and discovering a way of interpreting to his patients their manner of handling his earlier interpretative efforts.

Psychopathology and Interpretation

In addition to the strains just described, the agapaic capacity of the analyst is tested by those responses of patients to his interpretations that are specific to their dominant psychopathology. Such are the responses from patients suffering from early narcissistic personality damage and from persecutory anxiety belonging to fixations at the paranoid–schizoid position and, in general, from identifications with early states of hunger, rage and guilt. In the first case the patient, deeply involved in "heroic" do-it-yourself psychology, feels compelled to ignore his analyst's interpretations. This involves the analyst in having to suffer frustration of his spontaneous wish to be responded to meaningfully and in having to content himself with inserting unobtrusive remarks into the narcissistic thought-flow of his patient. In the other cases, the patient needs to reject as persecutory any interpretation that clashes with his own expectations. Or again, any interpretations carrying the smallest hint of mutative content will be rejected out of anticipatory terror in face of any change even though sensed as good. Or the patients, rage-filled and guilt-ridden, may block interpretations because they are sensed to be as devastatingly critical and condemnatory of them as they are, in fact, of themselves. These transactions will often carry some kind of cost to the personality of the analyst, though any skills he can muster in response to such challenges may be richly consolatory even if not always successful.

The Timing and Language of Interpretation

As a bonus for allowing himself a personal involvement in his patient's *ontos* and growth, the analyst may gain an increased sensitivity in the timing of his transference interpretations. Racker (1968), for instance, has shown a way in which the occasions when complementary or concordant counter-transference feelings in the analyst get activated may be taken as indicating the time for beginning transference-interpretations. Of course, such sensitivity to the problem of timing not only increases with practice during the lifetime of an analyst but also develops similarly in the course of each particular analysis as patient and therapist get to know each other as real persons.

Finally, it would be appropriate to mention here the affirmation made by the psychoanalyst Balint (1968) that the particular language and frame of reference of a psychoanalyst must inevitably influence the way in which a patient comes to understand himself. This agrees with Jung's emphasis upon the importance of the personality and real attitudes of the analyst for the outcome of the treatment. In other words, however much the analyst attempts with success to speak the language of the patient and to empathize with his situation etc., his own personality remains an essential factor. It is hence safe to say that the final outcome of the treatment, containing as it does elements that belong to both patient and analyst as individuals, will itself have a unique quality about it.

The description I have undertaken in this chapter of the part played by the analyst as a person in therapy seems to have reached sufficient complexity to make a drawing together of the theme desirable.

My thesis is that some of the contemporary literature of analytical psychology, psychoanalysis and analytical psychotherapy in general suggests that implicitly or explicitly a large number of therapists agree that while analytical interpretations are the central agent of real therapeutic advance, they need a setting, and a background, without which they are normally ineffective. This involves not only the personal skill and capacity to mobilize the analyst's predisposition to understand and analyse the transference/counter-transference situation but also a certain quality that may be taken as a twentieth century heir to an attitude originally expressed by the Hippocratic Oath and the Pauline concept of agape, whereby the analyst is personally and individually involved in the treatment. These qualities need a setting of limitation, continuity, reliability and ritual, within which the patient can respond meaningfully to the analyst's interpretations, which in turn may be regarded as essentially an expression of the analyst as a person. Under these conditions there can come into play the kind of good enough parenting that is appropriate to the age of the patient and suitably designated as "analyst-parenting". This may enable symbolic processes of regression, death and rebirth or repair and growth to take place in relative security. Varying degrees of integration and individuation are observable as by-products of this kind of work. These cannot, however, be achieved by aim-directed striving. Furthermore, interpretations are often understood half-consciously by patients to be a function of the analyst's personality and can also be treated by them both negatively and positively as part-object representations of the analyst himself. Agapaic attitudes in this area are therapeutically effective and the timing, and language of interpretation are discussed as important functions of agape. The fact that the analytic process is worked out as between two unique individuals and emerges as a unique experiment in integration promotes that side of personal development that may be called *individuation*.

Chapter Four

Resistance and counter-resistance

We have considered some of the qualities of the *analyst's* personality that make for successful treatment and suggested what his function mainly is. It seems appropriate now to investigate aspects of the *patient's* response, and in this chapter I shall first of all examine this response in terms of the meaning, mode and indeed therapeutic function of his resistance. Equal in significance, though not always recognized as such, are both resistance and counter-resistance phenomena on the part of the analyst.

I therefore propose to cover the following topics in this chapter. In Part One I shall sketch out topics like the paradox and problematic aspects of resistance, together with an etymological note. I shall then trace the history of the concept both in psychoanalysis and in analytical psychology. In Part Two I shall try to cover a number of topics subsumed under the notion of the patient's resistance to involvement in anything like a personal response to his analyst as a person. This will be considered in terms of primary and secondary resistance and will include a study of envy of the analyst, fear of penetration by and fear of damage by the analyst, together with a note on the therapeutic failure to resolve resistance. In Part Three, I shall describe the phenomenon of resistance on the part of the *analyst*, to be discussed under five headings: non-neurotic resistance, neurotic resistance, reactive counter-resistance, complementary counter-resistance, and concordant counter-resistance. I shall conclude the chapter by attempting to compress into a short statement the story of the vicissitudes, even revolutions, that have occurred in the history of the struggle of both analysts and patients with the challenging phenomena of resistance and counter-resistance. In doing this I hope that the connection between this subject and that of *individuation* will be clearly shown.

PART ONE

The Paradox of Resistance

The paradox of resisting the very experience we long for seems to be a perennial problem of the human condition. The weak resist the strong, the foolish the wise, the ignorant the learned, the empty the full, the isolated and unloving the loving, while the sick reject the healers and vice versa. The problem is exacerbated by the fact that the resistance is affirming something very useful and, in truth, carries within itself something just as important as the need for health, strength, wisdom, knowledge, fullness and love. If this is the case with the world at large, so much the more is the problem an hourly one with analysts and patients because, despite their request for help, patients find that they resist it. We are all the time involved in resistance on the part of patients, or in counter-resistance, meaning resistance experienced by the analyst to his patients' material, whether activated by the resistance of the patient or a function of his own resistance either to the patient's personality as a whole or to specific problems in the patient that have remained unsolved in the analyst's own personality.

The ubiquituous aspect of this problem has in the past stimulated the production of many papers, largely by psychoanalysts, so that apologies could be due for yet further attention to the subject as late as 1981. The fact remains, however, that papers are still being written on the subject. Recently I have found that Roy Schafer's paper "The idea of resistance" (Schafer, 1973) represents a distinct advance in psychoanalytic thought of the more classical type. Furthermore, Racker on "Counter-resistance and interpretation" proved to be exciting reading (Racker, 1968). On the Jungian side, apart from Fordham's work (Fordham, 1957), there is an interesting paper by Dieckmann that describes the neurotic resistance on the part of the analyst to his patient's material. This was uncovered, in the first place, by the patient's resistance to his interpretations and then corrected by compensatory thought arising from more unconscious levels in the analyst which enabled him to reassess the material he had hitherto needed, for neurotic reasons, to misunderstand (Dieckmann, 1971). Papers like these have caused me to consider afresh the subject of resistance and counter-resistance from a Jungian point of view, particularly in London, where the topic has not been publicly discussed for a number of years.

In doing this, I am hoping that we may go further in distinguishing these concepts from those connected with defences on the one hand and transference/counter-transference on the other. I hope, too, that we may be able to refine our concept of resistance/counter-resistance, so that it can be understood to refer to a process that essentially arises within analytical treatment as such and strictly belongs to it. This may preserve us from using the word "resistance" in an obscuring or punning way. An example of this can be seen in the well-known situation whereby psychoanalysts in the past were tempted to ascribe to resistance all criticisms of their metapsychological formulations by the adherents of other disciplines.

The Etymology of the Word "Resistance"

The word "resistance" began to be used by Freud to describe certain phenomena experienced in psychoanalytical treatment. In view of this usage and for the sake of comparison, it may be profitable to consider the etymology of the word.

According to Partridge (1958), the root verb is "to sist". This means "to cause to stand". Therefore, to "resist" means "to cause to stand back", or "to stand against", "withstand" or "oppose".

The next step is to consider the word "stand". Here we find a number of significances. Thus in Indo-European languages we find meanings clustering round the root "sta"—*s, t, a.* The basis of this is "to hold oneself upright", with cognates like "status", "to stand upright" and significantly, "to pause or tarry awhile". Greek, similarly, produces cognates like "stasis", a "stop or stoppage", a "situation", a "condition", a "building", a "stage"—and interestingly enough, an "ecstasy" (ec-stasis = to put out of place or derange), and a "system". Nor should we forget "homeostasis"—a standing "alike" or in equilibrium.

Such a cluster of meanings as this provides us indeed with a veritable analyst's picnic. To "resist" is coming to mean to "stand and hold oneself upright", maintaining a status or a system, bringing about a stasis, a stoppage, a pause, thereby withstanding someone or something and causing them to "stand back"—with a hint of ecstasy withal. And when we have added *"prostates"*, a stander before, with a line to "prostate", and "stele", an upright gravestone or pillar, we are right into the phallic content of the verb "to resist".

All these physically based origins of the word suggest that a patient's unconscious feeling might be formulated as follows.

At this point of resistance in my analysis, I will allow no potency, no penetration, and no orgasm in my analyst. I will remain intact, organized, tensed, aim-directed, a system, upright and together. Implicit in this "stance" is the fact that there is another being, in whom I am interested and in whom I have aroused interest, alertness—even insight into my condition. But now, this person is going to be withstood and allowed no real personal entry for fear that my present working system may be disturbed, modified, or, even worse, destroyed.

An ecstatic abandonment to resistance, paradoxical but clinically observable, is being substituted for the offer of good intercourse, lest there be disappointment, flaws, an absence of good experience or a disturbance of longed for homeostasis.

It seems indubitable that even this superficial glance into the etymology of the word "resistance" may be regarded as having yielded a rich feast of meaning for analysts, and we may celebrate their insight in laying such emphasis upon the concept of resistance in their work. It demonstrates a certain link with the past, for we are here dealing with meanings developed long before analysts were thought of. This exercise, taught us by Leopold Stein, of relinking abstract words, used in psychology, with the physical experiences to which they originally refer facilitates a sharpening and deepening of analytic insight (Stein, 1962).

Resistance in Psychoanalysis

Our understanding of the development of the concept of resistance in psychoanalysis owes a great deal to the work of Sandler, Dare and Holder. Their sketch of this development over the past 80 years shows that the concept, arising, as it did, out of the daily struggle of psychoanalysts with their patients, should be regarded as *clinical* rather than *psychological* (Sandler *et al.*, 1973). By this I think they mean that the concept was, so to speak, forced upon analysts by sheer practical experience and necessity. The patients would not do what their analysts asked of them and refused what their analysts said or interpreted. The early Freud, in the first decade of this century, found that his patients, whether they were hysterical, obsessional or paranoid, resisted his request that they should freely associate. When he considered why they should behave so inconveniently, especially after having asked him to treat them, he concluded that their response was based upon two considerations. They feared that they would suffer from unpleasant affects like shame, self-reproach, psychical pain and the feeling of being harmed. They also feared that they would find themselves at the mercy of inner impulses and wishes. Freud, furthermore, thought that resistance, being unconscious, could be implemented by the use of repression and various types of distortion functioning as its disguise. At that early date, indeed, resistances were not distinguished clearly from the defences that Anna Freud would be describing thirty-odd years later. As a step towards this kind of differentiation, however, Freud had, by 1909, worked out that there could be a concept of constant resistance, as if this might be regarded as part of a patient's character structure, and, furthermore, normal to the analytic process (Freud, 1909).

It was three years later that Freud developed the enormously important first notions of transference resistance (Freud, 1912). The analytic process, he discovered, led to the revival of early experiences, as a result of which the patient began to focus upon the person of the analyst and make love demands of the sort that involved a flouting of the analytic "rules" and an ignoring of his interpretations. That "love" began to be interpreted by him as an expression of resistance to the analysis, although later work with regressed patients has shown this to be not always so. Accordingly, Freud formulated the notion of two types of resistance: (1) transference-resistance, manifesting itself as extremely variable; and (2) repression-resistance, regarded as ever-present and invariable.

The assimilation of these views and their application to clinical practice was followed by virtual silence in the literature for fourteen years, which of course included World War I. Then in 1926, Freud produced a further list of five types of resistance, designated as follows:

(1) *Repression* resistances.

(2) *Transference* resistances.

(3) Resistance to any analysis that might threaten the *epinosic or secondary* gains offered by the symptom. Thus if the illness itself promises a primary or paranosic gain through flight from the struggle of life, then any care and attention that others might devote to the sick person represents for him a secondary gain— seductive indeed to a patient already impoverished by the illness itself.

(4) *Id* resistances, whereby the id elements of patients resist any alteration to the mode or form of primary instinctual expression as well as any idea of learning about and developing an ego position towards id processes, let alone subjecting them to analysis.

(5) *Super-ego* resistances to all attempts at improvement or recovery because of the relief this would provide through modification of the self-punishment and disapproval that originate from super-ego sources in the psyche (Freud, 1926).

A further decade's work finds Anna Freud, in 1936, distilling out from the study of resistances her well-known list of the defences of the ego, with no clear distinction between *resistance* and *defences* yet adduced (Freud, A., 1936). This notion was further developed by Hartmann (1951) and Glover (1955) and the ego-psychologists; earlier, Wilhelm Reich had been taking up the early notion of constant resistance and working it into his concept of the *armour-plated character structure* with all its problems of rigidity (Reich, 1928).

Three years later, in 1939, Helen Deutsch made her own list of resistances:

(1) *Intellectualizing* resistances, in which the intellectual study of psychoanalysis was being used to promote "head-resistance", thus keeping the patient above or beyond the emotional experiences of pain and change. This, of course, was a study of a mode or method of resistance.

(2) It was similarly a question of mode or method in the second on her list, namely, *transference* resistance.

(3) The third on her list centred on the *content* of resistance, i.e. it operated against certain recollections from childhood that patients feared would revive terror and pain (Deutsch, 1939).

It was at this time, also, and once more before the onset of a war, namely World War II, that the distinction between defences and resistances began to be clearly recognized. It began to be perceived that defences played an important in-built part in the total psychological structure of an individual. Resistances, on the other hand, had a quite different function. They were mobilized by the patient against any effort of the analyst that might make for disequilibrium or disturbance to the psychic status quo of the patient—even if he longed for the change that might be brought about by the integration of hitherto unrecognized parts of his personality.

World War II, and the ten years following it, saw another silence on the subject of resistance, and then in 1955, Glover wrote about resistances in a more sophisticated way (Glover, 1955). He concentrated less on the aims of resistance and more on describing degrees, modes and methods of resistance as employed by the patient. He described first *obvious or crass* resistances—like breaking off analysis, lateness, missing sessions, some sorts of silence, circumlocution, rejection, deafness, misunderstanding everything the analyst says, pretending to be stupid, falling asleep etc.

A second mode of resistance he called *unobtrusive* resistance. The most famous examples are noticable compliance, including immediate agreement with everything the analyst says and bringing material which is thought to be liked by the analyst.

Very quietly, these resistances, to the extent that they are absolute and unconscious, undermine the whole analytic process in a subtle way by distorting the patient as if he were a non-person, and leaving the analyst with an uncomfortable feeling and sense of isolation and unreality.

Experience of these two modes of resistance has become so well-known to analysts that it is of interest to realize that Glover's formulation was made as late as 1955.

In order to complete our picture of the development in more classical psychoanalysis I have taken the liberty of reducing the main propositions of Sandler, Dane and Holder (Sandler *et al.*, 1973) to four main groupings.

In group one, they include resistances arising out of *faulty procedures* and technical measures on the part of the analyst. Today we would probably concentrate more on the analyst's personal failure of consciousness resulting in inappropriate responses to his patient. The latter's resistance would simply represent self-defence against potential harm from his analyst, with the result that the progress of the analysis gets held up until matters are put right.

In group two, we find emphasis upon resistance based upon the patient's fixated longings for gratification, aroused by and, indeed, provided by the analyst's sympathy and receptive powers and focused upon in preference to his analytic aims. These are the *transference* resistances. Added to this is resistance to analysis based upon fear that the patient will lose a loved object, the analyst, if the analysis should come to its longed for but feared successful termination. Clinical experience suggests that, with reasonable good fortune, these resistances may be analysed and lessened, if not resolved.

In group three, we find types of resistance arising out of *incapacity to change*. One of these may be called difficulties over unlearning. The other may be regarded as due to extreme fixity and rigidity as described by Reich. The prognosis for group three resistances is sometimes a poor one—in analytic terms.

In group four we find all those *repression* resistances due to fears that adaptations of the personality that have hitherto worked moderately well will fall under threat of destruction and dissolution, so that the patient, after analysis, will be worse off than he was before he began. This may include a loss of secondary gains, of id and super-ego satisfactions, and possibly of personal relationships, however unsatisfactory. Finally, characters noticeably organized round the idea of a rather precariously sustained self-esteem can become resistant through fear of their destruction by the analyst. In this group, the resistances are considered to be reasonably manageable by skilled analysts.

This, then, completes a sketch of the history of resistance in orthodox psychoanalysis—a history of deepening penetration and increased discrimination and yet a history somewhat limited in the scope of its understanding. This limitation seems to centre on too low a regard not only for the real personal relationship between the analyst and the patient but also for the nature of resistance. The impression given is of a patient bringing a complaint, asking for help and then being discovered to be resistant both to doing free association and to taking any real notice of the weight of an observing analyst's interpretations. These latter (made, incidentally, from a cool point of view) seem to be understood as verbal propositions about the patient's condition and reckoned by the analyst to be more or less "true". The patient is expected therefore to make use of them for purposes of self improvement—unless he severely resists. Plausible enough, many might think; nevertheless from the standpoint of today this classical notion about psychoanalysis suffers from serious deficiencies. It is weak in its understanding of the real and transformative relationship between the patient and his analyst, whether the latter is experienced by the former as part-object or whole object. It is inadequately explicit over the homeostatic functions of resistances in preserving the wholeness of the patient's personality. It is deficient in recognizing the altered significance of resistance in the case of patients who need to regress to the early months of infancy. Recent work by Shafer, Racker and Winnicott have opened out these hitherto neglected areas and have made analysis available to numbers of patients hitherto considered incapable of response to it. It is to these writers that I propose now to turn my attention.

Resistance in the Work of Schafer and Racker

Thus Roy Schafer (1973) writes significantly of resistance much more in terms of an "activity" gone in for by a person (the patient) towards another person (the analyst) and vice versa. The patient is a person caught in a self-contradiction, because while asking another person (the analyst) to help him, he finds that he is resisting that very person willy-nilly and despite himself. Furthermore, Schafer argues correctly that the idea that resistance represents defiance of paternal authority is quite inadequate to the facts because maternal authority plays just as important a part (Schafer, 1973). Much analysis is concerned with processes belonging to pre-genital life and is involved in understanding how the patient reacts to the way in which the mother/analyst manages his feeding needs; how the patient experiences the breast and nipple and the flow of milk; how he can enjoy himself at the breast well enough or, on the other hand, not at all; how the mother/analyst cleans up his bottom and handles his motions or his constipations—or earlier still (I am paraphrasing Schafer) how the patient handles his fears of devouring or of being devoured, of fusing with or disintegrating in relation to the analyst experienced as an archaic mother.

We can see here that Schafer, influenced, surely, by Kleinian formulations of part and whole object psychology in infancy, does go a long way towards understanding the patient's experience of the real person of the analyst as a psychosomatically based being whose interpretations are essentially an expression of his personality. My own comment is that interpretations are getting near to being understood as actions of an analyst involved in an instinctually based agapaic relation with the patient (see Chapter 3) rather than as a purveyor of interpretative propositions, and hence exercising the ''real'' authority that enables and facilitates growth rather than ''formal'' authority that confines itself to pattern imposition (Lambert, 1973).

From the specifically Jungian point of view, however, we may think that Schafer's point about the analysis of resistance is one of great importance, for he is saying that, thereby, the affirmative reasons for the patients' mounting opposition to his analyst may be understood. I quote:

> While mounting this opposition has its negative aspects, such as denial, avoidance, dread, disclaimed action and primitive reductionism in understanding, it also has its affirmative, even constructive aspects, such as maintaining relationships, being faithful to ideals, maintaining pride and autonomy and achieving mastery (Schafer, 1973).

This account of developments in psychoanalysis must surely show how near it has arrived to positions held strongly by Jung and his successors. For resistance has been brought by Schafer more closely into connection with both the realization and the defence of the self as a whole within a personal relationship. He writes that ''the so-called analysis of resistance has become for us the analysis of the total personality'' (Schafer, 1973).

A similar implication may be found in Heinrich Racker's work on resistance and counter-resistance. He points out that real counter-resistance on the part of the analyst is experienced when he feels he has an interpretation to make but yet finds himself blocking and unable to make it. The analyst rationalizes that he would wound the patient and hinder the analysis. For instance, he can now see that the patient feels hatred, malice and resentment against him but is keeping himself unconscious of these feelings. For Racker it can mean that often when the analyst's counter-resistance to interpreting such feelings is strong, it may be taken as an indication that something has been left out. What then becomes necessary is that he should be able to make an interpretation of the sort which indicates his understanding that the patient finds himself in a painful and embarrassing conflict and resists because, despite the fact that he knows in so many ways his love for his analyst, he also finds himself full of fear of and hatred towards him for various reasons. When the patient knows from the analyst's interpretation that his love as well as his hate is recognized by the analyst, the resistance becomes modified; likewise the analyst's counter-resistance (Racker, 1968). Here again we find a psychoanalyst affirming that there is a kind of resistance that has the long-term aim of protecting the wholeness of the personality.

Winnicott and the Apparent ''Resistance'' of the Regressed Patient

The emphasis of Schafer and Racker upon the interaction between the personalities of both the patient and the analyst as whole people has, as we have seen, ushered a revolutionary notion into classical psychoanalysis. Even more revolutionary in an extensive way, however, is the work of Winnicott on the problem of a ''false self'' which both protects and threatens the integrity and growth of the ''postulated true self''.

In patients with this kind of problem, a significance attaches to their resistance that is quite different from that attached to resistance in classicial psychoanalysis. The latter has generally assumed in the patient both a reasonably intact self and a sound enough working ego—a condition which enables the patient to consider, accept, reject, or adapt to his purposes his analyst's interpretations. In view of this, resistance has been considered as something to be overcome even though needing to be analysed. Winnicott, however, focused on those patients in whom there had been gross deprivation, if not privation, of a good enough holding mother in early infancy. Such people can survive only through a spontaneous development of false self and false ego organization that protects but encapsulates their true self which is maintained in an immature condition. This non-development of true personality often produces in people a deep sense of dissatisfaction and of unreality in their lives which forces them to seek psychotherapeutic help. It is in such patients that Winnicott has discerned two modes of apparent ''resistance'' to traditional interpretations, both of which seem to express a ''defence of the true self'' in a way that is comparable with Fordham's ''defences of the self'' (Fordham, 1934). In these patients it would be wrong, unacceptable and damaging if the analyst were to understand their behaviours as classical resistance. One form emerged from Winnicott in his work with "squiggles" and his well-known observations of the infants to whom he offered spatulas to play with when seated on their mothers' knees (Winnicott, 1941). He has described what he calls the "period of hesitation" after the first contact with the spatula and before the infants contacted their feelings about it and entered into a kind of intimacy with it.

This process, he showed, could be understood as being expressed in resistance-like activity of regressed patients towards their analysts during similar "periods of hesitation" prior to venturing on "kinds of intimacy". Any attempt to eliminate such hesitation by disapproval or interpretations about resistance would be damaging because, paradoxically, for the patient to try to repress this hesitancy would represent a real hidden resistance.

We can introduce Winnicott's second form by the old joke about the supposed reaction of country folk to the sight of a stranger in their midst. They used to be credited with the well-known phrase "''Ere's a furriner. 'Eave 'arf a brick at 'un''. There are echoes of this in Winnicott's description of the process whereby the infant during his early months develops his capacity to find an object through aggression and attack. He needs space and time in which to discover and learn the difference between being identified with a totally subjective experience whereby everything, including objects, is "me" and a state in which the objectivity and "not me-ness" of objects is fully experienced. The latter is achieved if he is consistently held by the maternal object while he delusionally "attacks" and "destroys" it. He wishes to see whether it survives the attack—an event that establishes for the baby its distinctiveness and otherness. It is only after this that the infant can move on to an ability to use an object (Winnicott, 1945, 1969). Above all, it is within a situation of playing and being played with (Winnicott, 1969) that these experimental moves can be made.

One of Winnicott's contributions has been to help analysts to understand that patients who suffer from very early deprivation—not privation—of a holding mother, and who apply for analysis, do so with an unconscious hope. This is to find an environment that holds, perdures and survives id-originated destructive attacks, for it is of this experience that they have been deprived after having had some of it when they were babies. Such patients have been subject to over-impingement, through lack of protection by the maternal holding environment from intense stimulation, to such an extent that the postulated true self has remained in a primitive condition and unable to find and create objects. Their maternal object had not been reliably "there" to be the object of attempted destruction, to survive and gradually become an object of concern in a situation of ego-relatedness. Such over-impinged-upon babies become exclusively reactive to stimuli and develop a false self which is an extension of both "shell" and environment at the almost total expense of the "inner core". They are not psychotic but have strong anti-social tendencies. Though they make demands, they are not able to ask to be allowed to regress, but they can grow and develop in an environment that understands this and appropriately meets their needs.

As the problem arises at a time when ego-development is rudimentary, they can make nothing of ordinary analytic interpretations and need to treat them as objects to destroy. They treat the analyst as the original maternal holding environment or seek a transitional object in his room. If he fails to meet them through holding, through remaining in being, by being at their disposal and surviving attack and insult, their growth processes stop, accompanied not by rage but by a renewed sense of futility. If he succeeds, they will move past mere destructiveness. Even as he survives, they may sense his stored hate (Winnicott, 1947). Gradually they move on, first, past destructiveness, then rage, and then on to concern and care for the analyst. As this takes place, they become able to benefit from ordinary analytic interpretation, to feel more real inside and to enjoy, with their developing true self, id-feelings and impulses through ego-relatedness to their analyst and others. They have thus learned to use their analyst as a real personal object.

At first these patients appear totally resistant to all normal analytic and interpretative processes. The paradox, however, is that they are not resistant at all in the deepest sense. They are really at a stage where the actual relationship with the environment is crucial, where the situation is presymbolic and where the true self and ego are not developed enough to understand and make use of interpretations, or to experience symbolism. As a result, any conformity with or acceptance of the normal analytic and interpretative situation by them would actually represent a collusion of the false self with environmental expectations (Khan, 1975). It would be behaviour of the latter sort that would represent resistance, for by it the real issue of being a person involved with and in another person would be dodged.

Jung's View of Resistance

The way is now open to gather together some of the contributions made to the subject by Jung and place them side by side with those of the psychoanalysts. Jung's remarks on resistance are scattered mainly in Volumes 4, 16 and 17 of the Collected Works and he uses resistance in several senses:

(1) In a number of passages he makes no distinction between resistance and repression of certain contents of the psyche, and he can talk of a "continual mood of resistance" (Jung, 1925) in respect of sexual matters—in a sense that is interchangeable with repression.

(2) In other places resistance is to the analytic method or the analyst (Jung, 1913a), or to the analyst's work (Jung, 1931), or to the idea of needing to resolve an infantile attitude to the analyst as a loved or hated father (Jung, 1913a), or to admitting to the analyst numerous perverse phantasies (Jung, 1913b), or to any recovery from illness, or to any movement into heterosexual life by, for example, a homosexual boy (Jung, 1925).

(3) Again, in many of these passages, we find in Jung an assertion of the importance of the personality of the analyst, or his work, together with the notion of resistance as resistance to him—heavily weighted, however, by the father transference.

(4) One thing stands out clearly in Jung; he took resistance very seriously. There are, for instance, warnings against arousing it unnecessarily, and he writes that dreams are useful to analyse "provided you keep away from all theoretical assumptions as they only arouse unnecessary resistance in the patient" (Jung, 1925). Indeed a whole series of passages suggest suitable attitudes on the analyst's part towards the phenomenon of resistance. Although Jung can write, perhaps with tongue in cheek, about the analyst having "forbearance enough to *melt* the strongest resistance", he can also write that he always takes up any sign of resistance and that he never breaks it down (Jung, 1925). So far from trying to melt or break down resistance, he is rather inclined to emphasize a type of resistance that is parallel to, but not the same as, that mentioned above by Sandler, Dare and Holder, namely, resistance to faulty procedures and technical methods on the part of the analyst.

Jung's emphasis is more on faulty attitudes rather than on practices or techniques. Thus, in 1929, when he was considering how to get the hang of the case and in particular how to judge when to apply a Freudian or an Adlerian viewpoint, he writes: "When in a quandary, the resistances of the patient may be valuable signposts. I am inclined to take deep-seated resistances seriously at first, paradoxical as this may sound, for I am convinced that the doctor does not necessarily know better than the patient's own psychic constitution—of which the patient himself may be quite unconscious" (Jung, 1931a).

Again, by 1951, he writes that adequate self-criticism should be exercised by the psychotherapist "when he comes up against insuperable resistances in the patient that may possibly be justified" (Jung, 1951). He should remember that "there is no single theory in the whole field of practical psychology that cannot on occasion prove basically wrong. In particular, the view that the patient's resistances are in no circumstances justified is completely fallacious. The resistance might very well prove that the treatment rests on false premises'' (Jung, 1951, p.21).

There is, however, another important statement of Jung's in which the resistance is considered to have arisen for different reasons and which should be given serious weight. This is found in the introduction to *The Psychology of the Transference* (Jung, 1946), where Jung claims to be dealing with what he calls ''the onset of the transference'' in the context of which he writes of ''the union of opposites'' or ''the royal marriage'' of alchemy—powerful archetypal contents that may be activated in an analysis. At this point it is incest feelings that are in question and issue in a kind of symbolic copulation between patient and analyst. Out of this intercourse there may be ''issue''—the child, the self—a real, though not necessarily similar, change in both patient and analyst.

At the beginning of this kind of process it is not unusual to experience collision, chaos or darkness. It is at this point that Jung emphasizes the emergence of resistances. He holds that a lengthy analysis, concerned with what he calls the stage of rapprochement, may be needed to come first. At this point, also, I would like to point out the strength and emotionality of Jung's language; he writes that this may be so particularly in the case when the patient shows violent resistances coupled with fear of the activated contents of the unconscious. There is good reason and ample justification for these resistances and they should never, under any circumstances, be ridden over roughshod or otherwise argued out of existence. Nor should they be belittled, disparaged or made ridiculous; on the contrary, they should be taken with the utmost seriousness as a vitally important defence mechanism against overpowering contents which are often very difficult to control. The general rule should be that the weakness of the conscious attitude is proportional to the strength of the resistance. Therefore when there are strong resistances, the conscious rapport with the patient must be carefully watched, and in certain cases his conscious attitude must be supported to such a degree that, in view of later developments, one would be bound to charge oneself with the grossest inconsistency (Jung, 1946).

Incidentally, we can infer from the use of such strong language and strong prohibitions that the intensity of his patients' resistances must have irritated Jung so much that his emotions could only just be controlled. Indeed, his ability to exercise such control must have arisen from his feeling for the phenomenon of homeostasis in the psyche. Thus, familiarity with the play of opposites enabled him to be, on the whole, less suspicious of resistance than were the early psychoanalysts, prior to the emergence of therapists like Schafer, Racker, Winnicott and others.

By 1945 then, Jung had, through his interest in the incestuous royal marriage motif, brought to a high degree of intensity that emphasis upon the importance of the integration of the analyst as a person that he had begun to make sixteen years earlier in 1929 in *Problems of Modern Psychotherapy* (Jung, 1931). By 1945 the mutual interpenetrability of patient and analyst was seen to carry a heavy charge of powerful archetypal transferences and counter-transferences needing deep analysis. The resistance seems to be taking two levels. One level is that of frightening and intense transference, but another remains even after transference has been analysed. Now it is the change occurring as a result of the real analytic intercourse that is feared.

Jung, in other words, goes further in 1945 than Schafer does in 1973. For Schafer, the patient resists the thorough disturbance of the total pattern of his personality as a whole that may be brought about in him as a result of his analysis. For Jung, however, there is an intercourse in which the change involved is not only a resetting of the whole personality of the patient and a bringing forth of hitherto unconscious capabilities but also a really new development symbolized by the image of a child—a development in which the analyst, as a person, is deeply implicated as well as the patient. While the patient–analyst involvement has undoubtedly archetypal determinants, the new development is almost certainly a unique event and a function of the interplay of two whole persons.

Jung's emphasis upon the child as a symbol of the emergent self is comparable with, though more all-embracing than, Winnicott's salving and nurturing of the true self of his patients within the therapeutic relationship, when their deprivation has been of adequate early mothering. Light has been thrown upon the care required as a result of work done on the "primal scene" by Meltzer (1973) and others. This has shown how relationships within the family, particularly between the mother and father, profoundly shape or distort the individual's archetypal image of the original family matrix out of which the child emerges into adult growth. It is as if the patient and the analyst, through work upon their relationship, can repair the original damaged and damaging primal scene and thus facilitate a rebirth and development of the true self of the patient in a less damaged and more positive way.

Finally, Jung's understanding of resistance includes an insight that partially overlaps Freud's concept of "id-resistance" but goes beyond it in a unique way. In *Answer to Job* Jung dramatically describes the moment when Jahweh began to wish to become incarnate—to become man (Jung, 1954). This is an image and may be conceptualized in terms of the idea that there can be a movement of the unconscious, *qua* the matrix out of which the capacity for ego-consciousness of the personality can emerge, towards becoming conscious. It thus would become subject to the limitations of space and time and personal life (see Neumann, 1954, pp.335-9; Williams, 1963). Archetypal contents can thereby be transformed from postulated states of potentiality into realizations—to the benefit of the personality as a whole. Jung sensed a conflict here as a result of evidence that the unconscious, which he obviously related to his No. 2 personality, is also resistant to such a process. This is expressed in *Answer to Job* in terms of the incarnation being only partial because the good son, Christ, alone was involved. As a result the bad son, Satan, remained unincarnate, a spirit, not subject (unlike Christ) to the manifold limitations of human personality even to the point of temporary destruction through crucifixion (Lambert, 1977).

Jung's insight is often confirmed by analysts who can sometimes meet in their patients powerful forces that brook no interference from consciousness and remain blindly determined to have their way even at the cost of endangering the personality of the patient as a whole. It is probable that this resistance is never completely modified, but it seems to be exacerbated in people whose personalities, in the first months of infancy, have been continually shattered by cross-currents of titanic emotion. Their ego-weakness is due to an experience of unreliability, absence etc. on the part of their mothers, in whom an ample supply of ego-conscious care and reliable holding is essential if their babies are to weather the emotional storms of early life. At the same time we need to remember Jung's strong historical sense. He thought that, in the mainstream of Hebrew–Christian historical development, certain contents had, so to speak, to await their turn over the centuries before they could come into consciousness. It was as if preparation had to be made before some new development could tolerate coming into the open or indeed be tolerated by the old. This is sometimes true in personal historical development as well. The rub often is that, side by side with the gain involved, pain connected with an element of limitation is part of the price to be paid when an unconscious content is to be integrated into consciousness.

Summary

The Psychoanalytic Development

In psychoanalysis the development of the concept of resistance has proceeded in the following order:

(1) Resistance is a defence against anticipated emotional discomfort expressed by a refusal of the method of free association, a refusal of interpretations and adherence to "loving" transference used as a defence against free associating or the giving of any serious consideration to the analyst's interpretations.

(2) Resistance is mobilized as a defence against the loss of primary and secondary gains from illness and against any modification of the power of id and super-ego.

(3) Resistance uses the defences described by Anna Freud against interpretations that will, it is feared, as likely as not disturb the status quo or the basic equilibrium of the patient.

(4) Resistance is described by Glover in terms of methods employed by the patient and is defined as (*a*) crass resistance and (*b*) unobtrusive resistance. The latter would also include the "head-resistance" first described by Helen Deutsch.

(5) Object-relations theory and the work of Klein and Winnicott direct the study of resistance into analysis of the transference which will indicate whether or not the patient can tolerate an analysis of his relation to his analyst in terms of experiencing him as a part-object and, later, as a whole person.

(6) Resistance is defined by Schafer as the patient's response not only to paternal but also maternal authority, as well as to any activity of the analyst that might disturb the "conscious" totality of the patient's personality. The analysis of the patient's resistance should give full recognition to its affirmative as well as to its negative aspects.

(7) Racker's study of resistance/counter-resistance brings out the importance of the analyst's counter-resistance in helping him to understand the resistance of the patient, particularly when it operates as a support to integrative processes within the latter's personality as a whole.

(8) Winnicott, indebted to both psychoanalysis and Kleinian psychology, has shown how different is the significance of resistance in the case of deeply regressed patients where the release and nurture of the true self is essential. At this point the paradox is that to resist the normal interpretative efforts of the analyst may indicate a real cooperation with him at the level that matters.

Jung's View of Resistance

Jung's description of resistance is less full and differentiated than Freud's: he does not distinguish defence from resistance and sometimes speaks of a continuance of the latter as a life-style. Nevertheless, early in his development we find him emphasizing resistance to the analyst as a person. This personal aspect pervades the whole of Jung, as does the tremendous importance of resistance and the need not to attempt to break down the resistance but rather respect it. His emphasis was that resistance is often an indication that a faulty attitude or approach or view of the patient's problem is being held or made by the analyst. He also respected the patient's resistance to the transference when it was archetypally determined and felt to be overwhelming.

Jung, as is often the case, is strong where psychoanalysis has been slower and more fumbling—namely in terms of his emphasis on the resistance as that of one person, the patient, to another, the analyst, and on the need to respect and carefully analyse the homeostatic and other aspects of resistance. He is less strong in the detailed study of resistance, in terms of method and content, that has been carried out by the psychoanalysts. On the other hand, his emphasis on the resistance of aspects of unconscious archetypal potentiality to analysis and conscious realization represents a unique contribution to the subject and affords a wide field for further detailed study and research.

PART TWO

Resistance to the Analyst as a Person

I now move on to the second and less historical part of this study which will concentrate on some aspects of resistance that are very much concerned with those resistances on the part of a patient to his analyst as a person which, however complicated by transference/counter-transference considerations, tend to belong to interpersonal relationships as such. I refer to the phenomena of (1) the patient's envy of his analyst and (2) the patient's fear of penetration by another person, his analyst, resulting either in feared damage or feared new growth. As a corollary of this type of resistance, I shall suggest that a distinction should be made between what I propose to call primary resistance and secondary resistance. All this will be illustrated by case histories. Finally, I shall describe the main aspects of counter-resistance.

Resistance and Envy of the Analyst

Melanie Klein, Wilfred Bion and other Kleinians have called the attention of analysts to the phenomenon of the envy, more or less nihilistic, which overwhelms some patients in respect of the health, the professional skills, even the therapeutic gifts of their analysts (Klein, 1957; Bion, 1962). This involves the patients in having to destroy the efficacy of their analysts' interpretative interventions and penetrations or, when the envy is in-turned, in having to destroy their own capacities to receive and use the efforts of their analysts to their own benefit.

Envy of that kind originates from infantile levels of the patients which have been activated by the analysis and which need to be understood. At such levels we are dealing with envy of the breast, the breast–penis or the penis, i.e. part-objects representing the whole person of the mother/father analyst. The breast and penis are felt to be full of goodness and overflowing but, owing to almost inevitable limitations in their availability, may also be experienced by the baby to be withholding. As a result, envious destructive rage against these part-objects produces the illusion that they are damaged or destroyed.

The extent and potency of this kind of envy are well illustrated in the case of a patient who had experienced delay in establishing a firm working relationship to the breast during the first month of his life owing to the virtual absence of his mother. When she was able to take him on, she did her best to meet his needs but set up a pattern of compensatorily "smothering" and "stuffing" him during his childhood. He experienced much greed, rage and depressive anxiety. In his childhood, and later, these feelings had made him feel very much a bad person—a horrible "shitty little runt"—liable to be bullied by the other boys. As he grew up into manhood, however, the patient discovered in himself capacities to be genuinely witty, kind, intelligent, humane and clean.

These qualities doubtless developed as a reaction formation, but, despite their being defensively employed, they were in fact really his and not false. Nevertheless, the inner delusionary feeling was that of being a nasty little throw-out—a piece of shit—and he had to doubt and denigrate his gifts.

The pressure of this inner delusion activated strong envy and feelings of rivalry, coupled with considerable perfectionism. Out of this grew envy-originated idealizations about me as analyst. In phantasy and dreams he thought of me as coming from a highly distinguished family—artists, cabinet ministers, aristocracy; I had a large estate in the country and lived in a mansion; I had to be wise, able, together in myself, and a compendium of manly capabilities.

Though he made progress in his analysis, he was not altogether satisfied and felt that he could never make real use of my interpretations, and so he would obsessionally rehearse them lest he forget them, as if they were life-giving propositions from on high. As a result he tended to feel that he was not changed as much as he should have been. Further analysis revealed the fact that he felt he needed to keep me at a distance as a person. His envy of the breast, activated by the absence of his mother, was coupled with a terrified envy of the strength, ability and occasional violence of the males in his family. The resulting depression left him feeling weak, empty, worthless and "wet"—feelings that were activated in connection with me. He had to resist my penetrative work because he would be too small to tolerate my big prick in his anus; worse still, he would be found by me to be nasty and shitty inside. This would make me cast him out, as indeed he felt in a delusionary way he had been all his life.

This envious idealization of myself and others made him feel so unworthy and demoralized that he became vigilant to discover flaws and in particular any character defects in such people that could be used as the justification for rageful attacks upon them. The patient's resulting fear of intimacy expressed itself not only in strong, though subtle, resistance but also in an intense feeling of isolation attended by an activist urge to seek concrete homosexual relations in order to by-pass its pain.

When his envy, as well as the delusions engendered by it, became better understood, the patient became more able really to test me out and to assess whether my reality could justify him in taking the risk to enter into a closer and more real analytical symbolic intercourse with me. He no longer needed to deal with me as an envied, dangerous, self-withholding provider of intellectualistic analytic propositions of which he was unable to make much use.

The patient's genuine strengths, abilities and excellent qualities were related to his love of and quite considerable admiration for his father, who was in many ways a sound man but, according to his son, had been weakened by the mother, who subjected him to continual criticism of a castrating and egotistical sort. The son felt that his father was far too compliant and unable to stand up to his wife.

As a result, the internal parental objects worked out as hampering rather than strengthening. There was an internalized bad shitty breast of a maternal sort and a father figure that was strong, able and competent but weakened by a real doubt about potency. The fear was that the internal father object would succumb to the onslaughts of the internal shitty mother or bad breast.

This produced a double attitude on the patient's part towards me. It was all right for me to know him, provided that I did not get close and penetrate him. If that happened, I would know of the inner shittiness and, as a result, reject and despise him. The transference therefore took on a twofold form. In its first aspect, the patient identified with his shitty side in an exaggerated and rather archetypical way, while he identified me with an idealized archetypical expression of the potent good father. In other words, in the dynamic distribution of qualities, he transferred the shitty female feeling on to himself and the potent good father feelings on to me.

The second aspect of the transference arose out of his internal conflict. In this, a potent side of himself, though despising the shitty side, tended to feel overwhelmed by it. It rather wished to have nothing to do with it and to live on the surface of things. This last aspect was transferred on to me, and I was thought of by him as likely in the same shallow way to reject him utterly if I were to meet this shitty side. I would want to have nothing to do with it but, perhaps worse, like the weak side of his father, I might succumb under its pressure and be destroyed. In either event, the resultant pain was feared and felt to be intolerable. The internal image of the split parental primal scene produced in him an inner split, a splitting process in the transference and a split between a longing for a good family life and a tendency to reject it as a nightmare.

It was this transference that produced what I would like to call *secondary resistance*. It is based upon transference and is not to be confused with transference resistance. This secondary resistance involves a high level of illusion, if not delusion, but it is, I believe, effectively analysable by an analyst with agape and respect for the patient's nature and potential self.

Primary resistance, on the other hand, arises in a person in whom the deprived infant within experiences intense fear of savage annihilation from without. It is an extreme extension of the natural, cautious resistance that is involved before permitting a personal interpenetration to take place between two persons. This is not generally undertaken lightly because it can lead to deep involvement, to potential change and, as Jung has uniquely emphasized, to new developments that can best be symbolized by the figure of a child. It is likely, therefore, that many analyses raise questions of secondary resistance mainly, while primary resistance plays a lesser part, owing to the fact that, often, movements into conjunctio experiences of the depth envisaged by Jung are unlikely to become a living issue.

Resistance and the Fear of Penetration

Another kind of resistance, also heavily laden with transference experiences, seems to be connected with taking the analyst's interpretations in a very concrete way, as if they were penetrations by a totally foreign body that could not be tolerated for long. The mildest of these resistances is the simple necessity to prove the analyst wrong, not by considering the reasons why the analyst makes the interpretations but by adducing irrelevant counter-arguments or seeking subtly to shift the premises of the discussion. Another method is to get rid of the foreign body by an act of extrusion. If an interpretation of an "as if" type is made—or one that is describing some new feeling or emotion, the patient, rather than work at chewing and digesting this new thing, will go away and "act it out" in order, quite unconsciously, to show by its results how bad and foreign to his true welfare it is.

A special example of this is where a patient, who used to be noticeable for his acting out and also for his envy, was recently describing to me a number of feelings and attitudes he was experiencing in respect of his City firm, its partners, and his near colleagues within it, as well as towards the economic difficulties that people in the City were experiencing. He was doing this in a markedly relaxed way, despite the real economic crisis. Indeed, he was showing himself less identified than usual with his long-established feelings of paranoid suspicion towards his colleagues, based, as they were, on homosexual rivalry and suppressed passive homosexual longings. Previously he could always dig out plenty of evidence both of "disaster round the corner" in the economic situation and of the dislike and ostracizing suspicion of him that gripped his colleagues. At the end of the session in question I made a comment, not really an interpretation, that he seemed to be discovering himself to be less anxious these days despite the real dangers of the economic situation and despite the fact that some of his colleagues had been made redundant.

After this there was a gap of a weekend and a day during which, as it turned out, he managed to catch a streaming cold. He arrived for the next session full of envious suspicion of his colleagues, anxiety over the incompetence of his immediate boss, and renewed panic over the economic situation. So much for my summing-up comment in the previous session!

Reporting the renewal of his uncomfortable feelings, he began to wonder why he had got into such a state after his last session and volunteered the phantasy that he had had to throw my comments out and prove them wrong. He felt that the basis of this was envy and a feeling that I had put something into him that might have been good for me but was bad for him.

I think that his idea was a sound one. Even if I had made a balanced interpretation like "You seem to have managed successfully to combine envious anxious feelings with more realistic less 'disaster-laden' ones and to have handled the tension caused by this in a way that was less painful", his reaction would probably have been the same. I think that at that juncture he would still have had to reject it as if it represented a penetrative bodily action of a homosexual sort on my part. His envy of me as a repository of "good" experience forced him to feel that if I said anything "good" about him, it was "superficial and unreal", so he threw it out. On the other hand, if I said something "bad" about him, then he felt that that was real and concrete and he tended to act it out as though forced by my "buggery" to do so.

Of course, this resistance of his to me was never absolute, for he himself was possessed of a realistic streak of self-preservation which had generally helped him not to blunder into quite disastrous situations. It counteracted some of the effects of the years of envy that had made him dangerously used to feeling bad inside and "forced" to act this out, while feeling very unsafe if "by chance" anything good happened to him.

Resistance and Fear of Damage by the Analyst

The expectation that the analyst will damage the patient takes on a number of forms. For instance, the analyst may be expected to bring about in the patient dreaded states of disintegration (Bion, 1962), when in fact it may only be deintegration, in Fordham's sense. Or again the analyst will be feared lest he is but one more of a long line of people who will let you down if you become attached to them. More grossly still, the analyst is really only an exploiter of other people's illness and distress.

In all these cases, resistance appears to be a mixture of primary and secondary resistance. Thus the secondary resistances, arising out of transference/counter-transference illusions and delusions, require analysis prior to arriving at the real existential problems of allowing oneself involvement in another person, particularly when the patient has suffered a series of traumata in real relationships in his history.

I propose at this point to illustrate something of this by describing an analytic session.

The patient, a young woman from a rather conventional family which defended itself against consciousness of real emotional problems in relationships, very often presented herself in a somewhat aggressive way. For example, she arrived for the session in question with an expression that was subtly sulky, surly, even dumbly insolent. Perhaps, of course, I was mistaken and the expression on her face was not in line with her feelings. Perhaps it was only a fashionable trendy expression and not to be given much weight.

Anyway, she plomped on to the couch silently and lay still for five minutes or so, remaining silent. She interrupted this to ask about an extra session which she had thought might be available. She dallied with the idea, but it happened that this would have meant coming twice in one day, or perhaps exchanging the session for the one she thought was free—all subject, of course, to my agreement. I felt resistant to this for reasons that became clearer to me as the session went on. Accordingly, knowing that it would be slightly provocative, I replied, "Well, twice in a day is not often indicated, except when patients are feeling really bad and cannot stand a longer gap—or when there are other special circumstances." In myself I reckoned that she was not in that sort of need, that she was not serious about asking for another session and that she was "having me on". So I had tried out that provocative remark to see what would come out.

At this point, there was a silence and then she started to tease me, saying, "Well, much as I love you, I think that one session will be enough!" There was more silence and then another tease: "Of course, I could work up some sort of crisis for you and then I could come!" A further silence ensued, and then "Anyway, you ought to give me the experience of coming twice in one day so that I would know not only by hearsay."

I replied that I would not, but that she was having a nice time teasing me. She half agreed with half a smile. There was more silence. Then she said "I don't know what I should say next." I said "Another tease." Again she smiled, agreed, was silent and then said: "I think I am not in the mood to stay today", and continued silent. I observed that she did not seem to be particularly interested in this mood. She replied, "I'm supposed to be interested in it then? But all I want is to be off." I said, "Well, it's lots of fun, this teasing, but I think it might be covering something up." After a silence, she changed her mood and said, "Well, it reminds me of sometimes wanting suddenly to leave my lover. Sometimes I wanted to stay forever. Sometimes I wanted to get

away—inexplicably. He used to say, 'It's one of your funny moods.'"
I said, "You, both of you, gave up trying to understand them." She
replied, "Well, I felt just now as I did then, when I wanted to go away.
I used suddenly to feel the pressure of his personality and his demands
and felt that I couldn't stand it any longer even though I wanted to
stay."

To explain the reference, I ought to say that the lover was one of
those people who had picked up a number of analytic ideas and phrases
and, according to her description of the matter, used interpretations
upon her in a most intrusive way. He would do this, she considered, in
order to break her down, play upon her masochism and force her to
meet his demands. She said that the interpretations could be very
interesting but that they were also felt by her to be a terrible burden. "I
didn't want all this analysis," she used to feel. "Which, by the way," I
pointed out, "was gratuitous. You hadn't asked for it." The other
thing about her lover had been an unusual demandingness for instant
sympathy, presence and sex, whatever she was doing and whatever her
commitments. Before they finally parted, she had become afraid that
he would destroy her.

She then continued, in the session I am describing, with the
comment, "Maybe I didn't like it about not coming twice in one day,
not because I particularly wanted to, but because it also reminded me
of not being able to see him any time I fancied. He had a busy life, like
you." I agreed: "That seems pretty plausible and must make coming
here remind you of being with him." She said, "Yes, and the trouble is
that actually you look rather like him." All this was confirming what
had been counter-resistance feelings in me (see pp. 79 ff.), and so I
now felt free to make a long interpretation of a more penetrative sort as
follows: "The difficulty really is that this analysis with me is reminding
you of the way in which he practised a kind of enforced analysis, which
was unasked for and felt as intrusive. It seems that side by side with the
richness of the experience you had with your lover, you also suffered
damage and loss, and endured demands that felt so oppressive that an
almost blind revulsive resistance would possess you, even though a
masochistic desire to surrender would force you to come back to him,
so that it is this that comes over you from time to time when you come
to me." She agreed to this with some relief and left more relaxed and
also less resistant for the time being.

This is obviously a resistance that has been exacerbated by the once-
bitten-twice-shy experience—not that the lover was the first to be felt to
be terribly demanding. Indeed, many-times-bitten, many-times-shy
describes better what was a progressively intensifying experience. The
patient's parents, though loving and to the best of their ability really

caring, were nevertheless experienced as demanding, as well as being on bad terms with each other. At an early age she was sent to boarding school, perhaps because of the situation at home. The teachers were felt to be strict and repressively demanding, though, for all that, she enjoyed work, games and the arts. A typical memory of this period was sitting in school looking through the window and longing to go outside and away into the open air, an experience often repeated in the consulting room.

At adolescence she went to a school where the headmistress was experienced as sympathetic, easy to talk to and possessed of common sense. This tempered the underlying rebellion, with the result that a reasonable fulfilment in school life from then onwards masked the underlying trouble. With adulthood there emerged a somewhat aggressive, self-willed, though moody yet acceptable, personality, albeit there was hidden within a longing for love and dependency and for the feelings of power proper to an infant whose needs are being adequately met.

This what was, in principle, a warm personality could give the impression of having very little sense of relationship, give-and-take and consideration, while at the same time swinging between "being hooked upon someone", as she called it, and compulsively breaking away from the addiction.

In situations where disputes or differences of opinion arose, this patient could present herself in a light that made some people feel that she functioned entirely egotistically. She would state categorically a position that had been somewhat prematurely arrived at and then try to push it through with the threat of walking out if the other party did not accede to the demand. Furthermore, all this tended to be done without real discussion and analysis of the feeling. Thus an almost strong and formidable impression was given, even though underneath there was neediness and a passion for loving of a highly dependent, yet rebellious, sort. In terms of Jung's function type psychology, the feeling of this patient is probably introverted, although superficially it would appear to be the opposite.

It was natural, therefore, that she resisted me as her analyst and that this was based upon the fear that I would overpower her by my interpretative presence, hamper her freedom by enforcing attendance at sessions, get her addicted to me and then destroy her or, worse still, let her down by disappearing or getting ill or dying, a theme with variations discernible all through her history. Her resistance therefore expressed an exaggerated affirmation of her existence, a function of survival, a resultant of a series of situations of "getting hooked", being exploited and suffering for it. She therefore needed to test me out as to whether I was really different from what she experienced in her parents, her teachers and lovers, and whether I could really understand her nature and her needs. Only after prolonged reality testing of me could she begin to take the risk of making a relationship with me.

The resistance arose spontaneously to protect her against a need for love so strong that it could foster credulity and the risk that her introverted feeling would fasten upon an unsuitable object in an addictive way. Despite appearances to the contrary, this patient could not be accurately classed as one of Winnicott's "false self" patients, because she always needed more than just "management" in Winnicott's sense, because she could benefit from analytic interpretations, and because she was capable of experiencing her real feelings to a considerable degree—even though from time to time she dissociated from them and half-persuaded herself of the total validity of the false defensive ones.

Failure in the Analysis and Resolution of Resistance

One of the problems that seriously exercise analysts is that of resistance which does not submit to analysis even when the point has been reached where the value of the resistance has been fully acknowledged. In Chapter 2 (p. 22). I referred to Michael Fordham's paper describing a patient's resistance to a fundamental analytical point that caused her, after many years of analysis, to defy all efforts at interpretation despite progress having been made in general health. It involved an ending that in view of the treatment having lasted for so long a time was hard to bear. Sometimes the issue arises with patients seeking analyses ostensibly over a sexual problem. The latter is not solved, even though the patient improves in terms of increased contentment, relaxation and reduction of anxiety. Analysts sometimes meet factors that seem so strong, although not very meaningful, as to justify the use of the notion of "causation". The patient is *caused* to leave the problem unsolved, perhaps because it would, if solved, seem to him to collide with other aims and considerations that imperiously demand total obedience. In the case referred to, Fordham describes how he, as an analyst, gave notice that if the point at issue could not be resolved, the analysis would have to be brought to an end. Resistance can seem sometimes autonomous, even impersonal, and far transcending a mere clash of wills, so that there is nothing that either analyst or patient can do.

The practical clinical problem for an analyst, who is involved in his patient's development and whose acts of patience and acceptance have multiplied themselves "unto seventy times seven", is when to stop and call it a day. He is likely to be assailed by two systems of guilt. The first centres round the notion of uncaring abandonment, the second around obstinate pride that can persist in continuing even past the point where further analytic activity could prove to be mutually destructive.

When termination, as true ending (Fordham, 1978), cannot be achieved, then an existential decision about termination, as a cut, has to be made in which an element of guilt must be tolerated as part of that human condition so vividly and poetically described in Jung's famous last paragraph in his *Answer to Job*.

For all this, however, a last word needs to be said in connection with guilt. Guilt generally suggests that unconsciousness is present somewhere in the analyst's awareness of the situation, even after a prolonged attempt at analysis. Such guilt certainly stimulates a good deal of thought and much clinical discussion, arising as it does out of the fact that analysts tend to be cautious and loathe to admit either that the patient seems unanalysable or that they as analysis have failed. Of course the practical risks of failure, with all the loss of time and money involved, can be modified by refining diagnostic tools for the selection of patients suitable for analysis, but this sometimes leaves unsolved the problem of the unsuitability for analysis of certain individuals and the question of what has happened to them to make this so. One source of help that can be gained from past experience suggests that, as time goes on from decade to decade, advances are made that open analysis to people hitherto thought to be unsuitable. The consolation, such as it is, offered by these facts is that analysts are inevitably limited by being born into the conditions of time and space at a certain point in history, that coming to terms with this is part of the problem of mental health, and that a measure of failure is built in to the human condition. Guilt needs modification if analysts are to serve their patients well. Nevertheless some guilt needs to be tolerated as a spur to improving the quality of their work.

PART THREE

Counter-Resistance

The case described in detail on pp. 75–78 leads me on easily to a short discussion of counter-resistance. I noticed this phenomenon to be operating in myself in the early months of the patient's analysis. The form that it took was that I experienced a resistance to making penetrative interpretations for some time. It also took me some time to get the hang of the case in depth and as a whole. Interpretations came out a bit laboriously and I felt annoyed that she was so resistant: she would shift the premises of a discussion; she could be blind to links; she could tease; she could falsely present herself as a shallow person without knowing consciously that she was doing so. I could say silently to myself, "She damn well won't let me interpret. All right, I damn well won't make the effort and she can go to hell." This counter-resistant and retaliatory response inside me turned out to be a reverberation to her retaliatory tendencies, but of course it was not acted out. It began to occur to me that this was not the whole truth about her and that I was identifying with her resistance and not recognizing at first its validity. This, in a way, could be called (to borrow an adjective from Racker) my complementary counter-resistance, coupled with a certain amount of neurotic retaliatory counter-resistance against this "bad mum" who would not let me be a "nice neat analyst".

As time went on, however, I began to see that her resistance was forcing me to attempt to improve as an analyst so that I could better understand the resistance as part of the whole and thus become more concordant with it. While not much liking the power-driven unrelated and orgiastic aspects of her personality, I could empathize into her situation and, as described in the session, could manage an interpretation that was appropriate for the time being.

We are now, I think, in a position to build upon Racker's introductory sketch of counter-resistance, which was cut short unfortunately, by his untimely death (Racker, 1968). My present view is that the analyst's resistance to his patient can be grouped together under five headings.

(1) The non-neurotic resistance.
(2) The neurotic resistance.
(3) The reactive counter-resistance.
(4) The complementary counter-resistance.
(5) The concordant counter-resistance.

The Non-neurotic Resistance of the Analyst

Resistance to involvement at a deep level with the personality of another person may be regarded as an aspect of normal psychodynamics. In instinctual communities, it gets expressed in a certain reticence towards strangers—if not hostility. A reaction formation may sometimes be expressed in terms of an over-open hospitality to strangers, but seldom can such a degree of openness be expressive of depth. A sophisticated analyst as well, as a result of his own analysis, will surely have accepted this preliminary caution as normal to the human condition. On the other hand, during the time when he is considering working with a patient and the patient is considering working with him, he is using this caution to help him to become clearer in his own mind as to whether he is willing to attempt the setting up of a therapeutic alliance with this individual or not. In doing so, he is beginning to mobilize what Racker terms a disposition to open himself to undertaking the analysis of another person. This caution may be regarded as part of the non-neurotic resistance to the patient experienced as a stranger and hence an unknown quantity. Naturally this resistance lessens as the analyst gets to know the patient and finds the situation manageable.

There is another aspect of the analyst's resistance that may be classed as non-neurotic, at least at the beginning of his career, because it is based upon the strangeness of the experience. This has been well thought out by two young psychotherapists in training (Copans and Singer, 1979), who have commented at some length on the resistances discovered in themselves as beginners—which no doubt are well enough known to seasoned therapists as well. The resistances they refer to are of a generalized kind and are based upon sheer anxiety. I would classify this as non-neurotic, for it is, in the beginning, a reaction to a more or less unknown enterprise, involving a feared limitation by and vulnerability to the creative and destructive forces that could be released by their therapeutic efforts. This resistance can certainly be modified by the analysis and training but it is activated by the fact of being faced by the palpable existence of the patient as such. Often, and it can be quite a surprise to the beginner, he finds himself fearing entanglement or being swamped by the horrific experiences of his patients. If his early cases turn out to be difficult, he can find himself fearing inadequacy in meeting both their criticisms and those of the patient's friends and relatives, and, often exaggeratedly so, the criticisms of his own peers and supervisors. Such fears are mainly inner phantasies, and a well-supported trainee is likely to realize this quite soon and will be able to resist the temptation to act avoidance out in gross ways.

The Neurotic Resistance of the Analyst

Some subtler forms of resistance may still arise. The analyst may unconsciously avoid really being with his patients or really listening to them. He may unconsciously keep them at arm's length by losing them inside some chosen therapeutic model that has been suspiciously easy to set up. Experience shows that the main safeguard against responses of this sort, neurotic as they are, is the analysis of the beginner analyst and the skilled supervision of his work.

The most striking instance of the neurotic resistance of the analyst to his patient occurs when he entirely misses a point in his patient's material, particularly when it is a point with which he is normally well acquainted. It can be also the case when the point is quite new to him and has so far been successfully resisted throughout the analyst's life. Supervisors of trainee analysts are sometimes in a position to observe this in their supervisees and it is well-known that the things that are missed are sometimes brought by the trainees back into their own analyses. Dieckmann's paper shows how resistance within himself to a theme of separation at a particular phase of his life made him take for a time similar material in his patient as illustrating the theme of fratricide instead. Jung himself describes conscious resistance to infantile regressive material (Jung, 1913). "The analyst," he writes, "must not shudder at dirty work."

The Reactive Counter-Resistance

Reactive counter-resistance seems to arise out of annoyance at a patient's continued resistance. Talion responses take place within the analyst's feelings and he may even find himself, in a driven way rather than as a policy, ceasing to make interpretations, mainly in order to punish the resistant patient. The acting out of this tends to be counter-productive. It is obviously preferable to register it, to integrate the emotion thus generated, and to use it for deepened investigation of the patient's resistance. I certainly experienced this annoyance in the case of the last patient described.

The Complementary Counter-Resistance

This seems to arise when the analyst finds himself in a state of identity with internal, often parental, objects inside the patient. These internal parental objects often resist analytic understanding on the part of both patient and analyst and cling to old-fashioned rationalization. The parental internal objects in the last patient were clearly rather stereotyped, conventional and non-understanding, as well as non-analytic. I experienced this as a feeling, for a time, of surprise at the nature of the patient's resistance, but later, and more significantly, as a feeling in myself of resentful thick-headedness about her difficulties. This thick-headedness was a feeling more appropriate to her parents than to me—at least in the analytic context.

The Concordant Counter-Resistance

The concordant counter-resistance is achieved when the analyst begins to understand the patient's resistance and to be able to make interpretations that are complete enough to do justice to the whole situation of the patient and so become acceptable. I experienced this with the patient in the session discussed on pp. 75–78. When we got the clue that justified and made sense of the patient's resistance, there was relief in it for both of us.

The Subjective Experience of Counter-Resistance

Some of the subjective experiences of the analyst in counter-resistance may be listed as follows:

(1) The analyst experiences angry, frustrated feelings coupled with feelings of revenge.

(2) If an interpretation is being contemplated, the words expressing it seem almost to stick in the analyst's mouth.

(3) This seems to be accompanied by a feeling that it is premature to venture an interpretation because it is felt that:

(a) the interpretation would damage the patient or increase negative resistance;

(b) the patient would need preparation before being able to receive interpretations;

(c) the analyst would be the object of scorn on the patient's part for being unscientific or just "thick";

(d) in the minds of some sophisticated patients, the analyst would appear to be dull, boring, bourgeois, inadequate or just crassly undergifted. Indeed, he sometimes actually feels himself to be so.

In all this, it is likely that the analyst is feeling the more unconscious aspects of his patient's resistance and much depends upon the analyst's ability to understand in full how and why these are so strong. The hesitation to make interpretations under these circumstances may be understood as appropriate procedure, particularly with reference to the difficult problem of *timing* in interpretation. Counter-resistance and its subjective components as listed can give the analyst a clue as to when to keep off interpretation. We say that the time is not right. The patient is not ready. The analyst is not in a sure and concordant position on the basis of which to act interpretatively. Indeed, if anything, he is in danger of going in for one of Bion's "psi" interpretations, i.e.

something is done interpretatively by the analyst in order to discharge and relieve himself of feelings of anxiety, discomfort, alarm and shame about the patient's situation and his feelings of responsibility about it as his analyst.

Counter-resistance hesitations may be distinguished from other situations where it is also an analytical virtue not to interpret. The analyst sometimes needs to content himself with silently forming hypotheses about the drift of the patient's development and to wait until a process has been completed within the patient without interference. We need to give the patient breathing space, to avoid fussiness, not to "jog his elbow", above all to avoid being too "knowing". An example of this has been provided by Massud Khan (Khan, 1974), who described the case of a silent adolescent who was enabled to communicate verbally only after a considerable period of silence during which his analyst had to go in for a judicious withholding of therapeutic intervention, whether through excessive interpretation or reassurance, coupled with a "sentient, concentrated, alert attention"—a listening with "mind and body". Too much weight given to the importance of our activity as such may cause us both to under-respect the spontaneity of growth process in the patient and to pretend to a more holistic understanding of the patient's situation than is likely to be the case.

These last considerations have a part to play in the special case of counter-resistance hesitation as well, though this latter hesitation may be regarded as a stimulus to waiting for increased information and perception of the kind of interpretation the patient needs.

Conclusions

In this chapter I have worked out some of the ways in which our understanding of the phenomenon of resistance has undergone a number of historical changes.

It seems that we have reached a point where there could be some agreement that resistance is essentially the activity of one person in relation to another person, or an image of a person, whereby the resisting person takes up a stance, maintains a system, a stasis, a pause or a hold-up. He holds himself up like a pillar—with undertones of phallicism and ecstasy. Thereby he opposes the other person and causes him to stand back. The pause and the phallic ecstatic element suggest an excited wish behind the resistance that is sustained at least until the other person has been fully tested out.

A hypothetical formulation might be that the "system" or "stasis" elements in resistance arise from the rigidities inherent in a contrived or indeed "false" ego, while the "pause" or "hold-up" elements might stem from true ego-self sources. By contrast, the "ecstatic" and "phallic" dynamisms provide the libidinal drive behind resistance for its own sake and gratification. In some patients there can appear at times to be half-conscious excited wishes of this sort that they allow to run away with their personalities. Such Dionysian type elements can be understood as manic compensation for unexperienced and damned-up potential in people whose capacities for living experience have suffered frustration and damage. Unfortunately, when this has not been perceived and analysed, their potential personal relationship to their analyst and their long-term development are at risk.

A formulation such as this seems to represent a point towards which a history of the concept in all psychotherapy of an analytical sort seems to have moved. Originally resistance was considered in terms of fears of pain and shame involved in submitting to analysis. This moved on to a study of the modes and methods of resistance. In expanding the subject of a consideration of what the resistance is defending, the study has moved on to an investigation of the interpersonal process whereby what is being resisted is both the impact of or penetration by another person and the threat this seems to pose to the integrity of the self.

My illustrations from patients' material were intended to illustrate more concretely how envy, often overwhelming, together with memories of past damaging intrusion and anticipatory fear of devastating penetration, can cause patients to resist the personal influence of their analysts. These considerations make it easy to distinguish resistance from defences by virtue of the fact that in resistance the wholeness of the patient's personality and its present organization are felt to be under threat by the analyst. In the case of defences, on the contrary, the subject is defending himself against the pressure of a part of himself that is either feared or disliked. For example, as Fordham has shown, these parts thought of as "bad" parts are "perceived" by the patient, through projective identification, to belong to the analyst—often in an attempt to safeguard the patient's "good" parts from attack or destruction by the "bad" ones (Fordham, 1978). With Winnicott's deeply regressed patients, however, the distinction between defences and resistances ceases to be relevant; a blind push for survival in the face of threatened annihilation is the order of the day. Prior to treatment through analysis, the false self and ego, together with whatever there may be of a rudimentary real ego, seem to cooperate to provide protection against feared disaster. After therapy gets going, clinical evidence suggests that the resistance-defence put up by the false self works either through uncomprehending compliance with interpretations or by rejection of them as absurd. The true self, on the other hand, with enough hope in it to seek analytic psychotherapy at all, employs resistance-defence to reject all therapeutic efforts save those that seem to meet the over-riding need for "first months of life" care.

Resistance can be divided into two types. Secondary resistance is very heavily saturated by archetypally originated infantile transferences. Primary resistance involves the direct resistances of a person to the possibility that a changed, if not quite new, development of life might be brought about by an interpretative and interpenetrative relationship with another person. A deeply conservative force is at work, which is in a way justified until reality testing has taken place or, when necessary, the patient's capacity to carry out reality testing has been facilitated. Of course, secondary resistance has a basis in primary resistance but it is heavily influenced by the infantile experiences and the personal history of the patient, which in turn determine to a great extent the archetypal configurations involved.

Two phenomena that look like an infantile expression of a primary type of resistance have been uncovered by Winnicott. Patients who regress to the point where their dependence upon the maternal environment is nearly absolute and who have been interrupted in the early process of finding and creating the maternal object either (1) go in for a "moment of hesitation" prior to experimenting with a "kind of intimacy" with the analyst or (2) seem to resist endlessly all normal analytical and interpretative processes. This they need to do in the service of the true self because of their need to reproduce with the analyst something in symbolical terms as close as possible to the experience of the early months. Here the attempted destruction of the maternal object, her survival, the objectivity of her reality and the birth of concern and care for her represent the real point at issue—a critical one for the establishment of the infant self's sense of security. In such cases, the real resistance would paradoxically be expressed in any acceptance by the patient of the normal analytical procedures and interpretations. This would in fact only collude with the purposes of the false self.

The insistence of Winnicott's patients upon the recovery and release of the "true self" may be seen to make links with Jung's work on the symbolic imagery of the "child" of the conjunctio. The latter possibility may arise from a transformation of the strong incestuous drive that can arise in certain forms of analysis. In this case, however, resistances can arise either through a refusal of the pains of the frustration of acted out sexuality or through fear of the possibility of a radical rebirth as something that might unsettle or even revolutionize established patterns of self-realization and living.

The emergence of such new life can represent a further development of the individuation process, and it is in relation to this that the analysis of resistance can play a very important part. It implies, of course, the analysis of the transference. This not only promotes integration of the patient's personality owing to the fact that content projected on to the analyst can be withdrawn from him and built into the consciousness and personality of the patient but also promotes the development and integration of capacities for interpersonal relationship by means of the analytic work done on the encounter between the patient and the analyst as real persons. It is certainly in the unique analytical relationship with the "other" person, the analyst, that the uniqueness and potential individuation of a person may be promoted, whereby he "becomes a psychological 'in-dividual'" as Jung puts it, that is, a separate indivisible unit or "whole"—or again "a single homogeneous being [which] embraces our innermost, last and incomparable uniqueness" (Jung, 1963).

The individuation process appears to be a potentiality in persons that urgently insists upon realization. Perhaps it is the deepest significance of resistance and counter-resistance to be both symptom and agent of just this.

Chapter Five

Archetypes, object-relations and internal objects

To consider the part played by the analyst's personality and the significance of the many forms of resistance that emerge in the patient – analyst relationship leads me next to the study of the conditions that make possible the formation of object-relations and internal objects. In analytical psychology this can with profit be related to archetypal theory which, I shall argue, has a special contribution to make to the subject. The practical problem is that of a person being able to link the experienced objects of the personal and non-personal environment on the one hand with the appropriate internal, though objective, processes of the self on the other. There is a gain if this can be done in such a way that their reality in their own right can become a true psychological experience for the subject and hence can be appropriately related to by him because thereby greater objectivity and a fuller and deeper relationship can be attained.

Psychoanalytic theory, through the work of Klein, Fairbairn, Winnicott, Kohut and Kernberg and others has shifted part of its emphasis from the study of instinctual drives and their satisfactions as such to that of the human need to establish relations with other persons in the non-self world: mother, father, siblings, relations, friends and colleagues and so on. The ingredients of this study are centred round topics like the establishment of self-representations and object-representations and damage that can be suffered in the process.

This latter includes narcissistic personality damage, one result of which is that the individual thus damaged cannot have a realistic experience of himself or others and has perforce to live in a world of inflated and compensated images such as those of "grandiose self", coupled with a mirror transference to the analyst, or "idealized good or bad parents" coupled with an idealizing transference (Kohut, 1971).

Furthermore, a serious hold-up and damage can take place to the normal progress from what Kernberg (1974) calls the normal autism of the 4th to 12th week, where no differentiation between self and object is experienced, right on to a developed state at two years where there can develop an integrated self-concept and identity, and integration of good and bad self-representations and of good and bad object-representations. Finally there can take place damage to or frustration of the actual process of developing experientially object-recognition, object-testing and object-using as described by Winnicott (1941). On the side of analytical psychology, the damage to the deintegrative–reintegrative process described by Fordham (1976) may lead to similar results.

Most of these writers assume what has been called an "average expectable environment", though Klein seems to have focused less on this and more on the spontaneous emergence of unconscious infantile phantasies, often projected on to the environment and then re-introjected to form objects little related to external reality. It was perhaps Winnicott who most emphasized the importance of the objective environment as actually supplied by mother, father, siblings, and others. This either facilitates or hampers in quite detailed ways the infant's capacity to negotiate his passage from auto-eroticism to object-relations formation and the development of a sense of object constancy. Somewhat in contrast with this is the systematic work of Fairbairn and others like Rycroft around the question of the disposal of internal objects by the infant once the formation of such objects has been achieved. They are designated by him as good, accepted objects or bad, rejected objects in accordance with early gratification or deprivation at the breast. In obsessional cases both good and bad objects are felt to be inside the patient. In hysteria the bad is kept outside and the good within. In phobic patients both good and bad objects are conceived of as outside; in paranoid patients the good object is conceived of as inside while the bad object is kept outside. It is difficult to underestimate the importance of these formulations, and they thoroughly deserve the attention given them by psychoanalysts and analytical psychologists. As a result they have greatly modified drive theory, linked it with objects and dispelled the suspicion that they were content to conceive of and study drives operating *in vacuo* and mainly simply seeking discharge.

The present chapter, then, will concentrate on the process of forming object relations with the person normally primary in the individual's life, namely the mother. A further limitation will be to confine the scope of the topic to that of the place of archetypes and archetypal images and themes (in Klein's terms, unconscious infantile phantasy) in the child's approach to the mother on the one hand, and the inaugurating and responsive presence and action of the mother on the other. When an object relation of this sort is successfully negotiated, there will be promoted in the infant an emotional security and ability to enter into real personal relationships that will serve him all his life—long after he has separated from his mother, whether psychologically or in terms of spatial and temporal distance, or as a result of her death. This survey necessitates the setting up of some simple working definitions of "archetypes", "archetypal images", "object relations", "internal objects" and "innate release mechanisms". It will attempt to demonstrate some of their interrelationships.

First, then, the archetypes. I shall, with Stein (1958), take an archetype to be an example of a theoretical entity, i.e. a postulate found to be useful in understanding and handling natural phenomena, in this case, in the human psyche. Jung's postulate, based on countless observations, is that there is present in the psyche a predisposed potential to expect that real objects when presented to the individual can be experienced in accordance with certain forms, patterns, or images—to be found, we may add, in the "average expectable environment". It is also thought that although this predisposition can propel the human child from within to move in the direction of finding external realities that correspond to his archetypal expectations, it is nevertheless also an essential task for parents, educators, and cultural agencies in general, to present infants, children and adults, young and old, with objects appropriate to their archetypal expectations at each phase in their lives. It seems essential that these objects can be tangled with, indeed grappled with, as we shall elaborate upon later. This is a very different experience from perceiving objects only as images.

Jung distinguishes the archetypal "image" from the dynamic archetype "*an sich*" that "sets to work ... ordering the conscious material into definite figures" (Jung, 1942). It would seem that the phrase "conscious material" surely refers to the object in contrast to the archetype. It would seem, too, that the notion of the presentation of an object seems to combine the two complementary meanings of the word "object". It is something thrown on to the senses, i.e. a stimulus. It is also something one throws things on to. Thus the archetypal predisposition awaits the presentation to or stimulus of the senses by the object, after which it throws on to the object a meaning that is archetypal. There comes into being a real object that can be internalized and become a real "internal object", not a phantasy or image only, unbased on reality an archetypal object.

When it comes to the presentation of the mother to her newly hatched, or newly born, we are familiar with the phenomenon of the innate release mechanism (see Fordham, 1957). For instance, ducklings attach themselves to the first object that looks like a mother duck, whether it is a real duck or a wooden one. Furthermore, apart from the well known Harlow experiments with rhesus monkeys, who attach themselves to fur-covered frames as if to their mothers' furry bodies, we are well aware of the release of the baby gull into feeding activity when it sees the red spot on the underside of the mother-gull's beak. Similarly the human baby, under normal circumstances, latches on to the nipple when presented with the breast—within a very short time after birth, as if predisposed to do so, given the stimulus. In each case, the presentation of the appropriate object seems to inaugurate into action a predisposition to attachment or feeding behaviour.

In addition, Melanie Klein (1932) has introduced us to the complexities of part-object psychology in which the part-object represents the whole-object, whether it is the breast or breast–penis representing the mother or, later, the penis representing the father. Out of the perception of body-parts there then arise phantasies of the good nourishing breast, the withholding breast, the punitive breast etc. Later, in adult life, we may still find ourselves the heirs of part-object psychology and describing one personal quality of the mother i.e. her physical ugliness, or her primitiveness, or again her beauty, or kindness—as if it summed her up as a whole. Even after the growth of perception enables the infant or child to see the mother as a whole person, a similar tendency can be observed. This is expressed in archetypal images like the bliss-giving mother with whom one wishes to feel fused, the good gracious mother, the spiritual mother, the castrating mother, the devouring mother, the withholding mother, the abandoning mother, the witch mother, the bad sexual mother, and the jealous mother. All these images really refer to part-views of the mother, organized no doubt by archetypes and sometimes focused on one and the same mother-person, but more often distributed among a number of different women, selected (to use Kleinian terms) as if in accord with predetermined unconscious infantile phantasies.

How does this come about? I adhere to Fordham's view that it is a function of deintegrative processes within the original self which appears at birth, or even quite early *in utero*, to be a more or less undifferentiated integrate (Fordham, 1976). This integrative, deintegrative and reintegrative process looks like an innate capacity of the self. At birth, or possibly even before, certain archetypal potentialities in the child separate out—like latching on to the breast, sucking, crying with discomfort, discovering parts of the mother like her breast, face, teeth, eyes and, gradually, varying parts of the baby's own body. The self ceases to be an undifferentiated integrate and progressively unpacks into its archetypal elements. These expectations become activated in response to appropriate objects and, owing to the fact that there is always a certain clash between expectations and reality, bits of ego-consciousness develop around the parts of the baby's body involved. As a result, a certain charge of libido is directed towards the objects in question, and inaugurates the problematic process of relating to them.

What have we so far? We have first the object, breast, or later the mother as a whole, no doubt experienced largely as a configuration of sensations and colours, in connection with which certain subjective experiences take place, like gratification or displeasure and with whom feelings of fusion or identification, both projective and introjective, seem to come into being. Secondly we have a postulated archetypal predisposition to release a tendency to relate to that object and to organize it and selectively shape it in accordance with the archetypal theme in question.

This leads to a process, described by Neumann as "secondary personalization" (1954) but containing a difficulty highlighted for us by Winnicott. It is the problem of how the baby—or if delayed, the child—can get the sense of something more, namely the inner reality of the object, in contrast to an external or even an hallucinatory view of it. Winnicott (1969) can make a psychological distinction between a "subjective object" and the "object objectively perceived", in terms incidentally that further illuminate the Jungian distinction between archetypally originated images and the real concrete objects to which they refer. It should incidentally be emphasized that for the purposes of psychotherapy that distinction does not require demonstration in epistomological terms, for it refers to naive subjective experiences of the object—an experience that may be regarded as part of what adds up to make emotional health.

The importance of this realization lies in the fact that the release of the capacity to form relationships with objects experienced as real is not only vital for the individual's survival, nourishment and creativity of all sorts, but is also closely connected with the development of his ability to feel real and substantial within himself. Furthermore this capacity to distinguish between inner and outer reality and to relate the two together is an essential function of the self operating through ego-consciousness.

How does the baby learn to develop an experience both of himself and of the not-me? It is Winnicott's researches that have supplied a new dimension to our Jungian contribution. He has shown in some detail how this experience emerges spontaneously out of co-operation between (1) the efforts of the real mother and (2) complementary activity on the part of the child.

The function of the real mother is a dual one (Winnicott, 1963). She is to be an "environment-mother" and an "object mother". It is for her to look after the environment and help him to feel contained and also to hold her baby in such a way that he does not feel "over-impinged" upon, by her or any other object. In this way, he can leave the environment to her and thus be freed from the anxiety and rage that can so quickly overwhelm him if his needs are not met and alternative hallucinatory satisfactions fail. The instinctual mother also attempts, spontaneously enough, to maintain herself for her baby as a constant and enduring object—really there, whatever the experience of the baby. This furthers two of her maternal aims. The first is to facilitate the child in maintaining object-constancy—a fundamental achievement closely connected with developing an intact ego, as Fred Plaut has recently elaborated upon in "A note on object constancy or constant object" (1975). The importance of this could be that otherwise the baby may, in his struggle with object fragments, become fixed in a serious splitting process, for if the good and the bad experiences induced are too intense and too extremely polarized, he not only splits the mother into many mothers—good ones and bad ones—but he also splits inside himself thus entailing libido-loss through conflict. The mother's second aim is to be present and to maintain herself "in being" as an object to meet the child's unconscious phantasies (Klein) or his archetypal expectations (Fordham). Winnicott could speak paradoxically of a useful illusion on the part of the baby that he "creates the breast" or "creates the mother" (Winnicott, 1951, pp. 238 ff.). Of course the breast and mother are already in existence, but not yet as an inner experience in the child's psyche. He needs time and space, breathing space, within which to play and to experiment with his archetypal expectations in relation to the real object, and thus to form in his own mind a convincingly real breast or mother—neither overweighted by the archetypal image, nor undernourished by a rather dead piece of concrete fact.

The child's contribution, on the other hand, is distinctly active, as has been described by Winnicott in several papers. In consultations with mothers and babies—thousands of them in his lifetime—he would present a spatula to the baby seated on his mother's lap (Winnicott, 1941). A typical sequence is observable. The baby reaches towards the spatula and then at once withdraws, apparently needing space and time for hesitation. He then takes it again, plays with it and "destroys" it in phantasy, perhaps by banging. He then seems to renew the object and finds that it still has survived and really exists. During the play he offers to feed the mother and the doctor with the spatula and enjoys their reciprocal play with him. Finally he throws it down (often, it should be added, with laughter or rage) when "enough is enough". Or he gets on to the floor and takes it up again. Winnicott became impressed by this repeated sequence, for it seemed to him to represent essential experimental moves prior to the baby's becoming able to enjoy and relate to the spatula. A central point in this play is to attack the object in order to see whether it survives the destruction and has a life of its own, and thereby to discover its usage potential—noise-making, feeding, disposability, etc.

Winnicott moved on in his paper "Primitive emotional development" (1945) to study the "complementary" experience that can develop between the child and his mother. This can be succinctly described: a child with instinctual urges and predatory ideas meets a mother able to provide milk and wishing to be attacked by a hungry baby. Under her care their aims can sometimes come so near together that moments of illusion occur, and as Winnicott points out, the baby may be balanced between taking the breast either as his own hallucination or as something belonging to external reality and involving the "non-*me*ness" or "otherness" of the object. As adults say, "It might be too good to be true—or it might after all really be true." Winnicott (1969) made a radical distinction between "object-relating", which is based upon subjective responses, and object-usage", which involves the effort to consider the nature of the object *qua* object. The capacity for object-usage can begin with the breast and the mother and then move on to "object-usage" in the wider world, or it may need to be learnt in analysis through "use" of the analyst as an object. Light is also shed on this activity by studying the infant's relationship to the "transitional object" (1951). A bit of cloth, blanket, or dirty old doll is "found" by the infant: it is an object and not just his hallucination. He then assumes absolute rights over it, so that it must not change without his permission: he pours upon it his instinctual love and hate. He attacks and mutilates it—and finds it survives as a reality with its warmth, texture and vitality. It persists thus until it is spontaneously de-cathected, emptied of meaning and discarded.

Winnicott argues that the experience of this gets diffused into the cultural world—a space between inner psychic reality and the external world. The "thingness" of the transitional object can help the child to differentiate a growing "inner reality" from a "not-self" world that is also gradually becoming sensed by him, and to work upon their interrelationship in cultural, religious and artistic terms. To return to the individual once more, we may say that, in a way, the transitional object may serve to symbolize the self under its aspects of integrating inner and outer experience into a whole—as Fordham has suggested (1969).

The royal road to the capacity to relate to real people may now be formulated as follows: as a result of play, experiment, violence and love, the child, with a co-operative mother that "remains in being", can marry together various archetypal expectations from within with a real mother object. He thus achieves a basis for real relationships with objects that are not distorted by delusional phantasy arising from archetypal sources. These relationships may be good enough, or too bad, or good and bad, but they are real rather than idealized and may be designated *archetypal objects*.

Once object-relationships have been established it becomes possible to take inside or internalize these composite but real objects. They become the internal archetypal objects that play, for weal or for woe, such an important part in the inner life of the individual. They determine the nature of his responses in real relationships in the outer world and can be a comfort to him when he is alone—or a curse.

Being alone, of course, represents a nightmarish experience for many patients. They feel depressive anxiety. It seems clear that no suitable internal mother-object serves them or gives them any support, strength or comfort. They feel half dead in an empty destroyed world, devoid of objects. In a paper entitled "The capacity to be alone" (1958), Winnicott describes the function of internal objects in what he describes as the "capacity" to be alone. This is to be regarded as a positive experience rather than a merely negative one, like defiance, or the fear of loneliness, or a persecuted wish to be alone and away from it all, or even heroic notions like that of the "nobility" of the solitary human being. His view was that there is one basic human experience "and without a sufficiency of it, the capacity to be alone does not come about; this experience is that of being alone, as an infant and small child, in the presence of mother—a paradox; it is the experience of being alone when someone else is present" (Winnicott, 1958, p.30). The experience referred to is that of the baby lying quietly, safely contained in the cot or pram, within earshot of his mother working about the place and holding the situation. This facilitates a condition in which the baby can relax, be unintegrated, and flounder, without any part of him having to look after the situation. This relaxation depends upon his feeling protected from "impingement" upon his inner core from without and from the consequent "threat of annihilation" (Winnicott, 1956) accompanied as it must be by fear and terror. It is in fact this threat that contributes, particularly when internalized, to the rage and terror experienced by him if left alone or living alone for any length of time. He feels isolated in a dead, unpeopled world, and a prey to unnamable terror. His internal objects lack anything that is holding, strengthening, comforting and present. If, on the contrary, the infant has been met often enough and long enough in his expectation of a holding mother that "remains in being", while keeping a watch on the situation, he can then relax, with a feeling of safety, into phantasy and an experience of himself. Winnicott sensitively describes a kind of enjoyment that can then become available to him. In this quiet state, also enlarged upon by Louis Zinkin (1978), the stage is set for the emergence of an id-impulse or sensation, probably in connection with the mother, that will feel real and satisfying. It will come to a kind of climax, called by Winnicott and other psychoanalysts, an "ego-orgasm"—not, be it noted, an "id-orgasm". It is a personal experience that strengthens the ego, giving the child a sense of personal substance and identity. After sufficient experiences of this sort have been experienced, then the individual can introject the ego-supportive mother as an internal object and enjoy being alone for varying lengths of time without frequent reference to his actual mother. In terms of Fordham and Winnicott, the child has moved through a number of stages. First, an actual breast or an actual mother is presented to him. Then, archetypally predisposed as he is to deintegrate and to respond actively to this stimulus, he grapples with the real breast and the real mother and after much play, experiment, love and hate marries his archetypal expectation to the real breast or mother. He "creates" the object for himself and for his use. He finally introjects this, after repeated experience, so that it becomes an internal object and a potent part of his psychology—for good or ill. The movement is from archetypal imagery on to object-relations and the formation of internal archetypal objects. Thus the archetype, hitherto only a predisposition, has nourished an effective inner capacity and results in a piece of creation on the part of the child. (I need hardly mention that I am taking the word "mother" to cover the personal or substitute mother, the nurse, "containing groups" like the family, the school, the church, the club, the town, the community, neighbourhood, nation and even the "world" or "cosmos"—everything real that is creative/destructive, nourishing/withdrawing, containing/excluding, etc., etc.)

This account of the interrelationship of archetypes, object-relations, object-formation and internal archetypal objects carries implications for clinical practice. Two groups of patients are involved. First, there are the somewhat schizoid patients whose grasp of the objective reality of the presence of other living three-dimensional people is weaker than usual, so that, sometimes grossly, sometimes subtly, other people can seem no more than configurations of lines, colours and movements and identifiable shapes—or be perceived as archetypally originated images but scarcely as archetypal objects.

The problems of such patients are best met by a regular, frequent, reliable and continuous treatment, if they can tolerate it, as this opens out to them an opportunity to explore the reality of the analyst. At first, less frequent sessions may be indicated for those patients who are unusually terrified of impingement by the analyst upon their private self. Overall, however, they are unlikely to be able to come to grips with the reality of the analyst as a parent-object unless they see him frequently. Otherwise delusionary phantasies may effloresce during the intervals between sessions.

Secondly, there are patients whose object-relations have been governed by mainly negative experiences of the breast or mother as presented to them in infancy. I list some of the negative experiences: difficult and unduly protracted deliveries; awkward and painful holding; prematurely timetabled infant care, sometimes with no reference to the infant's spontaneously emergent needs; unreliability and/or absence of the mother; being left unattended for long periods, often to cry themselves to sleep; schizoid or depressed withdrawal on the part of the mother; not being allowed to cry much because of parental mistaking all crying to be a signal of distress. Under such circumstances, then, archetypal images of mothers, whether abandoning, frustrating, suffocating, torturing, delaying, tantalizing, or neglectful, may overwhelm them and provoke in them infantile rage and violent retaliatory impulse. Their match with the breast or the mother is accompanied by a clash that is painful enough to establish a continuum of relationships with bad objects. As a result, mainly bad objects become internalized and over-determine all their expectations and experiences of life in the future.

For such patients also, analysis needs to be frequent—to give the analyst–patient pair a fair chance to work systematically through transference/counter-transference and to open out the way, through the sufficiently reliable, faithful "agapaic work" (see pp. 34 f.) of the analyst, to activate hitherto unawakened archetypes in the patient and to relate them to the reality of an analyst experienced as a good and bad, perhaps good enough, but at least a reliably present parent–analyst. Once more, new internal objects of a good enough sort may be able to be established to redress the balance in the patient's psyche and to enable him to realize more positive sides of his nature in what now seems to him to be a perhaps more positive world, not wholly dangerous or destructive. There are further practical reasons for frequent sessions. First, gaps of several days are extremely painful and difficult to bear for patients doing such work. Secondly, such pain, if prolonged, tends to make it likely that they will build up fresh defences that will impede the work of analysis.

My simple theoretical set-up has now been described—or at least the barest bones of it. I would now like to give a clinical example of this, slanted to illustrate the theme.

Case History

My patient, Tom, opened his analysis with the following complaints:

(1) He suffered from emotional restlessness, and difficulties about finding a suitable work-environment. He was in the world of finance, but felt isolated and spurned by professional colleagues in his small work group.

(2) He had unsatisfying relationships with women, whom he idealized but feared and even loathed.

(3) He felt the cold to the extent of needing eight blankets and two eiderdowns on his bed in the winter. Furthermore, numerous colds and constant bouts of winter 'flu had made him fear he would lose his job.

To his first session he brought a dream. He was on a trawler in the North Atlantic surrounded by icebergs. Because of dangerous underwater ice, there was nothing to do but stop the engines and wait. He thought this meant that his work-relationships felt ice-cold and persecutory and that he had better call a halt and enter analysis. At a later point in his treatment, he saw the stopping of the engines as a paralysis of thought and emotion that he experienced when in unsympathetic company. Later still, he noted that people were being taken by him impersonally—as icebergs and that he thought of himself as a machine controlled by a mind. We may imagine from this that Tom suffered from a failing environment.

He was in his early thirties, unmarried and living alone—only occasionally seeing his parents and one or two friends. He felt himself disliked as odd by his colleagues, whom he saw, with envy, as easy-going, clever and not very responsible—often doing minimal work with maximal show. His bosses, he felt, did not appreciate the hours of conscientious work he put in, both in the office and at home. He feared involuntary and explosive bowel-motions when away from home, so that, as he arrived for sessions, he feared he would soil himself on my doorstep before he could get through the door and rush to the lavatory.

Sexually, he masturbated a good deal, often to phantasies of whipping healthy, strongly built whores, whereas the few women he knew tended to be sick or disturbed. If they were not so, he constantly scanned them for blemishes. He also feared that he was really, deep down, homosexual in a way that would be apparent to others.

His life, in general, was felt to consist of hard grinding work, about which, however, he would generate images. He likened himself to the driver of an express train crossing the heartland of the USA. Or he was the captain on the bridge of an ocean liner ploughing through an Atlantic storm, while the rest of the ship's company were enjoying themselves at dinner, with dancing and music, in the warm lighted saloons below. These people he envied—for their women, their "man's talk", their insouciance. It always seemed to him that it was very hard to gather up the resources of energy or skill needed to do his work or keep well. Indeed he felt the same insufficiency on the part of his family, his firm and his profession, and also of English people as a whole. Furthermore, while longing to be at the top of his profession, he half-unconsciously ensured failure, just as during the war he had refused opportunities to be trained as an officer in the Navy, feeling very unhappy that he could not tolerate the responsibility involved.

Tom, thus, was lost in phantasy and though seeming very practical and down to earth was in fact isolated from objects in themselves. This drove him into attempts to be "knowing" and "insightful" about himself and others, but his judgements were superficial, at the best phenomenological, and nearly always cynically unkind. He used the surface aspects of a person, including himself, to describe the whole. His paranoid ruminations led him into serious delusions about the nature of other people. He often felt slighted, talked about behind his back, and hence felt angry and explosive. His defence was to become obsessional in his profession and to make sure that his house was kept polished and clean, both before and after his marriage, which took place some years after entering into analysis. Tom thus presented as a markedly obsessional and anal personality beset by a number of homosexual paranoidal and delusional systems. He was over-concerned with survival, unable to use his powers to the full, and sad about the dearth of mutually invigorating personal relationships. It will be clear that his relationships both to himself (a machine) and to others (icebergs, or uncaring and successful playboys) were heavily saturated by archetypal imagery. It was felt by him to be a serious problem because he felt too shy and indeed too paralysed to be able to test out his "objects" in everyday life by attempting much in the way of relating to them.

Tom's feelings about himself can also be laid side by side with some of the realities of his appearance, his family matrix and history and his day-to-day situation.

In appearance, Tom, despite his asthmatic bronchitis, was a strong sturdy man. He would walk for miles, with a steady stride, leaning slightly backwards with an internal image of himself as if he were like a ship pounding forward nearly head on to a heavy wind. His head was square and his face unsmiling, grim, and drawn. When he came into my room he hardly looked to the right or to the left, as if blind and deaf to looks feelings or words emanating from me. He seldom let on to noticing me much, save for anything that would confirm his anxieties, envy or rivalry, though later evidence suggests that his range of observation was a good deal wider. His aim-directedness drove him with such impetus that he would bang through doors and even brush my door-opener aside (before the days of entry-phones, I may say!). He looked like a man whose object-relations had been rendered inflexibly unadapted by a heavy load of archetypal content, and upon whom hostile internal objects made constant demands. It was partly because of this latter factor as well as a number of others that, despite his grim and at times unprepossessing look, I found myself in sympathy with him and slowly developed a liking for him. That was something he could activate in others as well, though he seemed unusually unaware of this capacity.

Tom's history had been an uncomfortable one. His mother and father were first cousins; his original cultures Prussian, Levantine and, through maternal connections on both sides, half-English.

His mother, known to have suffered maternal deprivation, was a chronic asthmatic—never quite "with him". In his infancy, her milk supply had failed and caused a crisis of near-starvation in him. Later, understandably, she "stuffed" him with food, over-cosseted him and often took him with her to spas in search of a healthy environment. His father, tough but anxious, had failed in business, largely through rigidity and lack of adaptation. He retired young, to look after the invalid mother; he drove Tom intellectually to win scholarships to boarding school and university, with threats that he would end up in the gutter if he did not work; he threatened him too with violence, especially if he did not do his mathematics on Sundays! Actually his father meant well by him for he wished to save him from the "disasters" he imagined to be always round the corner, and, maybe, from a fate similar to his.

Tom had a younger brother who, he thought, was easy-going, charming and successful. He never seemed to do any work, and, when young, interfered with Tom's toys. Tom's sister he considered to be privileged, "as girls are", with an easy life, doted upon by father.

So Tom was not able to make satisfactory object relations in his family, through vigorous impact, through play or through experiments of all sorts. As a result, they were not so much real people as figures, saturated by archetypal phantasy.

Tom's analysis required that I be a safe, reliable, continuous, and holding object and parent-analyst, able to do reconstruction within the transference/counter-transference situation. It was indeed quite possible to reconstruct the relationship with his mother, e.g. out of the following evidence: (1) his feeling of the insufficiency of resources in himself, in his firm, in England and, transferentially, in me through "my incapacity" to really help; (2) his need to have a sick woman and to scan healthy ones for blemishes; (3) his phantasies of a fresh strong woman, even a whore, whom he could whip and have intercourse with. Transferentially he could sometimes give me a word-whipping for something wrong or "foolish" I had said, and he was always on the look-out for signs of illness in me. The suggested reconstruction is that he had not been able in childhood to get the sense of a "real" mother who was there to meet his needs. On the contrary, he had always seemed fated to a reversal, necessitating that he treat her as an invalid. Because of this, he had not been able to attack (whip) her or test out her survival capacity. Thus the real experience of his mother, including his emotional and phantasy response to her, had triggered off archetypal phantasies like that of the empty withholding breast, the sick, disabled distant mother and later the stuffing mother. His consequent rage generated further archetypal phantasies of the loathsome and robbing mother as a result of which, in order to survive, he had endlessly to work like Sisyphus, with inadequate resources in a perpetual grind. It also landed him in hating women and yet all the while dreaming of a good one somewhere to be found.

Reconstruction with the father-object revealed little sense of his father as a real person. His internal object was the taskmaster-father who is never satisfied, who devours him out of anxiety and who confirms the Sisyphus feeling that even grinding work can, with luck, do no more than stave off ultimate disaster and exhaustion. Transferentially, this meant that he felt that I lived off his substance and relentlessly required of him the grinding work of journeying to sessions and working to pay for them—with only very slow progress for his pains. At the office, he believed the same of his boss.

Reconstruction with the brother revealed an image of a shallow charming playboy who always got away with it. Tom's envy of his brother's capacity for taking holidays and securing relaxation fostered in him a sense of unfairness that he was denied such delights. Workwise, his colleagues were seen in this light as well, while, transferentially, I seemed too easy, too optimistic, an "india-rubber man" with a lot of resilience, and far too fortunate in life. There was some shadow in this, for Tom took the matter of his holidays very seriously and often longed for a shallower, less demanding and sybaritic way of life for himself.

Reconstruction with the sister showed an envy for women resulting in a longing for a relaxed passive homosexual dependent relationship with a man who would be less anxious and less sadistic than his father or his boss or, in some of his moods, myself. At the same time he was often able to experience such feelings with me in the transference during sessions.

Summing up, we may say that Tom's experience of his family, though doubtless factually well based, had activated an archetypally saturated phantasy life, to the exclusion of real archetypal object-relations. The internal objects formed were of a distinctly delusional sort that falsified his work and domestic experiences to a degree that filled him with terror and rage, expressed in psycho-somatic functional disorder.

As the analysis proceeded, he was able to get at my reality and test me out over each one of the transferential distortions I have mentioned. He got to know me as someone much less demanding and devouring than his father, and he extended this principle to considering his boss to be not so demanding a tyrant either. He got to know me also as one able to feed and sustain him to quite a degree, and effectively, unlike his mother as he had experienced her in, perhaps, exaggeratedly archetypal terms. After careful scanning he decided that I was no more an invalid than I was a stuffer. He could also see how the projection of the failing internal mother object on to the firm, his profession and even England was not fully supported by the facts.

He came to the conclusion too that I was not merely just an india-rubber ball man, full of easy resilience, like the image developed of his brother. He discovered this of his actual brother as well, and indeed of the colleagues in his work who had seemed so similar. That modified his homosexual rivalry on the one hand, and eased him over his fear of passive dependent homosexuality on the other.

Finally, reconstruction of his envy for the privileges of women loved by their fathers facilitated a modification of his despair that he could never relax, for he became just about able to experience relaxation as a result of ceasing to struggle against relaxed passive homosexual feelings both with me and his colleagues.

Above all, perhaps, he came to recognize that the best results in his work-field were not necessarily secured by the external grinding work of Sisyphus. On the contrary he could see that it demanded much more play, more relaxation and more friendliness to release the creative imagination essential to its success.

Tom's case illustrates the analyst's function as a real person in this kind of analytic treatment, which is after all a suitable situation within which his delusional systems could be identified, named and tested out. In Tom's case, the actual persons in his original family tended to activate archetypal configurations in the "primal scene". The transference of them on to me made it possible to analyse their origins so that in the end they could be compared with the real mother, father, sister and brother involved. This also enabled him to perceive the reality of his wife whom he had married during his analysis, together with that of his son whom he learnt to love. Friends and colleagues as well were experienced in a less delusional way. Furthermore, he could assess how his criticisms, fears and dislike of aspects of family life had been transferred to me and indeed to analysts in general, for he had had the idea that analysts tend to criticize and break up family life.

In his relationship with me, Tom could push, pull and criticize me, though with considerable anxiety. He thus could begin to assess more accurately my reality which I did not try to obscure from him by the unremitting use of screen-technique. This enabled him to begin to notice features of me other than those picked up by his transference, so that the ruling archetypal images and internal objects were modified together with a lessening of delusion in his relationship with me. Moreover, he did not only project upon me but he "used" me as a lavatory-analyst, a listening and sympathetic father-analyst, a relaxed homosexual father–brother–colleague person, and a "purveyor of wisdom" who sometimes seemed annoyingly right. He could also experience in connection with me envy, rivalry, love, hate, and a sense of outrage, almost, that I could survive in life. My function was to "remain in being" through all this, so that he could form an object-relationship with me and take me in as an internal object.

In my naive experience of Tom I found him to some extent a grinding, tiring patient owing to his long periods of unrelatedness. From a complementary standpoint, I felt from time to time, just as his mother must have felt, that I could not help him much (see pp. 149 ff.). I thought I felt, as his father did, irked by his aim-directed fear that rendered him sometimes paralysed and inflexible in feeling and thought. I could imagine how his brother felt when I wished that Tom could appreciate my "quick-witted interpretations" for which he could sometimes make me feel almost guilty and facile. Putting myself also in his sister's shoes, I could imagine that he made her feel how easy her life was—as he could make me feel, despite the long hours I worked as an analyst. However, as Tom's object relationships and internal objects shifted and became less persecutory, I found no difficulty in feeling that his presence was much more agreeable and enjoyable, and the greater ease with which he could deploy his homosexual feelings greatly modified the strain.

Tom reached a point where he could enjoy a reasonably satisfactory family life, a cessation of compulsive masturbation, and a reasonably creative output in works felt by him to be recognized by his bosses and colleagues. His cynical, destructive and persecuted attitude to these people was sufficiently reduced to enable him to experience a sense of belonging. This does not mean that his problems were all solved. He could still fall a victim to his complexes, but the attacks tended not to last very long and his more benign and constructive objects could remain relatively intact.

The case history of Tom, like most case histories of treatments in which psychological progress can be discerned, is among other things an illustration of the individuation process with special reference to improved object-relations with both himself and other people. There is no space in which to expatiate on many other aspects of his situation, but perhaps enough has been described to indicate that Tom has changed from being a rather "odd" person to becoming a more individuated person. Despite having the same parents his siblings turned out very different. Characterologically they were both less tensed and possibly less gifted. Tom, as the oldest child, combined an "enhanced" sense of responsibility both towards the siblings to come and towards the sick mother. A tough, gifted boy, for all his bronchitic asthma, he as the eldest was expected very much of in an ambitious way by his anxious and progressively less successful father, so that in different ways both parents relied upon him to an unusual degree. Coupled with this was his resentment at the births of the younger siblings and his envy at the easier lives he was certain they had been given by the parents. Guilt about the anger, resentment, envy and rivalry that had been aroused in him produced a sense of isolation from others together with proliferation of phantasy about his own situation and about the attitudes of others towards him and about the content of their inner life.

The analysis in general, and in particular the feeling of being understood, enabled him to be much more realistic about himself and others and to understand his life as a whole. As a result the striving near-defeated side modified. He felt less odd and gradually more centred, more full of himself and hence less an oppressed prey to impersonal archetypal phantasy.

Tom's case illustrates, among other topics, the thesis that improved object-relations with self and others are an essential aspect of the individuation process. This is partly because the real nature of persons is highly individual and unique unless it is obscured by collective patterning and becomes stereotyped, whether this stems from archetypal elements from within or from social and familial pressure from without—or indeed a combination of the two. It is also because improved object-relations force the individual to withdraw the projections of parts of himself from others and to own them as his. This promotes integration and renders a person in-dividual, i.e. no longer divided, but one. The analysis of a patient's object-relations and history within the transference clears the way for the emergence of individuation—a process, it must be repeated, that is spontaneous rather than contrived, though one where the patient is in need of containment, support and validation by his analyst.

Chapter Six

Reconstruction

Introduction

My description of the basic elements involved in the process of analysis, repair and individuation has so far sketched out topics such as the personality of the analyst, some responses of the patient and particularly those connected with resistance and counter-resistance, and the establishment by the patient of object relationships and internal objects and the dependence of this upon the presence of the therapist under the special conditions of the therapeutic set-up.

Sound object relating, however, involves an appropriate feeling and cognitive response on the part of the subject to the reality of the object in the here and now and *at this particular moment of time* rather than to an over-subjectivized image of it that has been *heavily influenced by the experiences of the past*. Such a relatively simple-sounding phrase covers a multitude of analytic problems such as: (1) the tendency of the patient to respond to present situations with a degree of emotional intensity that is grossly and exaggeratedly inappropriate by any objective standard of judgement; (2) a distorted and one-sided characterological development, fixated at some earlier point in his history, and crippling the patient's handling of the day-to-day problems of adult life; (3) difficulties about living in an appropriate span of "present time". A patient may be "frightened out of his life" by traumatic experiences in the past and "overwhelmed by anticipatory fears of horror" in the future. As a result he cannot live in the present either. There is little libido available for a real experience of the living moment in a continuum comprised of the immediate past, the present and the proximate future. The experience of time for him loses significance, datability, expansiveness and its public character (Boss, 1979). The result is a hold-up of the growth that arises out of the past or might be inaugurated in the present.

106

Reconstruction in the Now of the Transference

One of the advantages of the analytical set-up is that this sort of problem tends to be reproduced in the wide area of interaction between the patient and the therapist and can be studied and handled as if in a state of pure culture.

The following example is illustrative of this point. A patient, on her way to the first session after a week's break during which I was not seeing patients, stopped to do some shopping. When she returned to her car, she was unable to start it and, to cap it all, the ignition key jammed. A nearby garage announced that the mechanism was broken and would take a week to repair. The session was to begin in twenty minutes time. My patient telephoned me but could get no answer. The house happened to be empty at the time save for myself, who was seeing a patient, while the telephone naturally was switched off in the consulting room. In a rising rage, if not panic, she persevered with ringing until about five minutes before the session was to begin. She then did not ring again during her session time, although I would of course have been free to receive the call. When she did not arrive, I telephoned her after twenty-five minutes, as I wondered whether there had been a mistake. I got an angry reply to say that her car had broken down, she could get no reply on the telephone and had returned home. She then wrote a letter saying that I could never be got at by phone, that the whole thing was impossible, and that perhaps she should not come again, until I was free to receive her. In response, I telephoned and confirmed the next session.

When she arrived for this, she was nearly speechless with fury but could just manage to say how everything was now totally changed and how after three years she no longer believed in her therapy. After this kind of absolute statement, the angry phantasies began to be expressed in a rather heartbroken way. She knew that I could have been writing during the holiday break, so she became sure that neither I nor my household really wanted her to bother me and that it would be much better if she were told straight that she was not wanted and she could go away until she was. It was horrible to be tolerated only as a matter of duty.

I remarked that she was thinking of me as being very divided in my mind to be functioning like that. She replied that it had always been like that at home. They said one thing and acted the opposite. Prior to this incident she had often described to me her feeling-toned experience of her primary family, always with a factual care that seemed plausible. Great love was professed but she could never get access to her parents. Her father was irascible, infantile and tyrannical and professed a special relationship with God. Her mother had to keep the household together and to get enough money for the relatively simple needs of the family had to write articles for the weeklies. This involved a considerable expenditure of time, so that she could not be disturbed. Physical signs of affection were always in short supply, and hugs from mother, though genuine in feeling, were limited to the few occasions when she had free time. My patient said that she "knew when she was not wanted", but her parents never said so straight. The children competed for whatever overt expression of love and approval there was, but according to my patient, her two sisters had more success in gaining it—through their academic and artistic success. For her part, my patient mainly felt deprived, angry, and heartbroken, in addition to finding herself slowed down in her thinking, thick in the head, and relatively unsuccessful. She even managed to gain a reputation—that nobody else wanted and her sisters had succeeded in avoiding—of being "the fool of the family", a title that in my view was essentially unjustified.

At this point, she suddenly said that the fury she had felt with me had now become a cold fury—just like the cold fury she had felt when as a little girl she awoke one summer night feeling terribly cold because she only had one blanket. She lay for a long time icy cold and furious with her mother for not providing more blankets. Finally she got up quietly and put on some day clothes. I remarked that it was interesting that she did not think either of going to the linen cupboard and finding a blanket there or, more likely still, of going to her parents' bedroom. After all, most parents would want to meet her need and warm their little girl—maybe in their bed. Her reply was that it would have been quite unthinkable to wake them or even to make a noise and thatanyway this incident was but one of many similar ones. Indeed the suggestion that she might have gone to them was far too good to be believable or true. She added that she had found her therapy also too good to be true and that it couldn't last this way. It felt like a fairy-tale that was now ended.

In subsequent sessions, she remembered how her father's work as a minister of religion had always taken absolute precedence in the household. He was to be available to his people and was not to be interrupted in his study. Likewise mother would openly long for peace and quiet and complained of ceaseless interruptions when she was struggling to write.

My patient expatiated more upon her childhood longings to be hugged and physically made a fuss of. They were mainly frustrated, as the family was physically undemonstrative save in terms of violence. Furthermore she remembered that in the middle of her rage with me she had developed a phantasy that I would be wanting to get rid of her because she had heard that fees in London, where I also worked, were higher than those she was paying in the provinces where I was seeing her. This linked with her childhood view that money loomed large in her mother's activities, by contrast to her father's apparent incapacity to deal with it.

I have indicated at some length the main points of the patient's communication to me during a short period after the emotional disturbance just described. The whole incident may be regarded as illustrative of the emergence of powerful emotions, belonging to the past, into the therapeutic relationship in a way that was striking to the patient and demonstrated to her the degree to which unconsciousness of them had handicapped her for most of her life. The analytic implications are worth spelling out.

(1) My patient had, in accordance with her ascetic do-it-yourself psychology, not registered very much her feelings about one fact, namely that I had not been available to her for a week. The incident with the car took place on the way to the first session after the break. The frustration over her car and the unanswered telephone call had released, to her surprise, an enormous rage and other disturbances quite disproportionate to the seriousness of the incident itself.

(2) The extent of that disproportionate response makes it likely that the disturbance was about something very deep or connected with a level of great vulnerability in early life. The word "deep" here could refer not only to the past but also to the archetypal factors released in early life and becoming increasingly dominant at largely unconscious levels.

(3) The anger at my inaccessibility for a week was made up of more than an adult response of irritation and represented a reactivation of her anger with both her parents for their different kinds of inaccessibility to her when she was a dependent child. Her anger with her depriving mother and her violent and frustrating father was in a way impotent as if directed towards giants. It was fear-filled and heartbroken—a function of shattering disappointment. A child's response to such a parental environment is to develop, as a first line of defence, idealized images of "good parents". However, when this kind of defensive manoeuvre repeatedly proved ineffective, apathy and bitterness set in. In the case of her treatment something of the image of the idealized good parent had been revived once more in connection with me—only once more to be dashed to the ground in the incident just described.

(4) The unconscious need to bring these feelings into the therapy was further implemented by a fresh and temporary emergence of that paralysis of thinking process already mentioned as a feature of her childhood experience. This is evidenced by her not being able to phone

me during the time of her session and, perhaps, by her being unable to make alternative plans to reach me. The paralysis of thought made it easy for her to feel without any doubt that I, like her parents, was really inaccessible and that I was being protected from her and other patients by my family, just as she had wished to protect her father likewise. Moreover she could feel that, like her mother, I was busy writing and that just as it was in the case of both her parents, according to her view of them, my concern was not genuine and I was in reality only attending to her out of duty and, like her mother, busily "making money" in order to live.

(5) These experiences with her parents had not only activated but had also been shaped and intensified by archetypal predispositions to experience parent figures under stereotyped forms, like those of the powerful mother as the giver and withholder of life, and the violent, frustrating father as a primitive Ouranos, Saturn—or even Jahweh, with whom her father was especially identified. Indeed these had become archetypal images (see p. 90), heavily saturated by collective archetypal content by comparison with and distorting in her eyes the individual actuality of her parents. It was these internal objects projected on to me that were causing her such an intensity of emotional distress and were so much in need of understanding.

(6) When we consider the complicated background of my patient, remembered by her in bits and pieces and certainly not as an interconnected pattern, the contribution made by the analytic setting stands out clearly. In the case of my patient a certain modification of her defence systems had begun to take place as a result of entering therapy, with the consequence that the intense emotional and attitudinal system of complexes was now able to come out in the analytic relationship much more fully and as a whole than ever before. To her, this was all the more striking for being in such apparent contrast with her positive and loving feelings for me, which had consisted partly of idealizations but also of feelings of genuine gratitude for my acceptance of her and for listening attentively to her communications. The upheaval, however, activated as it was in relation to me, connected her more vividly than ever before not just with bits but with the whole attitudinal under-current that had operated unconsciously for most of her life. This had subtly influenced her feelings about herself, distorted her personal relationships and considerably hampered her full fruition. She could now realize better how, as a result, the difficulties and disappointments of her past had made her regretful and sad at heart if not bitter and, in a blind sort of way, often grimly despairing.

(7) It is safe to say that real change was inaugurated by the unheaval. Instead of everything ending in separation and loneliness, it was becoming possible to discuss the matter in the open and for it to be analysed in detail—without destructive rancour but with maximal understanding. The emotional disturbances over the incident could settle down within her psyche over a period of a few weeks, as compared with happenings in her past that might have involved months of brooding, as if in a fog, over not properly understood wrongs and neglect. Thus in the past she had all too easily dropped, as if through a hole, into a kind of ground base of painful feeling that had developed in early childhood and had, in a cumulative way, gathered strength and reinforcement through the years. This ground base of feeling had, however, hitherto remained undifferentiated and unanalysed, owing to the fact that it was normally split off from everyday consciousness. The loss of libido thus suffered had had a twofold negative effect upon her personality. One was to render her positive approach to life tentative, unsure, cramped and only partially successful in the deployment of her undoubted gifts and talents. The other was to increase the stress involved in maintaining the high standards required of all its members by her family and lead to a paranoid suspicion of the motives of others, an expectation of them that was too high in its demands, and an obsessional imposition upon herself of very high standards of duty—in each case to a degree that exposed the vice of a potential virtue. In other words, the image of her environment that she had "created" (see p. 93) for herself was disappointingly at odds with her deepest longings and ideals. It always seemed to her to be frustrating and unmanageable and it reinforced feelings of pessimism and hopelessness that often swamped her aggression and left her feeling isolated and alone.

(8) This unhappy picture of her world had landed my patient into a kind of "do-it-yourself" psychology as a working plan for survival, but a plan that could not finally meet her need for warmth, dependence and help. A shift of attitude was needed and the incident described in this chapter was an enabling one. She could in a way experience her childhood feelings in the safe enough situation of an analytical relationship. She could understand them better through a reconstruction of their origins and an acceptance of them by both me and her as inevitable in the early part of her history. Furthermore she could become more used to the forms through which these feelings tended to express themselves in adult life, and hence discover ways in which the energy in them could be gradually transformed into an ability to experiment in more satisfactory ways with relationships in the

present—at first especially in relation to me. Her life could then be gradually freed from the dead grip of the past—a sentence that hints at the significant fact that reconstructive analysis can facilitate a kind of mourning process. Thereby the past may be allowed to die and be accepted as dead. Then it can become something to be grieved for, to be angry about, regretful over, and to be understood. Whatever is valuable in it can be digested and processed into the psychic metabolism. What is left goes out as waste. It is this process that releases libido for new life, new development and new relationships.

It might, incidentally, be noted here that when bereaved persons seek psychotherapeutic help, they sometimes quite spontaneously review their relationship with the dead person and also the life of the latter in a reconstructive way as a part of their mourning.

History and the Psychological Experience of Duration

The capacity to make reconstructions living rather than formal depends upon how vividly the naive sense of duration has been experienced by the therapist himself and how truly involved in the present he can be. He needs freedom from identification with his fear, love of, and adhesion to the past. He needs to have foresworn all pretensions to a tight control of the future and to have accepted how imperfectly, in principle and in fact, the present can be known.

Such desiderata if accepted are bound, however, to stimulate the general question as to how such a relatively relaxed attitude to the phenomenological experience of duration can become available to the inhabitants of "this dangerous world". Certainly the foundation of a sense of duration of this sort must be laid in infancy, and depends upon intelligent and careful nursing on the part of the mother in the daily detail of nursery life. This is because the very young child appears to have no sense of the passage of time or of the position of objects in the space around him. In consequence of this his needs have to be met during the early months of life as quickly as possible, for five minutes can seem an eternity, while objects absent or elsewhere seem not to exist. It seems that their introduction to space and time can become traumatically premature if young infants are kept waiting as if in a vacuum long after the point in time when a need has arisen, is being signalled, and in connection with which tension is rising. Such experiences can be felt as cruelty and be shatteringly frightening.

Provided, however, that the introduction to the experience of space and time is only very gradually made, then the present can become a good enough experience. As the infant's capacities for imprinting, for recall, and later for verbal communication, develop, then pleasant enough memories of the past, coupled with sanguine enough anticipations of a future, can get sufficiently established to make the experience of duration, and even of clock-time, an enjoyable one. In connection with this, it should be mentioned that certain correlations can be established between the naive experience of duration and a range of psychiatric entities. For example, in deep depression the subjective experience of duration seems as if a minute lasts almost an eternity, while in manic states duration is experienced as if like lightening. Also in states of disintegration the experience of duration seems broken up and meaningless.

It might indeed be argued that it is vicissitudes in good and bad experiences of duration, linked up with growing awareness of calendar time, that colour an individual's interest in more collective studies like history. The latter is, of course, introduced to individuals in a variety of ways. In traditional education it used to be seen as the political and military history of a culture. More recently the history of everyday things, on the one hand, or of the child's town or locality, on the other, is added or substituted. Much less often is personal history considered. While lovers and reasonably cooperative or close families often enjoy reminiscences together about happy and other events in their shared past, less often do they discover meaningful patternings as a whole in their individual personal lives.

By contrast, however, analysts with a sense of history are likely to be interested precisely in *(a)* the personal histories of their patients as it becomes possible to reconstruct them out of the mass of material which they bring to analysis and which includes memories, bits of behaviour and clues that arise out of their transferences and *(b)* the psychological and social history of the times during which patients are growing up. Under the second heading the more general question would be whether patients have been brought up within a family and a society where strong religious and cultural forces attempt to mould children in a pattern-imposing way, or whether they grew up in a permissive but caring or a permissive and neglectful environment, or according to some other pattern of child rearing. More specifically, consideration might be given to whether they were brought up in the days of Truby King, Benjamin Spock or some other fashionable system, or whether indeed their mothers in particular, but also their fathers, were reasonably instinctual people who could remember both the positive and the negative aspects of their childhood and so feel their way into meeting enough of their children's real needs.

Naturally enough, the sensitivity of analysts to history will be found to vary infinitely, as well as their sense of the present and the responses to it that might be considered appropriate enough. In addition, it is possible that the reconstructive aspect of analysis is but one of its arts and arises out of personal predilection and a gift which, incidentally, includes a capacity to change hypotheses and to be open to fresh evidence. For all this, however, it may be insisted that some generally acceptable points can be made about the kinds of clinical situation that might be expected to stimulate reconstructive responses, especially within the transference/counter-transference situation. These points will be considered on pp. 120 ff.

Reconstruction of the History of Analysis

A study of the literature on reconstruction in psychoanalysis and analytical psychology does not yield much of a harvest—a somewhat surprising fact in view of the extent to which it has been used in practice and the fact that it deserves investigation both into its scope and limitations and into the phenomenon that it arouses a fair degree of controversy among psychotherapists.

(a) Reconstruction in Psychoanalysis

We first meet the notion in Freud's well-known study of the Rat Man (1909) in which he used the word ''construction'' rather than ''reconstruction'' to express the idea. It was as late as 1937 that Freud specifically used the word ''reconstruction'', in an essay on technique in which he compares his work as an analyst with that of an archaeologist in the following terms:

> Both have an undisputed right to reconstruct by means of supplementing and combining the surviving remains. Both of them, moreover, are subject to many of the same difficulties and sources of error. The analyst works under more favourable conditions than the archeologist, since he has at his disposal material which can have no counterpart in excavations, such as the repetition of reactions dating from infancy and all that emerges in connexion with these repetitions through the transference (Freud, 1937, p.259).

Again, we actually find Klein in *Envy and Gratitude* affirming ''the right—indeed the necessity—to reconstruct from the material presented to us by our patients detail and data about earlier stages'' (Klein, 1957, p.1). This seems a significant statement in view of the impression sometimes gained from their literature that Kleinian analysts tend to give two-dimensional interpretations in terms of unconscious infantile phantasy, referring to the here and now and without reference to the dimension of the past. It is not clear in fact whether in their clinical practice the actual process of reconstruction, as against its end product, is conveyed to the patient or not.

A later writer, Rubinfine (1967), describes how the use of the couch can facilitate in patients, through their adoption of an horizontal position, the recovery of early states of feeling and primary-process thinking which greatly ease the work of reconstruction. He also draws the attention of psychoanalysts to Bartlett's theory of memory which elaborates the way in which a patient's unconscious memories of his pre-verbal experiences may be discovered to have become grouped under patterned modes of experiencing that colour all similar later experiences, including those of the present. We may think that these patterned modes look rather like some aspects of those complexes that an analyst, working with reconstruction, might wish to reduce to their elements in order to promote thereby a more satisfactory adaptation to the present realities of the patient's world.

In a preliminary paper on reconstruction Novey (1964) argued the case for understanding historical reconstruction to be an intrinsic part of the process of therapy, so that "an attempt is made to see the patient and have him see himself in some continuing context in which his present modes of experiencing and dealing with himself and others are a logical outgrowth" (Novey, 1964, p.279). In a significant, but little-known, later book published posthumously (1968), Novey pointed out that reconstructions may often be acceptable to a patient "whether or not they coincide with the actual course of prior events" (Novey, 1968, p.148). This is because "the original past events were experienced within the perceptual scope of the patient and were influenced, if not actually determined, by his affective states at the time" (Novey, 1968, p.148). Finally, Novey had no doubt at all that when a patient is capable of making use of reconstructions, their impact upon the way his "past is seen cannot be overestimated as a force determining the course of future events. The very concept of history as a predictive instrument suggests that today's view of history will influence tomorrow's course of events. The existence (for instance) of optimistic or pessimistic outlooks is significantly based on the appraisal of past events, and such mood states bear considerably on what will actually happen tomorrow" (Novey, 1968, p.149).

Klauber (1968) ascribes the psychoanalysts' "sense of conviction" about the validity of a historical reconstruction to "the judgement that a complex assessment of the interrelationship of psychological motives and external pressures has been satisfactorily achieved. This is a judgement of process rooted in the immediate or distant past of the individual and as such a judgement of historical type" (Klauber, 1968, p.83). Influenced by Croce and above all Collingwood, with his definition of the historical process as one "in which the past, so far as it is historically known, survives in the present" and his better-known phrase, "all history is contemporary history", Klauber attempts to assess accurately how this operates in the analytical session and warns against over-simplified expressions such as "repetition in the transference" (Klauber, 1968). He emphasizes that such a phrase is clearly a metaphor that does not describe accurately the transference transaction in which the patient experiences a relationship with his analyst in a way more suited to a relationship occurring in the past than to the realities of the present. Klauber writes that this is because "re-cathected by the desire for introspection and understanding in order to overcome frustration, the repressed memories now strive towards recall within the psycho-analytic session" (Klauber, 1968, p.86). Klauber's point seems to be that the special circumstances of the analytic set-up bring out more than mere repetitions of pattern observable in other areas of the patient's life, but that they accumulate evidences out of which reconstructions can be made.

Greenson (1978), though not writing at length about reconstruction, implies that it is so central that he can affirm that, in the end, all interpretations lead to the process of reconstruction. He especially emphasizes the notion that reconstruction stimulates the synthetic function of the *ego* into an increased power of recall of memories and in this a circular process may be observed. This we may understand as follows. Memories are being used for reconstruction, which in turn leads to further memory recall, which in its turn modifies the memories with which the process began. Greenson's final point is the interesting one that reconstruction of the historical development of the self-image is a matter of vital importance to the patient, particularly if some sort of continuum is to be discerned behind it (Greenson, 1978, pp. 249–250).

Greenson's view is an interesting one when compared with those of Blum (1980), who in a plea for reconstruction can complain, no doubt with reason, that it has tended to fall into disuse in recent psychoanalytic practice and literature. Brenman, on the other hand, takes reconstruction for granted as a valid analytical practice and seems to be in agreement with Greenson over the stimulus that reconstruction can give to the synthesizing elements of the ego. Thus he can use the striking phrase "reconstruction is of value as a means of rediscovering roots, past objects and lost parts of the self" (Brenman, 1980, p.53). The general analytical question raised by Greenson, however, is whether it is sufficient to say that all interpretations lead to reconstruction and whether it is an accurate description to say that the synthesizing or integrating function belongs to the ego. To take the second point first, there seems to be no reason to doubt that the ego possesses *some* integrative powers. Nevertheless analytical psychologists have long held the view that integrative potential resides in the self, i.e.

the personality as a whole. It is not a contrivance of the ego, though the realization in terms of flesh and blood, space and time, of the integrative potential of the self is assisted and guided by the ego. The first point—that all interpretations lead to reconstruction—seems to limit the scope of analysis unduly. Analytical psychologists in their actual clinical practice do have an interest, when enough reconstructive work has been done, in helping a patient by interpretations to experiment with new experiences and to release hitherto undeveloped potential. Although it is possible that such developments can take place spontaneously once sufficient reconstructive analysis has been done, we cannot be sure that "helping-hand interpretation" by the analyst of a post-reconstructive sort does not play a vital part in the opening out and realization of the self in the later phases of an analysis.

(b) Reconstruction in Analytical Psychology

Jung's attitude to reconstruction seems to many observers to have been, if not negative, at least ambivalent. Readers of his later work may be forgiven if they see very little sign of it, and it is very easy to miss the fact that between 1944 and 1961 he worked out, in a most original way, what amounts to a massive reconstruction of the Hebrew–Christian psycho-cultural tradition (Fordham, 1978; Lambert, 1976).

During the twenties of this century, however, Jung did deal with reconstruction to some extent under the heading of reductive analysis. In a well-known essay on "The therapeutic value of abreaction" (Jung, 1921-28) Jung wrote passionately enough to seem to be both against reductive analysis and for it! When he was writing against it he tended to criticize reductive analysis as if it were a kind of "nothing but" analysis. Severely, he writes

> the continual reduction of all projections to their origins ... never produces an adapted attitude to life, for it constantly destroys the patients' every attempt to build up a normal human relationship by resolving it back to its elements (Jung, 1921-28, p.135).

He follows this passage by listing the negative results: loss of moral intellectual and aesthetic values, brooding on the past, looking back wistfully on things that cannot be remedied, and finding the cause of one's inferiority in the dim bygone etc. It seems likely, however, that Jung must have been referring to clumsy analysts who obsessively harped on reduction and were unable to analyse the way in which their reductions could be taken into the defence-systems of their patients. It must be stated that such analysts would be involved in a problematical misunderstanding of the whole point and aims of reconstruction, certainly as described at the beginning of this chapter. Without massive qualification, therefore, Jung's judgement seems wrong, for much clinical experience suggests that reductive analysis, with reconstruction within the transference, can not only remove blocks to a patient's creative functioning in personal relationships, etc. in the present but also with the addition of some elucidatory interpretations of a here and now sort promote synthetic development and growth into the future. It cannot be denied that Jung is also concerned to emphasize this very point when in the same paper he can write: "As a result of reductive analysis, the patient is deprived of his faulty adaptation, and led back to his beginnings". Jung further adds that this process should enable the patient to

> turn to the doctor ... as an object of purely human relationship in which each individual is guaranteed his proper place. *Naturally this is impossible until all the projections have been consciously recognized; consequently they must be subjected to a reductive analysis before all else*, provided of course that the legitimacy and importance of the underlying claim to personal relationship is constantly borne in mind (Jung, 1921-28).

The two passages quoted above certainly lay great emphasis upon what Jung calls a "normal human relationship" or a "personal relationship", and the capacity for such is surely an essential part of an integrated, let alone individuated, person. It can only be repeated that in most cases the analysis of early relationship traumata should promote this capability as illustrated at the beginning of this chapter (see pp.107–112). Jung's need to emphasize this general point to the degree that he does makes one speculate about the purposes for which the reconstruction he came across during that period of his life was being used.

Apart from Jung, Fordham (1978) has contributed concisely to a number of aspects of the reconstructive process. Like Rubinfine, Fordham considers that reconstructive work, which represents an important aspect of the analysis of repression, "is best conducted with the patient on the couch" (Fordham, 1978, p.125). Then, granted such facilitating conditions, Fordham holds that reconstruction can fill in the gaps about very early periods in the patient's life, which are not easily accessible to memory, and can "extend the range of experience to parts of infancy where behaviour and physical acts have been more relevant than organized mental functioning" (p.126). Fordham also emphasizes the initially rather tentative approach needed when reconstruction is being carried out and illustrates the interaction between first reconstructions and the fresh material they can release within the transference (pp.126–128), thereby leading to revised reconstruction. A further implication of Fordham's work on this point is the value of persistent working on infancy, which has of course the advantage of familiarizing the patient with this side of his nature. "Thus, by relating the present to the past, the patient's ego is strengthened" (p.125). Furthermore, still as part of the process, the new positions thus getting established may have the effect of changing memories of the past, not only in a more negative but sometimes in a more positive direction, so that good things in the past also get remembered and thereby change the subjective colour of the present and the future (p.60). Finally Fordham (1978) has defined the kind of case where reconstructive analytic interpretations made to the patient "seem largely irrelevant, in other words, where impulses and preverbal communications become more important than insights or phantasies" (p.124). He goes on to give an account of how an analytically, and indeed reconstruction-orientated, therapist can handle regression to primitive and infantile impulsiveness on a pre-verbal level in cases where "self-feeling has not developed or has become seriously damaged and cannot be assumed" (p.128).

To complete this list, a paper by myself (Lambert, 1970) concentrated, apart from a long case history, on factors which practically compel analysts—or at least those with a sense of history—to consider patients' communications in a reconstructive way, whether the reconstruction is conveyed to the patient or not (see also pp. 121 ff.).

Having sketched out some of the ideas about reconstruction in the literature of psychoanalysis and analytical psychology, it is worth while summarizing the points made:

All the writers consider the use of the couch to be of assistance in the work of reconstruction, with the possible exception of Jung, who is known not to have used it in individuation cases, which he thought needed synthetic analysis and scarcely any reductive analysis at all.

Freud, Klein and probably Klauber, on the whole, think the therapeutic value of reconstruction to the patient is an explanatory one.

Novey seems to have had a strong belief in the therapeutic value of providing the patient with an historical survey of the development of his attitudes towards and responses to his environmental situation—personal and impersonal, and an understanding of how his present-day attitudes are influenced by these long-established positions.

Rubinfine's contribution is to propose a theory of memory, originated by Bartlett and illustrated by a case history in which the patient's memories of extremely strong affects, which had remained deeply repressed but centred around and subsumed under the idea of the birth of a younger male sibling, emerged in a dramatic "acting out'' in the end. What was significant was how the powerful affects involved had remained unconscious, though contained in a definite mode of handling experience, in spite of the fact that cognitive knowledge of the factual event was available to her.

Jung's ambivalence seemed, despite a strong affirmative of the necessity of reductive analysis, to centre round strong fears that it could seriously damage the patient's capacity for personal relationships of a ''human'' kind.

Fordham's contribution is particularly valuable in discriminating between the kind of case in which reconstructive analysis is relevant and therapeutically helpful and that in which it is ineffective, at least in the earlier parts of the treatment.

My own contribution expanded somewhat the considerations which are likely to alert a therapist into the direction of thinking in reconstructive terms, and in this chapter they will be restated in certain ways.

The Analyst's Reconstructive Response

(a) Some Clinical Indications for the Use of Reconstruction

It is probable that in the majority of clinical situations an experienced analyst gets, quickly enough for it to seem almost spontaneous, a sense of when it is appropriate to offer the patient reconstructive interpretations and when not. In the latter situation, the analyst's reconstructive responses will be kept to himself for the time being—maybe for a very long time—but he will need to attempt reconstructive insights for his own sake, so he can better orientate himself in the treatment of the case. This latter situation can arise because certain conditions in the patient need prior establishment before he can benefit from the insight offered—or even from the ''as if'' element of the transference/counter-transference situation within which it is being offered.

The conditions about which the assessment is being made concern the degree to which the patient shows signs of:

    (1) Possessing something like a central core of personality about which, though in certain ways more or less damaged, he can both make statements that are meaningful and remain not entirely swamped by compulsive and desperate complaints on his part about overwhelming symptoms, unbearable pain, and primitive impulses against which no defences, however rigid, have proved efficient or useful;

(2) Having some representational notion of a self with an inside and an outside—with contents that are good and bad;

(3) Being able to consider, however minimally, the reality of others and, in particular, of the interviewing analyst;

(4) Being able to think symbolically, at least in a rudimentary way, so that "as if" does not mean "the same as" or "quite different from" and irrelevant to the situation;

(5) Being able to demonstrate a certain interest in and curiosity about his psychological processes.

It must be repeated that we are here assessing matters of degree and that there are many borderline cases. It does mean, however, that for the patient reconstructions can be more useful where the five conditions just mentioned are fulfilled. Where they are not, other forms of analytically informed treatment will be required, as indicated by Fordham (1978).

(b) Reconstruction as an Aid to the Analyst

Whether or not reconstruction is useful to any particular patient, it does seem clear that in every case it is useful to the analyst. To begin with it would not be possible without some reconstruction to decide on its suitability in a particular case. Reconstruction is even more essential to the analyst for orientation purposes in cases who arrive deeply regressed and disintegrated and require in their treatment management and care rather than reconstructive analytical interpretations at that particular stage of their existence. If the analyst cannot make reconstructions for his own use, he is indeed in a difficult situation.

(c) The Process of Reconstruction

The analyst can find himself strongly moved, in the first instance, in the direction of reconstructive considerations when he judges that the patient's experience and behaviour are unadapted to the objects he is describing and are delusionary or off-beam. His emotions and affects seem disproportionate to the events he supposes himself to be reacting to. Reconstructive efforts are based upon the hypothesis that the patient is so saturated by the memory of cumulative patterns of experience in the past, though largely unconscious of them, as to be unable to react creatively to the present real situation out of his present position, talents, age, etc.

For example, a patient began to realize after nine months of analysis that his real feelings about his work group, and his own family (himself, his wife and children), together with his feelings about the relationship between myself and both him and his wife and family, were surprisingly unadapted to the realities of the actual situation.

He felt that the organization in which he worked was futile; that he was a stranger not fitting into it and feeling lost, yet, at the same time, that he had some special responsibility in it which he could not discover; that his boss was non-involved and ineffective and yet possessed a strange power, felt by my patient as mysterious and over the possession of which he knew himself to be full of envious feelings. He felt that his wife and children and himself were all shabby, undistinguished and nothing to be proud of. In any case he himself sometimes felt a stranger in his own home. He felt that I made him depressed and angry and yet I had a power of insight and could be helpful. Furthermore there seemed to exist a kind of alliance or even a love feeling between myself and his wife, whom incidentally I had never met, and this made him jealous and hostile towards her. He was, however, well able to distinguish between this ''feeling'' account of his life situation and the more ''factual'' realities of it.

The facts of his history were that his father was old, patriarchal-looking and, if anything, seemed ''too wise''. He also became, after a sporting accident, a chronic invalid. His mother was young and attractive, although when he was angry with her in his eyes she looked ''tarty''. Furthermore he did not feel at home in his family situation and to make things worse his sister, who was five years older and whose company he greatly enjoyed, was mainly away at boarding school so he saw very little of her. At the same time he, too, was at boarding school during his adolescence. Also, his mother seemed to expect him to take on responsibilities without the corresponding privileges owing to the invalidism of his very old father, although what they were supposed to be seemed unclear and how he could fulfil them was quite beyond his strength or comprehension. Thus, although his oedipal feelings about his mother were further activated by these expectations of hers, in the final analysis his old father's word in his ''wisdom'' was law.

This childhood was therefore unhappy and confused. He felt the family unsatisfactory and he was more aware of shame about it than pride in it. He discovered in his analysis, through reconstruction in the transference, how deeply this old-established family pattern was still being lived and felt by him. This hampered his work and his own family life, while profoundly affecting his transference relationship to me. If the unconscious pattern uncovered in the reconstruction is spelt out, we find the same thread running through his domestic life, his work, and his analytic experience;

(a) A feeling of shame which pervaded all three.

(b) Likewise a feeling of being a stranger in all three.

(c) Feelings of happiness, like those occasionally experienced with his sister, were in short rations.

(d) The jealous oedipal feelings towards his mother, whether for her faithless "tartiness" as expressed in her "promiscuous" attitudes or for her constant adherence to his father, also worked out in his feeling angrily deprived both at home and at work. Transferentially he could even generate a belief in a special understanding between his wife and myself, though part of him knew that this was nonsense.

(e) The depression over the age and weakness of his father, coupled nevertheless with the idea that his father might be too wise for him, reproduced itself in connection with both his bosses and myself.

(f) The certitude that in some way he was expected to be omnipotently responsible for everything, combined nevertheless with a sense of weakness and confusion, became noticeably reproduced not only at work but also in a way in his domestic situation and, subtly, in his response to me.

My patient's situation was very similar to that of Marshall McLuhan's modern people; "when faced with a totally new situation we tend always to attach ourselves to the objects, to the flavour of the most recent past. We look at the present through a rear-view mirror. We march backwards into the future . . . we approach the new with the psychological conditioning and sensory responses of the old" (McLuhan, 1967, pp.74, 75, 92).

One of the more obvious implications of the analyst's work in reconstruction is that in it, in a way that parallels the work of the archaeologist as quoted from Freud (p.114), he is functioning as an historian. He is a psycho-historian, strongly biased by his work with patients towards the historical biography of the recent past, although it seems that in some ways he is in a more favourable position than most historians thus engaged. It is true that the historian has records, documents, accounts of the impact of events upon the minds of the people of the time, assessments of the long and short-term effects of events upon later periods and even contemporary life. He also studies historical development. He has little opportunity, however, eliciting a response from the people involved in his historical studies let alone any opportunities for analytical listening.

The analyst, however, is dealing, generally speaking, with a past which is alive at the present moment and which determines the experience and behaviour of his patients as individuals in a way that is little changed from what it always was, save that it is expressed in more adult-sounding terms. As a historian he has a vast quantity of material at his disposal to work upon:

(1) Transference phenomena and memories of the recent and more distant past on the part of the patient, together with information obtained by the patient from his family and friends and passed on to the analyst;

(2) His own responses to the situation of the patient which arise out of his capacity to introject it and work upon it in the light of his own analysis and memories together with his general experience of the world. It is sometimes by means of this function as historian–analyst that the analyst may enable his patient to get the hang of his history, sometimes even to understand it completely anew and as a result to get a quite different feeling about the significance of single brute facts and the often repeated patterns of a neurotic life-history;

(3) His observations of the responses of his patient to his interpretative and other work. Thus his enterprise can be subjected to a check from a living person to a much greater degree than is normally available to a biographer.

Another important topic in reconstructive activity is that of the range of phenomena to be understood. This may be regarded as twofold. On the one hand, it includes a study of the environment of the patient as infant and child in terms of whether it is a more or less facilitating one (to use Winnicott's phrase). Certain historical events as well as certain often repeated patterns of events can be looked at in this light. On the other hand, reconstruction includes a study of the actual specific ways in which the patient began to react according to an habitual and set pattern. By implication it can also reveal what ways of reacting and what potentialities were never released and remained primitive and undeveloped. Reconstruction facilitates the analyst's and the patient's understanding of the type of relationship that developed between him and the personal matrix of his early years, in particular how his mother dealt with his inner world, his omnipotence, omniscience, aggressions and his basic needs. This includes the crucial question of whether the environment supported and confirmed his worst inner persecutory fears and anxieties in such a way that the child became unduly defensive and delusionary, with a resultant crippling of psychic potentiality, or whether it facilitated a progressive development of his capacity for reality-testing and the deployment of his slowly maturing personality and archetypal potential.

The final point I would like to make about the findings of reconstruction is that they often contribute an essential element to *mutative interpretation* which intends that personality change should follow as a result of its striking and convincing content (see p.48). Chapter seven is intended to show that the patterns of interrelationship that develop between the patient and his mainly personal environment in infancy and childhood are rendered much more consciously experienceable by being linked with the everyday experience of the transference/counter-transference situation. The ability to make creative connections of this sort belongs no doubt to the analytic art, and is based upon a fine balance being struck between observation, intuition and a sensitive nervous system in the therapist, together with a capacity for apt verbalization and the possession of a well-practised and well-tuned historical sense.

(d) The Therapeutic Results of Reconstruction

We have described some of the elements in the reconstructive process. It seems appropriate now to assess its possible therapeutic results in those cases which have been judged suitable in accordance with the criteria described on pp.120, 121. Reconstruction comes in at a level of the patient's infancy or childhood where a high degree of dependence upon adults is involved, coupled with a relative weakness in his ability to help himself in an adequate way. However, though reconstruction aims to link the patient with the experiences of his more or less disturbed childhood, the latter is unlikely to be able to do this at a deep level of feeling, unless the analyst is consistent, continuously reliable, and sufficiently available in terms of sessions to be for him a good enough holding analyst. Reconstruction is offered as part of the process whereby a patient may, if need be, re-experience his early self in a symbolical relationship in a more satisfactory way than had been the case originally. It is not that the analyst can become the mother of an infant and young child for a second time in the patient's life: this is clearly impossible. But the analyst can provide an accepting, non-moralizing, understanding and interpretative personal caring for a patient in a way that is appropriate to his situation as an adult.

Granted this good enough holding analyst (Winnicott, 1965, p.240), then his reconstructive efforts supply guiding lines for the patient in the transference situation for understanding why, granted his past, he could only experience life and behave in the unfruitful way that he does. It clears the way for experimentation with conditions as they really are in the here and now and for allowing himself to feel and experience life afresh out of the elements of his true self—first in the analytic situation and then in the outside world. It is also through reconstruction that the nature of his over-determined and negative defensive systems can become real to him. Finally, continuous steady and persistent reconstructive interpretations within the transference develop the capacity of the patient to experience and create certain radical differentiations that are a part of health, i.e. those between past and present, inner and outer experience, and self and the "not-self world" of other people and things, animate and inanimate.

Above all, perhaps, the work will foster the capacity of the patient to make object relationships. The analyst provides a substitute in suitable terms for the holding mother who gradually enables the young child to personalize, i.e. make his sexual and aggressive impulses his own instead of developing heavy defences against the fear of being swept away by blind autonomous impulse. In this way the patient is gradually released from the old maladapted ways of response and a new way of deploying his real personality in personal relationships becomes progressively possible.

A further therapeutic consequence of reconstruction is that it has become clearer with experience that in reductive analysis synthesis is in fact being served, as described by Jung in his famous statement: "The synthetic view asserts that certain parts of the personality which are capable of development are in an infantile state as though in the womb" (Jung, 1935, p.9). In other words, "the synthetic view" does not necessarily imply that "analysis" no longer operates and steps aside in favour of something called "synthesis". The patient, released from excessive anxiety and crippling defensiveness through reconstruction within the transference, begins to experience new feelings and potentialities (i.e. no longer quite "still in the womb"), and these in turn require support within the therapeutic relationship. In a way, this activity is comparable to that of the mother who knows how to go along with the developing powers of the infant and toddler, enabling him to experiment with them in reasonable security and with firm enough holding.

It is fair to say that a renewed link with infancy and childhood through the modification of defences, together with an allowing into realization of newly discovered and deployable capacities, represents a movement towards synthesis and integration in a patient's personality which develops spontaneously alongside the reconstructive and reductive analysis in the transference. Jung's distinction between "reductive" and "synthetic" interpretations seems to be based on practical considerations rather than theoretical ones. He writes, "Both interpretations can be shown to be correct. We might almost say that they amount to the same thing. But it makes an enormous difference in practice whether we interpret something regressively or progressively" (Jung, 1935, p.9). Again, we do not know quite why Jung used the word "regressive" with such apparently negative or least specialized overtones. It does not agree with the experience that reductive analysis done with care normally leads towards synthetic development and in that sense is progressive.

A final positive therapeutic gain from reconstructive analysis is that it can foster in the patient a sense of his life process as a dynamic whole—past, present and future. He can become aware of his tail, that is, the way in which things were in the early part of his life. He is thus enabled to develop a feeling for both the positive and the negative elements in his early personal matrix that is truer in the sense of being fairer and better balanced. He can understand better where his development went awry and the vicissitudes of distortion and repair, after which perhaps it recovered itself and went more according to the true or vice versa. He can have a future. If he can recover a satisfactory experience of duration and the movement from the past, through the present, and on to the future, then he may grasp a sense of undeveloped possibilities pressing for realization in the future. This sense of his history and potential adds security to the process whereby both synthesizing and progressive elements in the individual develop—at first within the therapeutic relationship and then, even more so, into the future after the analytical treatment has been terminated.

One of my editors has suggested to me that I have concentrated upon the reconstruction of infancy and childhood in this chapter to the neglect of reconstruction in dealing with traumatic events that occur at later points in the life of patients. This is a true observation apart, however, from the fact that I have referred to the reconstruction that sometimes takes place in a mourning process that follows upon a significant death that seriously wounds a patient (see p.112). I would agree that there is an important place for a kind of reconstruction from which bereaved spouses and sometimes elderly people can benefit, often in a very moving way. It certainly has a most relieving effect and clears the way gradually into renewed hope and a deepened philosophy of life. It almost certainly should play an enriching part in the analysis of people with second half of life problems. However, I have not always found it possible or desirable to avoid the reconstruction of early life in older people who have suffered traumata in middle life. Although such a procedure might sometimes intensify feelings of loss and despair, it can also relieve much guilt and shame by fostering the deeper understanding of their early relationships that older people are very well fitted for. One of the noticeable features of such cases can indeed be the way in which early disturbances can operate cumulatively right through a person's life. An analysis of the beginnings can shift the direction of the life and free it from much suffering.

(e) Some Dangers arising from the Neglect of Reconstruction

It would be unwise to confine our attention to the positive therapeutic gains that reconstruction is likely to achieve without considering the results of its neglect. The latter can be observed in certain quarters, not least in psychoanalysis, though in the London school of analytical psychology perhaps less so. Behind such neglect we may find a temperamental distaste for historical viewpoints, but, perhaps more, disillusionment as a result of the limitations inherent in reconstruction and the misuse of it through its application in unsuitable cases and settings. Where this is so, interpretations tend to be made in flat transference terms without reference to depth in the past and therefore without explanation of how the phenomena in question came into being. There is, however, some evidence to suggest that in cases where the transference relationship turns out to be heavily saturated by infantile and early childhood content such interpretations of the patient's transference in the here and now, without any reference to reconstructive insights, can lead to an enhancement of guilty and demoralized feelings in the patient. He can feel that the interpretation simply confirms his worst fears, namely, his complete inadequacy in a personal relationship with his analyst.

Without reconstruction there can be no lightening of the situation by an understanding that it is the child in him that he is experiencing in relationship to his analyst or again by any insight into the dynamics that landed that child into traumatized, confused and shattered experiences with his primary maternal object and the rest of the family, etc. In a demoralized way he identifies with the most unsatisfactory elements in his nature and can lapse into despair over them or fall back on classical defence systems against them. He loses his bearings through a blurring of the distinction between the present and the past, between the infantile end of his life spectrum and the adult, and between impulse and action.

Resistance to Reconstructive Analysis

The previous section on the neglect of reconstructive analysis suggests that resistances can develop in relationship to it. They may be considered in terms of the resistance of patients and the resistance of psychotherapists.

(a) The Resistance of Patients

At the beginning of this chapter we considered the clinical situation where reconstruction is irrelevant or inappropriate. One sign of this is that the patient's resistance takes the form of remaining entirely untouched by or totally opposed to reconstructive interpretations. However, though generally with less intensity, resistances to it are also encountered as part of the therapeutic interaction in cases where reconstruction is clinically appropriate. These resistances can take the form of verbal comment on the uselessness of reconstruction. They may indeed seem plausible, perhaps because the considerations adduced are not untrue, though scarcely relevant to the problem on hand. The content of the objections may be summarized as follows. The patient accuses the analyst of wanting to rub his nose in the past with all its fear, pain and emptiness. He is being made to look back, when he wishes to forget the past, live in the present and look forward into the future. The analyst is wanting to destroy his good feelings and make him miserable. This type of emotive response to past events and this reading of the analyst's motivations may of course be considered in transferential terms, though the implications of this will naturally be hard for the patient to accept. This is particularly so because it is difficult for the patient to distinguish between a *true* freedom from the grip of the past by analysis of it and a *false* freedom achieved through repression. He is likely to be unaware of the potential relief both from over-determined guilt and from unconscious compulsions to land himself into inexplicably difficult feelings and relationships that can be one of the rewards of reconstructive analysis. He therefore needs some taste of the relief thus obtainable. Apart from this, many patients are in unconscious despair of obtaining any real satisfaction in the present and future, and so they ask "What is the good of delving into the past? It does nothing for me." Obviously, however, in such cases it is their despair that needs to be brought into consciousness and analysed.

(b) The Resistance of Psychotherapists

There are psychotherapists who are very sensitive to the possibility that reconstructive analysis may be used by the therapist as an unsuitable defence against powerful negative, or positive transferences. The point here, however, is that any form of response may thus be used. The problem therefore lies rather in the therapist's personality, in which fear of strong transferences has not yet been sufficiently analysed. The difficulty is in fact about defences rather than reconstruction which could be employed after all as but one of the many possible defensive tools available.

Another criticism, and one that Jung was very much aware of, is that reconstruction is said to draw attention away from the present and future and to land the patient into obsessions about the past. The problem here is one of a mourning process that has become held up. The past cannot become the past as a subjective experience until it has been mourned. This is especially true with damaged or distorted pasts or with pasts where great happiness and fulfilment has been lost. Anyone who really loves the present and the future will know that their realization depends upon dealing with the past, mourning it and then letting it be the past. It then no longer hampers the present and the future and may with safety be simply remembered from time to time and, if necessary, lessons may be learnt and relearnt from it.

The more general criticism is that reconstruction is simply ineffective. Indeed this can be a true criticism if certain conditions are not fulfilled; the choice of suitable patients, the constant relating of the reconstruction to the transference/counter-transference situation, and the establishment of a suitable therapeutic container within which the reconstructive analysis is made.

Some Limitations of Reconstruction in Individual Analysis

The last three sections of this chapter, on the neglect of reconstruction and the resistance to it on the part of both patients and psycho-therapists respectively, suggest that a consideration of its limitations is desirable.

In undertaking this, it is necessary to repeat that its most fundamental limitation rests upon its inapplicability in cases where management and holding care are the order of the day. Apart from that, we need to remember that reconstruction of the psycho-history of an individual is unlikely ever to be complete or thoroughly sewn up. Experience shows that it remains for long a provisional process, often involving revisions and reassessments of childhood memories found later in some cases to be wildly inaccurate and hence often leading to the emergence of new attitudes towards the past. It is perhaps best understood as an attitudinal orientation that has been found to be useful in pragmatic terms, although based upon principle, in the sense that it involves an understanding of developmental process, of the nature of the family and other matrices, of the functioning of archetypes in childhood, and of the naive experience of duration and historical process.

Furthermore, the nature of the environmental provision afforded to the infant by his mother is much affected by the psycho-cultural patterns and current prejudices of society. This is particularly important when we consider which archetypal potentialities of the young self were supported and reinforced and which remained unrealized through lack of facilitation. The complexity of this is considerable when we consider the family as the matrix of the individual and the community or society as the matrix of the family, whether it be an extended family, a nuclear family, or a one-parent and possibly isolated family.

A final point about limitations in the ability of patients to handle reconstructive interpretations to their profit is likely to centre round the ways in which their approach may be influenced by their type and function considered in terms of Jung's well-known typology. It will be remembered that Jung postulated two types in accordance with the difference between basically introverted and basically extraverted approaches to reality, as well as four functions through which a person relates to the environment—thinking, feeling, sensation and intuition. In all sorts of complicated ways, some of these types and functions will be developed and dominant in a person and some of them inferior and kept in the background (Jung, 1921). It seems fairly clear that a person's sense of his history can be greatly influenced by the degree to which he is introverted or extraverted in his strongest functions. I think that intuitive people with imagination take kindly to reconstructions of their past psycho-history, while thinking-types may want to get it all too neatly sewn up. Sensation-types may find the historical approach unreal, while feeling types, with their clear-cut likes and dislikes, approval and disapproval, may as a result distort the facts and memories of their past in an unbalanced way. These are but a few of the possibilities inherent in the influence of typology. In any case a valuable analytic aim could be reconstruction of that early interaction between a person's constitution and his environment as a result of which the dominant type and/or function emerges as an end product. Such an analysis could serve to loosen his adhesion to, if not a static identification with, some particular pattern of type and function and hence to release him into a more dynamic and flexible deployment of his abilities.

Reconstruction and Individuation

We may sum up this whole examination of reconstruction by considering how reconstructive analysis promotes *individuation*. The most fundamental contribution is to provide for the individual a sense of his own unique history. This can promote a sense of significance, a heightening of consciousness, and an increased capacity to co-operate with that living and developing process that is himself. One of the adjuncts of this may be a discovery of the extent to which his capacity for relationships has hitherto been limited and the range of his perceptual span narrowed by fixation at immature levels of development that can, however, no longer serve his purposes.

Reconstruction thus clears the way for an establishment of more realistic object-relations and a more satisfying sense of the self. Although this no doubt renders a person less heavily defended in the crippling sense of the word, it opens him out to greater enhancement of life and, no doubt, as well, to greater wisdom and skill at self-protection in face of its real dangers.

In this way it helps to release the ongoing loosening and "unpacking" deintegrative – reintegrative process of the self (see pp.193 ff.), thus promoting the integration of the self realized in terms of flesh and blood, space and time. This in turn means the "un-dividedness of the individual and hence, paradoxically, the uniqueness of his contribution to the common life of the society of which he is a part and in which he shares" (Jung, 1963).

Chapter Seven

Transference, counter-transference and interpersonal relations

---

Introduction

It is a commonplace today to emphasize the importance of the patient–therapist relationship whether in the realm of medicine or that of the social worker. It is a field in which problems abound, especially in psychotherapy, which, however, is happily and unusually well-advantaged for their observation and study. Some of them are as follows:

(1) The problem of being able to interact with and trust a stranger over the intimate difficulties and sufferings of the psyche in the long term—not that, for some people, enlightening intro-ductions to their psychology may not be effected in a once-only meeting with a stranger. To achieve greater depth, however, the normal problems of unfamiliarity with new persons demand recognition and attention. Neurosis or psychosis apart, these resolve themselves in time into a positive and/or negative attitude as knowledge of and about the new person is acquired.

(2) The problem of distortions of perception, if not indeed of illusion and delusion, which can extend far beyond the normal problems of unfamiliarity and do interfere with the relationship potential that arises between patient and therapist as they seek to experience each other as real persons.

(3) Problems of personal idiosyncrasy, background, culture etc. arising within the real object-relations of the here and now, not only while but also after the distortions are being or have been analysed and worked through.

In the present book, we have elaborated upon a number of topics which, real enough in their own right, are yet also intimately bound up with the way in which the patient–therapist interaction may become a therapeutically beneficial one. In the first place, some definition was attempted of the *agapaic* predisposition the analyst needs to mobilize if he is to relate in a therapeutic way to patients in emotional turmoil and pain. This, naturally enough, leads on to an investigation of the multilayered problem of *resistance* in the patient, despite his longing for real object-relationships with another person in a way that implies an improved acquaintance with himself as a real person as well. Bound up with improved *object-relationships* is in its turn a release of the patient's going processes, fixated, as they so frequently are, at early levels in his past history. As a result, relationships with his therapist and, later, others can become more appropriate to the here and now, and it is for the achievement of such ends that close attention has been devoted to *reconstruction* and the experience of *duration*.

The Circular Relationship between Transference and Counter-transference and Personal Interaction

All the enquiries so far pursued in this book have already touched on and inevitably lead on to the problems of (1) transference and counter-transference and (2) the interactional dynamics of the patient–therapist relationship that both power it and maintain its momentum. A circular relationship between these two sets of phenomena is promoted by the fact that both patient and therapist can be drawn into feelings about each other of an intensity that is hard to bear, since the defence systems of both are undergoing a modification that is at least temporary. The patient fears he will be drawn, in relation to his analyst, into pain-filled conflicts between love and hate; between reluctance, embarrassment and guilt and feared desire for what is judged to be "forbidden fruit"; and between the infantile feelings that demand expression and his confessions of them as one adult to another adult person. The therapist, on his part, needs in an agapaic way to handle emotions aroused in him by his patient, to tolerate misrepresentation and abuse by him, and in addition to sacrifice the wish for quick definable therapeutic returns. In tension against this, continuity, regularity and reliability in the patient's sessions have to be maintained by him as well as a limitation of his concern to relatively few patients only, rather than the wide spreading of interest over many cases that is a temptation to some. Furthermore, in the meeting of these requirements and indeed those of the therapeutic holding process, an element of ritual is often discovered to have established itself in a spontaneous way and to need conscious support. Finally, the contrasting situations of both patient and therapist, however interesting and stimulating they may be, involve both of them, through their multilayered complexity, in a good deal of hard work, so that real fatigue is not unknown to both parties in the analytic transaction.

All this contains within itself a potential of anger, resentment, hatred, gratitude and love—ready to be activated largely in and through transference/counter-transference distortion. It is therefore to a considerable extent the transformative way in which the emotions involved are handled by both parties, but particularly so by the analyst, that determines whether the analytic result is to be creative and forward moving or a destructive hindrance to the on-going process.

Motivation in Patient and Therapist

To enter into such an enterprise, motivation needs to be strong. For the patient, at one end of the scale, the motivation can often be, sometimes after a breakdown, a nearly but not quite desperate experience of distress that verges on the unbearable but which is not felt to be open, in any acceptable way, to alleviation by drugs. At the other end, the motivation may be a positively passionate feeling for individuation and the self, sometimes even for its survival and autonomy where these are felt to be under threat from within or without. Naturally enough most patients come motivated at a point somewhere between these two extremes.

The analyst's motivation, on the other hand, is likely, at a deep level, to include gratitude, in Klein's sense of the word, to his own therapist and also to supervisors and colleagues. It will be part of his response to whatever they managed to do for him in the way of remaining with him, allowing varying measures of agapaic bonding with him to be established, and listening, tolerating, feeding and liberating him through interpretations. This is likely to be so, even if residual problems are not necessarily solved and still need a measure of toleration. After all, the nourishment to be derived from a non-moralistic agapaic response is considerable, particularly when the receiver of it has also been freed from a compulsion to destroy the experience by perfectionist criticism. Gratitude, then, when thus soundly based, provides a strong motivation to practise therapy, but it cannot be the only one. Other important motivations are: interest in and curiosity about the psychodynamics of people; empathy; and feelings of involvement, not only in the reparative work of therapy but also agapaically with patients as persons. These are present in varying degrees in would-be therapists, but a relatively high concentrate of these ingredients and the wish to employ them therapeutically appear to be a *sine qua non*. A further requisite is clearly a capacity to be alone with a series of individuals over long periods of time every day, five days a week. Also the periods of time must be frequent enough and long enough to foster the development of experience and competence. That the ability to sustain such perseverance is likely to have a positive vocational basis seems clear enough, and the effort is unlikely to be maintained if it goes against the grain. All this, plus a strong physical constitution, are likely to add up to the set of gifts and motivations needed to withstand the stresses of practice as an analyst.

By contrast with the motivational pattern thus described, other factors have been uncovered and judged inappropriate, such as a neurotic avoidance of the would-be therapist's own sickness and problems. For example, a do-it-yourself and somewhat heroic psychology can issue into pretensions to omnipotence, if not a quiet grandiosity. Such power drives are likely to be inimical to the individuation process, although in a patient they may be veiled in a seductive way. Another neurotic denial can be symptomatically expressed by an unconscious need to live much of one's life with disturbed people or, more sinister still, by a compulsion to drive other people mad. It is not unknown, for instance, for people to have become so adapted to living, in their primary family, with a member of it who was psychotic, that an unconscious wish may be discovered in them to reproduce this situation by a subtle driving of another person mad in their secondary family or other intimate relationships at a later date. Much simpler, but still neurotic, would be a compulsion to deny one's own depression, anxiety and other disturbances by treating them in others. Yet another would be to use the practice of analysis as a form of withdrawal into rumination and the avoidance of life processes. This would entail an unconscious and subtle avoidance of the difficulty of coming to grips with patients—a quite different matter from the quiet centering involved in working at grass roots level with them, in an agapaic way, for long periods of one's life.

Of course, such motivations and many others would come up in any competent analysis of candidates for training. It is important that it should do so for, apart from safeguarding prospective patients as well as professional standards, it is only humane to protect would-be analysts, discovered to be motivated thus at a deep and fixed level, from disappointment and heartbreak were they to go into practice.

Distortion in the Transference

It is clear then that patients and therapists with the strong motivations described above are coming together in an enterprise that seems essentially complementary. An added complication, however, is that a therapeutic relationship of this sort is nevertheless a thoroughly asymmetrical one. This is because of the wide gap that normally exists between the analytical experience of the two parties concerned and the fact that a high degree of dependence by the patient upon the analyst may be needed. The whole situation obviously creates a field of dynamic interplay that is full of powerful emotion likely to arise from deep levels of the psyche. Historically speaking, the therapeutic interaction soon turned out to be so full of seeming hazard and complication that in the early days Freud, while noticing transference phenomena, mainly understood them as hindrances to treatment and indeed, in some forms of the sexual transference, wholly inimical to it. I shall therefore move on to describing, first, transference in psychoanalysis and, secondly, transference in analytical psychology.

(a) Transference and psychoanalysis

Early in the history of psychoanalysis Freud (1895) recognized that in the course of an analysis feelings and experiences connected with persons in the past tended to be revived in connection with the doctor—in his view in a way detrimental to the treatment. Only by 1909 could he begin to see transference as a therapeutic agent (Freud, 1909)—in distinction incidentally from the "transference cure" (Freud, 1915a) brought about by love for the analyst. By 1912 "positive and negative" transferences in relation to the doctor could be seen, sometimes for defensive purposes, to be played off, one against the other, in either direction (Freud, 1912). In the same year, transferences specific to the patient's neurosis could be distinguished from transference arising, in general principle, out of the analytic process as such. Soon the "transference neurosis" (Freud 1914, 1920) was being distinguished, and through it the neurotic components of the patient's early relationships were seen to be moulding his relationship to the doctor as, in fact, a repeat—a new neurosis so it might be thought, although one felt by the patient to be a real new and contemporary experience and not a memory at all. This was about the time that the now somewhat discredited notion of "repetition compulsion" came into psychoanalysis. In 1936 Anna Freud introduced the notion of "transference of defence", for example as the repetition of hostility against the loved analyst, in the same way that the patient had used hostility as a defence against his love for his parents, which, it was feared, they might reject (Freud, A., 1936). Another of Anna Freud's contributions was the concept of "acting in the transference", which meant a patient's enactment towards other people in his outside environment of feelings and wishes aroused in him in connection with his analyst. She also generated the idea of "externalization", whereby the patient projects on to the analyst what are really unacknowledged parts of his personality, such as sexual wishes or a guilty super-ego-originated conscience. These need not necessarily or mainly be re-enactments of childhood patterns.

With the development of object-relations theory (see Chapter 5) psychoanalysis was able to give a better account of the transference transaction. It was realized that several complications could arise. The first was the "entrenched" nature of internal objects in the patient. Reconstructive analysis was needed to analyse what these internalized objects were composed of and the history of distortion in their formation. It became clear that difficulties in the relationship of the patient to internal objects could come out in the transference because the analyst was being treated feeling-wise as if he were one of them. What gets transferred are internal objects, often heavily saturated by the past and having a kind of sub-life of their own. Secondly, internalized part-objects (Klein) projected upon the analyst have the effect of seriously limiting and distorting the patient's experience and handling of him—or, indeed, of others. One bit of him is made to represent the whole of him and he becomes good or bad breast–penis, breast or penis. In Klein's terms, furthermore, analysts can become objects of envy, contempt and defiance, the targets of paranoid–schizoid retaliatory fears, and then objects undergoing repair of the damage the patients fear they have inflicted upon them. Patients can also make projective and introjective identifications in connection with their analysts—in states of unshakeable certitude.

Furthermore, in narcissistic personality disorder, a kind of transference has been found to develop in which the analyst as a real person is almost non-existent, as indeed might be expected. The transference is delusionary and twofold. On the one hand there develops a mirror transference of an omnipotent grandiose image of the self with an underside of weakness, uselessness and emptiness if not destructive rottenness. On the other hand there is a generalized transference of an idealized perfect good parent or a demonically bad one. The patient's real situation is one of isolation within a tremendously intensified and delusion-filled narcissistic self-love and self-hate. In borderline cases of this sort, difficulties for both patient and analyst abound. Transference interpretations seem useless and meaningless to the patient, and analysts are made to feel empty and ineffective.

As the psychoanalytic debate about transference proceeded, new areas were opened. For instance Strachey (1934) mounted a strong case for holding that the only really effective interpretations are transference interpretations. Another was that practically every communication about any subject or third party made by the patient to the analyst can be seen in an oblique way as transferential of early wishes and phantasies (Rosenfeld, 1965). It was not too long before the question was raised whether all relationships and attitudes of the patient, as much outside as inside the analytic situation, may not be understood in transferential terms as repetitions of past patterns of behaviour and experience (Greenson, 1965). However, most analysts would feel that this blurs useful distinctions, despite the fact, obvious enough to the practised observer, that unconscious transference phenomena continually affect if not hamper people's relationships in everyday life. Nevertheless the fact remains that within the analytical situation a greater degree of pure transference is made likely by the fact that in that situation opportunities for reality testing, at least in terms of knowledge about the therapist as compared with knowledge of him by acquaintance, are often more restricted. Furthermore, within the analytical situation a certain specificity of depth is more likely to develop, by contrast with general tendencies to experience the environment outside in terms of generalized and persisting character-traits, such as demandingness and provocativeness. Finally, in the purer forms of analytical treatment, transference illusions and manipulations of reality to promote their plausibility can be analysed by an analyst who, unlike people in the outer world, tends not to "feed in the facts" rather than make an interpretation and does not play into and live the projection out.

So far we have described some of the observations made within psychoanalysis of phenomena that may be subsumed under the title of the "neurotic transference", in which the patient is considered likely to become able in the end to understand the "as if" aspects of his illusions. He begins to be able to comprehend that in his transferences to his analyst the point at issue is much more what of himself he is seeing in his analyst than what he at first believes he perceives in his analyst, which may or may not be "true". When he reaches this point, he can benefit from reconstruction within the transference as described in the last chapter.

Another kind of transference, however, which has been described by psychoanalysts among others, is difficult to handle and indeed in the earlier days sometimes used to reduce them to thinking that the patient might be untreatable. Freud's (1915) early and famous account of it describes the identification of patients with their erotic or sexual aims. Their obsession was not analysis but love and sex, and Freud would describe such patients in terms of their "elemental passionateness" or as "children of nature". In such cases variations are enormous, and sometimes it is not really a question of transference at all. There was never any question of sessions being analytic; they were to be meeting places for the expression of love—mainly incestuous. Sometimes it was a matter of defending the analyst by exaggerated love, from an inner hatred that they feared would destroy him. In such cases, there may be transference of just such feelings for a parent who had been similarly protected in the past, but such transference obstacles are not the only ones to complicate matters, for a mass of psychoanalytic literature by Searles, Rosenfeld, Winnicott, Rappaport, Nunberg, Khan, Little and many others has developed around the notion of psychotic or *delusional* transference (Sandler *et al.*, 1973). Here we find a striking incapacity on the part of the patient to handle feelings, thoughts and wishes in connection with the analyst on an "as if" basis or on the basis of their inappropriateness to the present and their origination under the different conditions of infantile and child relationships. Of course there are variations in this incapacity, ranging from delusions about the part to delusions about the whole, and delusions that develop during the course of an analysis, or last for a period during it, or never clear up either in part or as a whole. The subject is enormous, and its relevance to the present chapter lies mainly in the fact that the relationship between therapist and patient, as a result of very early damage to the latter long before the establishment of anything like unit-status, is somewhat different. The treatment must be somewhat less analytical and less reconstructive in so far as interpretations offered to the patient are concerned—though not in so far as the therapist is concerned. His orientation depends upon his being able to form an accurate view of the very early developmental fixation points and damage that dominate the patient's life. In the treatment situation, the analyst's real feelings, his actions and his tones of voice all become important as well as his recognition of the patient's real sufferings. Much more than in the case of the neurotic transference, the analyst needs to offer some kind of symbolic or token care that may fill in something of what was missing right at the beginning of the patient's life.

The considerations we have just adduced need to be touched on mainly in order to avoid misunderstandings in a chapter that is attempting to relate transference/counter-transference to interactional dynamics. Thus we may perhaps now leave the topic of the delusional transference and try to sum up the beneficial contributions of psychoanalysis in the field of transference in general.

The first benefit is that transference understanding reveals to the patient something of his real primitive or infantile attitudes both to himself and to others. Because sometimes quite a split may be observed so that these attitudes are found to be in considerable contrast with those of his adult, civilized and reasonable self, this increased consciousness represents the first step in an integrative movement that will bring the two sides of his personality into a closer and mutually more workable relationship.

The second benefit of the psychoanalytic contribution through transference analysis is that it facilitates the development of a relationship between the patient and analyst as real persons—with all the therapeutic gain, emotional nourishment, and increase in self knowledge that sound object relationships can promote.

(b) Transference in analytical psychology

Transference was always regarded by Jung as fundamental to analytical psychotherapy (Jung, 1946). He experienced it as essentially a spontaneous event and was scornful of the idea that it could be required of a patient or manipulatively induced in him. When it happened, the basic mechanism involved was that of projection (Jung, 1946, p.70). He fully accepted that much of it represented the transferring into the analytical situation of feelings and experiences belonging to the past. He did not deny its content of infantile erotic or sexual feeling and he was well aware of the incest at its heart (Jung, 1946, p.173). He did wish to establish that in its content there are also to be discerned power drives, sometimes associated with sexuality and sometimes not (Jung, 1946, p.173), as well as hungry impulses to possess, fear, self-destructive impulses and negation of desire (Jung, 1946, p.173). There is not, however, much in his writings about the aspect of transference that has been called the *infantile transference*, the details of which, he tended to think, could be taken as read (Jung, 1946, p.165). He was really more interested in what has been called the *archetypal transference*, in which parts of the self, archetypal in nature and hitherto unrealized, would in the first instance be projected onto the analyst. He was strongly impressed by what he conceived of as the efforts of the self to press upon the attention of consciousness hitherto unrealized archetypal potential, such as the shadow, animus, anima, the wise old woman with her wisdom of the earth, and the wise old man with his cultural wisdom of the ages. These images, together with the feelings involved, would become projected on to the analyst in the first instance; a good example of this can be found in Charles's dream about the boatman (see p.184–5). Furthermore, the considerable complications involved in the projection of anima or animus may be meditated on in Jung's well-known figure of the intercrossing transference relationship (Jung, 1946, p.221).

Further work has been done by Fordham and many others on transference and published in the *Journal of Analytical Psychology*. Fordham (1957), for instance, has clearly distinguished two fundamental pairs of transference phenomena in relation to transference content. The first pair, as already mentioned, may be called the *infantile transference* and the *archetypal transference*. At first sight it seems to some people that they might be understood as contrasting strongly in a number of ways. Thus we could talk about the contrast between early beginnings and more or less very advanced end-product structures. We could contrast the relatively simple concerns of infantile and child life with survival and relationships within the family, on the one hand, with the complexity of archetypal potentials and realization in the full grown person on the other. In truth, however, there is plenty of common ground linking these two interests together through the fact that archetypal themes are to be found in childhood, while immaturities and infantilities are observable in the archetypal themes of adulthood and need to be allowed to be nurtured and to grow, as Jung constantly pointed out.

The second pair of transference phenomena in Fordham's work are the *illusional transference* as contrasted with the *delusional transference*. We have here, of course, in Jungian terms, what we have already described in the section on psychoanalysis: the difference between ability and inability to understand the "as if" quality of transference and the degree to which past experience can induce behaviour in the present which is inappropriate to present circumstances. Although there is plenty of evidence in the practice of analytical psychology to suggest the power of unconscious archetypal images and objects to create a delusional situation, it is also known that states of this sort are not necessarily permanently fixed and are often open in the long run to analysis.

Summing up the attitudes of analytical psychology in the special respect of this section of the present chapter, we find a resemblance to many aspects of traditional psychoanalysis, and as we have seen there is even something in common between Anna Freud's "externalisations" and some of the content of the archetypal transference in analytical psychology, though this statement should not be taken as playing down the significance of archetypes.

Transference/Counter-transference and Interaction

The account so far given of the transference in psychoanalysis and analytical psychology suggests that it is based upon a considerable element of abstraction and delimitation, for it has taken transference, so to speak, in isolation as if the therapist were more a passive recipient of projections than a partner in an interactional and reciprocal relation. So the account given represents a distortion of what many analysts would feel to be the true facts of the analytic situation. It is therefore necessary to attempt an account of the matter that demonstrates the relationship between the transference/counter-transference situation and the interaction of patient and therapist as real people, because consciousness of this interactional relationship has become more clear in recent years, both in psychoanalysis and in analytical psychology.

Transference/Counter-transference Interaction in Psychoanalysis

As I have indicated above, the subject of transference in psychoanalysis was at first treated mainly in isolation, and this was even more true with counter-transference. It was in 1910 that Freud first recognized some of the importance of the counter-transference and then mainly in terms of its dangers. There was then a silence of forty years in the psychoanalytical literature, with the exception of an article by Hann-Kende in 1936.

The subject was not reopened until the end of the 1940s, by writers like Lorand, Winnicott, Heimann, Margaret Little, Annie Reich, Gitelson, Weigert and Money-Kyrle. However, Volume 73 of the International Psycho-Analytical Library, *Transference and Counter-transference* by the late Heinrich Racker (1968), containing papers written by him mainly during the 1950s, represents to my knowledge the first systematic study of transference/counter-transference by a psychoanalyst, together with a fully worked out description of counter-transference therapy and an acceptance of its interactional dynamic.

Racker's parallel study sets out much of the detail of the interrelationship between transference and counter-transference, which he sums up in the apparently paradoxical phrase "transference is a function of the patient's transferences and the analyst's counter-transferences" (Racker, 1968, p.125). This is a variant on Hann-Kende's original definition of counter-transference as "a function of the transferences of the patient and of the analyst" (Hann-Kende, 1936). A phrase like that must still sound strange to many ears as a result of the two senses in which the word transference is being used, and to justify it Racker first sets out to define the nature of a therapeutic analytical situation. Thus he emphasizes that in it two persons are involved—each with a neurotic part and a healthy part, a past and a present, and a relation to phantasy and to reality. Each is both an adult and a child, having feelings towards each other of a child to a parent and a parent to a child.

This simple statement is open to various interpretations. It could tempt the superficial thought that what is sauce for the goose is sauce for the gander—as many defensively think. Such a thought seems inappropriate when applied to an asymmetrical relationship where the nature and purpose of the relationship demand greater responsibility and awareness, at least in some aspects, on the part of one member of the relationship than on the part of the other. I refer, of course, to the parent–child relationship, the teacher–pupil, the employer–employed and in certain areas, in a complementary way, in the husband–wife relationship. Without this greater consciousness on the part of one of the parties the relationship will go seriously wrong and come to a halt.

The analytic relationship is one of these relationships. It requires a considerably greater capability and know-how for the augmentation of consciousness on the part of the analyst, at least in the first instance, than could possibly be expected of the vast majority of patients. As Racker puts it, this difference is both quantitative and qualitative. The requirement is uncomfortably severe: to analyse effectively, the analyst must, in relation to his patients, be conscious of and emotionally comfortable with not only his own personal infantile and child dynamics but also the way in which the very analytic set-up itself induces in him regressive as well as responsible attitudes towards them. All this involves a kind of openness to himself and his internal objects that may result in both the patient and himself experiencing a long analysis in a beneficial way and in the patient in particular becoming increasingly able to deploy his personality within, and in time outside, the analytic situation.

Therefore in setting up a therapeutic situation the analyst commits himself to what Racker calls a "predisposition": "The intention to understand creates a certain predisposition to identify oneself with the analysand which is the basis of comprehension" (Racker, 1968, p.134).

I myself would add that as a part of the therapeutic set-up to be envisaged the analyst should strive to establish the conditions of the work in terms of time, place, number and length of sessions, fees and holidays in ways that can best promote a situation where the real interaction and the transference/counter-transference relationship can be profitably understood and used for therapeutic purposes. The responsibility is considerable, because the patient at the beginning of an analysis is often unconscious of the reasons for the therapeutic set-up suggested by the analyst. Of course, this is not always feasible in terms of both personal commitment and economics, but there are times when success in securing this depends upon the strength of the analyst's personal conviction.

The Neurotic Counter-transference in Psychoanalysis

We now pass on to the types of transference/counter-transference that can arise out of the analytic set-up and the analyst's predisposition. Here we find Racker distinguishing between the *neurotic counter-transference* (Racker, 1968, pp.91 ff.) and *counter-transference proper*. The former would develop were the analyst to become identified with his own infantile and child feelings in relation to the patient (Racker, 1968, p.106). There is a further complication if these infantile feelings focus much upon the opinions of the patient's relatives—or society—or the analyst's colleagues. In this case we have what Racker designates the *neurotic sub-transference* (Racker, 1968, p.114), which is likely to be intense to the degree that the analyst is a trainee or newly qualified and whether he admits it or not. The crucial point here does not rest upon the analyst's reacting to his patient from out of the infantile, the childlike and the primitive within himself, for these features are bound to be part of a total response to his patient. It rests, rather, upon whether the analyst *identifies* with these reactions and hence develops delusionary or disproportionate anxiety, anger, dependence, etc. in connection with his patient, as well as pathological defences against these feelings. The danger comes from unanalysed bits, unsolved problems, and emotionally insufficiently integrated early impulses.

One of Racker's contentions is that the very set-up of analysis, with its interdiction on many kinds of behaviour, including genital behaviour, can activate in the analyst a wide range of sexual and aggressive feelings towards his patients—if female as if towards his mother, if male as if towards his father. All kinds of oedipal feelings and oral, anal and phallic complications can get activated. Anger, hatred, rivalry, unconscious manipulation of the patient's relationships, love, submissiveness, manic excitement, depressive and paranoid responses can all serve to blind the analyst to the realities of the patient's position and damage his capacities to respond appropriately to the patient's need.

I cannot forbear from quoting Racker's generalized example. A male analyst becomes very angry with the avarice of a female patient. Intellectually he may be able to understand that she defends herself from him because he is felt by her to be the thieving analyst. An archaic, internal object, the rapacious mother, is being projected on to him. Emotionally, however, he may fail to respond adequately, either because he guiltily fears he might in fact be robbing his patient or because at that time, or perhaps often, he is overcome by oral resentment at the patient who, by rejecting him, has become for him his own robbing mother or perhaps the withholding breast. The neurotic counter-transference in this case renders him impotent as an analyst, during the time when he is identified, only temporarily it is hoped, with an unintegrated infantile response. On the other hand, if he can recover enough to have an emotional identification with the patient's threatened ego, he may be able to turn the neurotic counter-transference into what will shortly be discussed as a complementary counter-transference (Racker, 1968, pp.124-5).

The other danger of a neurotic counter-transference is that the analyst may graft upon or induce in his patient his own neurosis—an example being that of a young analyst, convinced that he should be independent when he has not yet reached that point, seeking to force his patient into acting a false independence when this is the last thing the patient should be attempting to do (Racker, 1968, pp.135-6).

Racker's concept of the neurotic counter-transference, with its notion of the primitive and infantile parts of the analyst being liable under the stress of certain circumstances to become activated, is indeed reminiscent of Jung's patient's dream of her former analyst clinging to her like a madman on the wrong side of the frontier (Jung, 1934, p.144). Jung's alarming example, assuming that the dream really was about the analyst, forces us to hope that analysts are better analysed today and hence not so liable to such disasters. A last point has to be considered, as I discovered when in concluding this paragraph I made some slips of the pen and wrote neurotic "transference" instead of neurotic "counter-transference". This made me wonder whether I unconsciously disapproved of neurotic counter-transference as if it were just the same as neurotic transference. I think, however, that the distinction remains valid. There is a quantitative and qualitative difference between a patient's transference to one normally more-or-less stable analyst and the response of an analyst who sometimes under stress and erosion from a number of disturbed patients may react neurotically to their transferences from time to time. Neurotic counter-transference is a more apt description and represents, normally speaking, a professional hazard. It is a neurotic counter-response to a transference from a patient rather than a neurotic transference on to a patient who has done nothing to provoke it.

Counter-transference Proper in Psychoanalysis

We can now pass on to the central point of Racker's paper and examine his contribution to the concept of counter-transference proper. He is concerned with the understanding of counter-transference from the point of view of the inner experience of the analyst and how his handling of it influences the transference of the patient. He therefore discriminates between two modes of it: one that is relatively steady and quiet; the other disturbing, dramatic, uncomfortable. The first he calls the *concordant* counter-transference, the second the *complementary* counter-transference. The two are interconnected and are based upon the development of the predisposition of the analyst to identify, in the first case, with the patient's ego and, in the second, with his internal objects.

The Concordant Counter-transference in Psychoanalysis

In the concordant counter-transference, the analyst identifies his ego with the patient's ego, and each part of his personality with the *(child ego)* corresponding part of the patient's personality (Racker, 1968, p.134). Racker himself explicitly confines this to ego, super-ego and id without mention of internal objects in this context, although of course internal objects have close connections with all three structures. The analyst who has made these identifications can become conscious of them to the extent of his own personal analysis and self-analysis. The identifications, Racker holds, come into being through introjection and projection, by which he means the resonance of the exterior in the interior leading to (*a*) the unconscious recognition that what belongs to another is one's own (through introjection I feel that this part of you is me) and (*b*) the unconscious equation of what is my own with what belongs to another (through projection I feel that this part of me is you). The phrase "concordant counter-transference" is used to stress the therapist's action in going along with the patient's dynamics with empathy and sympathy.

An interesting feature of this concept emerges in Racker's description of the way in which the concordance develops. It is the result of the analyst's predisposition to empathy with the patient whereby it turns out that an important aspect of the relation remains always in the following form: the analyst is the subject and the patient is the object of knowledge and concern. This annuls the "object relationship" *between* the patient and the analyst whereby there are two persons interacting. Thus there arises instead, as Racker puts it, an approximate union or identity between the various parts (experiences, impulses, defences) of the subject and the object (Racker, 1968, p.136). On this level, the patient and the analyst are in minimal tension over against each other and are in a state of maximal union.

It seems clear enough here that the therapeutic set-up envisaged includes the level of very early primitive aims, on the part of the infant to achieve a state of primary identity with the mother—a fusionary wish, in Fordham's terms. It provides a containing place for the anxieties of the very ill patient who is not only wishing to regress to the state of an "as if" primary identity with the mother – analyst but is actually beginning to be able to do so. And it is this very happening that can spontaneously generate in the analyst a growing concordant counter-transference.

Between the analyst and the patient, there can come into play the four mechanisms of defence against anxiety in early infancy described by Fordham in *Children as Individuals* (1969): projection, introjection, identification, and idealization. These experiences form the basis of the ability of the analyst and patient to develop between them a growing comprehension of the patient's problem, a process that is entirely in line with Jung's description of the union of like with like that fosters a situation whereby incest phantasies are "positively dragged into the light of day by the analytic method" (Jung, 1929, p.62).

The basic point here is that the concordant counter-transference arises, extends, and deepens uniquely within the analytic setting as such. Outside analysis, it can be observed in maternal care for the infant and young child, in the sympathy some teachers have for adolescents, and perhaps in states of being in love. Nevertheless the limitations of such types of concordance are well-known, leaving it fairly clear that the range and depth of the concordant counter-transference in the analyst can be quantitatively and qualitatively much greater.

We may add that the analyst's capacity for concordance rests upon his own experience of good enough handling by another when in a state of dependence. The motive power is gratitude and gratification in infancy which enables a person later to have concern for another that is real and not contrived. With the analyst, it is the experience and memory of his own analysis and the capacities for self-analysis started off by it that are determinative. Furthermore, it is likely that, whatever other fundamental aspects of counter-transference there may be, we shall find that it is out of his concordance that the analyst does his decisively creative work. We must add, however, that concordance is a growing process in a successful analysis—a growth in depth resting upon the successful resolution of the stresses involved in another kind of counter-transference.

The Complementary Counter-transference in Psychoanalysis

That other aspect of counter-transference Racker designates the "complementary counter-transference". It arises from the fact that despite the annulment in the analytic situation of the object relationship in principle there can yet appear a number of the aspects of an object relationship all the same. The analyst is still and always remains a total human being with a capacity for making object-relationships and experiencing the emotional responses proper to them as well as those that arise in states of identity. He may experience libidinal need of various sorts (Racker, 1968, p.105). He may feel ill-treated by his patient and experience outrage or anger. Again, he makes transferences on to or projects on to his patient as if the patient were an internal object of his own; and he may be open to the wide range of all-or-nothing infantile emotion already described under the heading of the neurotic counter-transference. Or again he may experience resistance to certain emotions in both his patients and himself—for instance to certain kinds of aggression. Furthermore, these feelings, as Fordham has pointed out, may be very intense indeed, especially if the treatment approaches psychotic areas of experience.

Out of all this a number of possible responses arise. At one end of the spectrum we find thoroughly neurotic counter-transferences. In the middle there arises the possibility of the analyst reacting to the experiences not so grossly but still in fact neurotically acting out within the analysis. At the other end, the analyst may be able to employ his counter-transference emotions as the stimulus to an effort to gain for himself information not only about the patient's transference, but also about his own state of identity with the patient's internal objects and his reverberations to the treatment meted out to them by the patient and vice versa. In the shorter or longer run, after this has become successfully accomplished, it becomes possible to renew his concordant counter-transference out of which he can make a therapeutically effective interpretation. The counter-transference involved is termed "complementary" and develops when, for a number of reasons, the patient treats the analyst as a projected internal object, with the result that in a complementary way the analyst feels treated as such and experiences emotions appropriate to such treatment (Racker, 1968, p.135). This is counter-transference proper, whereas if the analyst were to respond to such treatment as if his patient were one of his own internal objects in projection, then we should be dealing with a neurotic counter-transference. The mechanism involved in complementary counter-transference proper is that until he has become aware of it, the analyst is drawn into unconscious identification with an internal object or objects in the drama of the patient's inner life. With added consciousness, however, he can gain a sense of the internal conflicts of feeling going on more or less unconsciously in the patient.

Talion Law, Gratitude and the Therapeutic Interaction in Psychoanalysis

We have so far examined some of the dynamism inherent in the psychoanalytic situation as described by Racker when it is being considered as a whole situation within which various kinds of transference/counter-transference work together in a state of interaction. There are, however, deeper levels still and these relate to the personal integrity of the patient and, especially, the analyst as real persons. Racker has chosen, out of a number of factors, to describe one such level of interaction: the operation of the talion law in therapy. The essential points that he makes are as follows:

(1) Because the infantile and child parts of both the analyst and the patient are involved, the transference/counter-transference relationship tends to be profoundly influenced by the dynamism of the talion law. This, of course, is the primitive situation of "an eye for an eye, and a tooth for a tooth". In terms of the psyche it refers to the feelings that are aroused by love and hate, by cooperation and aggression—feelings that may be denied but are really there (Racker, 1968, pp.137–42).

(2) Simply put, the dynamism is activated by the fact that positive transference is answered by positive counter-transference and negative transference by negative counter-transference and, by implication, vice versa. The word transference is here used in not too precise a sense and in Racker's context seems to include the notion of a general affective attitude.

(3) In the actual analytical situation, however, I think that there are two types of progression in relation to the talion law.

The first is where the predisposition of the analyst to care for and understand the patient creates a superficial positive transference. This is answered by a deepening positive concordant counter-transference in the analyst that may render the patient secure enough to risk experiencing his latent hostile feelings as negative transference. This in turn activates negative elements in the analyst's complementary counter-transference, and here we get to the central point in the therapy from the point of view of the patient's relationship to his internal objects.

Two things can happen. In one case the analyst cannot understand his negative complementary counter-transference. He then either tries to suppress his feelings of hostility towards his patient, or he expresses it by more or less subtle and possibly unconscious ways, or he does it openly. In any case, the patient, who had projected his hostile internal object upon the analyst and unconsciously feels the analyst's hostility, introjects it again, not modified but enhanced and magnified. The outer world has only confirmed his delusionary inner world. This is the "vicious circle" of delusion that results from the straightforward operation of the talion law. In the other case the analyst manages to understand the complementary negative counter-transference and also to master his feelings in such a way as to be able to make useful interpretations out of a renewed concordant counter-transference. If he does so he may succeed in making a breach in the patient's vicious circle either in part or wholly, either temporary or long-lasting (Racker 1968, p.138). If he does so, the relief of the patient may be such, and his gratitude so great, that he may take a step towards a genuine and deep positive transference and an enhancement of his capacity for trust (see Plaut, 1966, pp.113-22). This promotes further openness to therapy.

The second type of analytic progression which we often find is that though there is a predisposition on the part of the analyst to understand, the patient at once brings a strongly enduring negative transference straight into the treatment, expressed by continuous hostile negation or masked by a compulsive positive over-estimation of the analyst. Then the analyst is involved from the first in negative complementary counter-transference and is landed with a lot of hard work in mastering this and turning it into understanding and beneficial interpretations. The breaching of the vicious circle is liable, as we all know, to be long and arduous. However any positive transference that thus develops out of it is likely to be deep seated and fruitful.

We may notice here that these considerations brought in by Racker are quite close in spirit to Jung, who seems to have considered that on a deep level a positive transference is important for success in therapy. The kind of positive transference envisaged is not of course an idealization or a one-sided denial of the negative, but is related to a repaired capacity to trust and to modify persecutory and paranoid delusions. Then the patient may be free to accept the reality of the analyst in his good and bad aspects, as well as his own good and bad aspects, and also the good and bad aspects of analysis itself. At this point something like health is being established, but it rests upon the agapaic ability of the analyst to contain the operation of the talion law and to modify the vicious circle caused by the fact that the outer world is seeming to the patient to confirm his worst fears.

The account given above of Racker's contribution shows that, within psychoanalysis, it has become possible to understand the analytic interaction as a whole and at a level of greater depth. In particular he has demonstrated further aspects of the dynamisms that keep the analytic process moving and ongoing. Implicit in Racker's account of this is a factor that he scarcely names—*gratitude* in both patient and analyst in their differing functions in the process. In this connection, I should add that it is to Melanie Klein (1957) that analysts owe a debt of gratitude for her work in drawing their attention to the experience of gratitude as an essential feature in personal development. It belongs to the movement of the generations. In normal development, when the infant's experience of having his needs met by his mother is satisfactory, gratitude spontaneously appears among a number of responses to his parents experienced as both good and bad. It is out of this gratitude that children in growing up can in turn do something for their children who are also the grandchildren of their parents.

In the analytic situation, where the repair of damage done to normal development is part of the therapeutic process, a similar pattern appears. Out of the transference/counter-transference, with its uncovering of the operation of the talion law, an appropriate interpretation that is truly non-punitive can activate gratitude in the patient who is worried by his destructivity and persecutory feelings—especially when these feelings are maiming the patient's capacity to make use of his analyst's interpretations. It may be considered that this non-punitive handling of destructivity can activate gratitude at the deepest levels—deeper even than those activated by patience in listening, steady concern and the putting at the disposal of the patient the accumulated knowledge and skill of the analyst.

If we consider the motivation of the analyst, we may think that it depends upon a sufficient experience of gratitude in himself for an appropriate handling of the talion law in the transference/counter-transference situation on the part of his own analyst and others concerned in his training as well as colleagues. Beyond that general gratitude, however, a gratitude in the analyst, specific to an individual treatment, arises in relation to the patient as well, as the latter becomes more and more able to make use of his analytical skills.

The problem of gratitude is not, however, an easy one. Analysts are forced to ask themselves whether the capacity for gratitude, a spontaneous emergent and not a contrivance of the "moral will", can be aborted or permanently damaged. Perhaps it is premature to attempt an answer, as no doubt much more understanding is needed of damage and repair at levels of infantile development prior to the point when gratitude is seen to emerge. Returning, however, to the actual analytic situation, I am inclined to the view that at least five levels or intensities of gratitude may be discerned in patients:

(1) There are patients who, while continually emphasizing the uselessness of analysis, tend to come to session after session rather than stop analysis. The continual return may suggest an action expressing, non-verbally and probably quite unconsciously, a rudimentary recognition that some kind of acceptance of their negativity as well as listening is being offered by the analyst on their behalf.

(2) A slightly more conscious level may be expressed in terms of a grudging recognition of services rendered coupled with the idea that "it is the least that can be done".

(3) The next level is a kind of half-gratitude suffused with tearful remembrance of a long, long wait before help came.

(4) Then there is something that may be felt by the patient as gratitude, except that it is not very lasting and gets rather soon diminished by perfectionist criticism.

(5) Finally we may discern a full and enjoyed feeling of gratitude that releases the personality of the patient into more creative and contributory work in the analysis while further bringing out creative responses in the analyst.

To sum up the psychoanalytic position arrived at by Racker, the ongoing momentum of the interaction behind the transference/counter-transference depends upon the integrative and, I would add, agapaic personality of the analyst to understand his neurotic counter-transference and to handle suitably those of his counter-transferences that are complementary to the patient's transferences of his internal objects on to himself. When the analyst can translate the libido in the strong affects thus aroused into a fresh concordant understanding, gratitude in the patient may motivate him into making fresh communications. Perhaps to complete the story we should add that this can only be achieved when the patient's envy of the skill, health and agapaic qualities of the analyst has been itself sufficiently analysed.

Counter-transference and Interaction in Analytical Psychology

Jung's contribution to the subject of counter-transference is dominated by his emphasis upon the interactional aspects of the patient–analyst relationship and his insistence upon the importance of the analyst's own analysis. These latter emphases began to emerge by the end of the 1920s, and it is therefore no surprise that at the same time he was observing that, in an encounter between two persons, who are not fixed and determinable quantities, "the counter-transference is evoked by the transference" (Jung, 1931, p.72), without reference, however, to the reverse of this. Counter-transference is also implicit in the same paper when he describes the activation of incest phantasies between analyst and patient (Jung, 1931, p.62), which necessarily contain transference and counter-transference as they belong in the first place to parent – child incestuous imagery. This gets activated by the appeal for help that is inherent in the analytical situation, "as if" it were the original situation in the infancy and childhood of both patient and, to a lesser extent, analyst.

Later, in *The Psychology of the Transference* (1946), Jung noted that "Freud had already discovered the phenomenon of the counter-transference" (p.171). Jung considered it along with Freud in the context of the possible deleterious effects of the therapeutic relationship upon the health of the analyst.

In the same treatise, Jung described an extremely complicated interpersonal interaction known as the intercrossing transference relationship or the marriage quaternity, as in alchemical thought. In the alchemical treatise known as the *Rosarium Philosophorum*, published in 1550 in Frankfurt and in 1593 in Basle, he found a series of pictures illustrating the relationship between the alchemist and his soror that seemed to him to anticipate the analytic processes of today. From the second picture of this series, called "The Marriage of the King and the Queen", he abstracted a diagram that could be thought of as expressive of the relationship between man and woman or patient and analyst as follows (Jung, 1946, p.221).

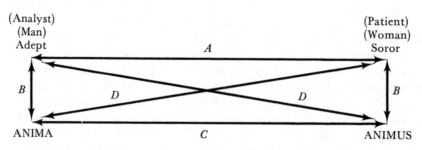

The direction of the arrows is meant to indicate mutual two-way attraction between masculine and feminine and between conscious and unconscious. Jung emphasizes that the diagram is a simplification, for the purpose of thought, of interchanges that are much more confused, complex and forever changing in content, but the four elements indicated by the letters *A, B, C* and *D* can be listed as follows:

(*A*) An uncomplicated personal relationship without reference to unconscious processes.

(*B*) A relationship of the man to his anima and of the woman to her animus.

(*C*) A relationship of anima to animus and vice versa.

(*D*) A relationship of the feminine animus to the man (which happens when the woman is identical with her animus) and of the masculine anima to the woman (which happens when the man is identical with his anima).

Jung is at pains to emphasize the difficulties inherent in the description and amplification of such a many-levelled process. It includes naively shallow surface *A* relationships and *B* relationships in which, either parallel to or totally split off from the surface, the parties are preoccupied with or are being deeply moulded by unconscious forces that are contrasexual in a complementary way. Under such circumstances, it is unlikely that the surface relationships will deepen and become meaningful. The two protagonists are otherwise engaged. When it comes to *C* relationships, in which the unconscious anima and unconscious animus engage each other, we find great difficulties occurring just because the dynamisms are not at all apparent. The most painful instance of this is the famous animus–anima wrangle, when a man and a woman get across each other in violent emotional ways that are meaningless, misleading and totally incomprehensible to the suffering and puzzled human beings involved. Jung's *D* relationship, however, can often be promising. It depends on the level of unconsciousness involved in such identifications or indeed on whether the anima and animus development has been minimal or again whether there is no integration of, but only states of identification between the man and his anima and between the woman and her animus. There can be quite good experiences of cooperation between the two human beings involved when the man can tolerate and appreciate the contributions of the woman's animus even if she is identified with it and vice versa. Unfortunately the contrary is often the case, so that infantile relationships of envy, contempt and defiance too often disturb and poison or destroy what might otherwise be a situation of mutual benefit. Recent advances in the understanding of early infantile developmental problems, however, have shed new light on some of the disturbances that arise in man–woman anima–animus interchanges. This has added something to what was adumbrated by Jung when he spoke of the presence of young and underdeveloped aspects of the psyche that demand attention, accompanied as they often are by what we now consider to be neurotic disturbance originating in early damage.

We may record too that in reconstructive analysis within the transference/counter-transference it is possible to analyse animus and anima end-product components into their elements in order to facilitate improved expression and integration of their content (see Chapter 6). For instance, an anima complex may have, as a result of early traumata, emerged as an end-product that is too neurotic, if not psychotic, for integration of it to be feasible without prior analysis for repair or release.

Another development that facilitates an improved grasp of the archetypal transference and counter-transference, as postulated by Jung in the marriage quaternity figure, is represented by the work on object relationships described in Chapter 4. If the archetypal object and later the internalized archetypal object are results of a kind of marriage (if not fusion) between archetypal expectation and the real presentation or situation corresponding to it, then by implication the function of the analyst and patient is not simply to be a screen to receive the projection of archetypal images. Their reality as people also becomes important, for out of the interplay between them as such and the archetypal content projected upon them, are then formed archetypal objects which inevitably, to some extent, contain elements of the analyst's personality and, for better or for worse, become powerful and stable factors in the psychology of patient and analyst.

A final point to be made in connection with Jung's marriage quaternity figure is that it seems to assume a symmetrical relationship between the two parties concerned. This may perhaps be so between the adept and his soror in the alchemical opus. It may often be so in the relationship between man and woman. However, for reasons already adduced (see p.144), it is unlikely to be so in the case of analyst and patient, at least under contemporary conditions, where an analyst has had long years of analysis, training, supervision and then a good measure of clinical experience. This, however, can operate to the advantage of the patient as his analyst can respect the asymmetry, and not force upon the patient knowledge that it would be premature for him to attempt to assimilate. Yet he can more or less understand what is going on in the marriage quaternity and hence can analyse it in a facilitating way that is unfortunately not available to an unanalysed pair struggling in the unconscious depths—if not darkness—of their relationship.

Apart from the more obvious transference/counter-transference implications in the motifs just mentioned there are other aspects of Jung's preoccupation with the patient – analyst interaction. First of all, he was convinced that therapy arose out of the mutual influence of two whole persons at a more mutually involved level than that envisaged in the early days by psychoanalysis. He could write about this in terms of a *dialectic* (Jung, 1935, p.3). He could use imagery like that of the *mixing of two chemical substances*, resulting in the transformation of two persons in a therapeutic relationship (Jung, 1929, pp.71-2). He could then envisage the asymmetry already mentioned by the use of a traditional image of healings whereby *the demon of sickness* can be overcome by the sufferer's transmission of his disease to a healthy person by whose powers it can then be subdued (Jung, 1929, p.72). If this, however, was to be effective, it was because of a *wounding of the healer* who, through his recovery, had now gained the power to heal (Jung, 1929, p.72).

It seems fairly clear that we are dealing here with holistic imagery of a symbolical sort that is striking indeed. Nevertheless it implies no denial of the relevance and usefulness of such modes of perception to insist that further detailed psychological investigation into the processes suggested by imagery of this sort is needed (see pp.16–19).

Finally mention should be made of the mobilization of libido envisaged by Jung in connection with the therapeutic interaction as described above. The incestuous libido is mainly activated by states of mutual attraction, a "pull from masculine to feminine and vice versa, and from the unconscious of one person to the conscious of the other" in the form of a marriage relationship, psychologically speaking. On a more superficial level other motivations are clearly observable like mother–infant and parent–child relationships in their infinite variety of possibility. It remains, however, likely that in many full analytical treatments something like Jung's conjunctio will take place, with the implication that something new will result from it, as if a birth takes place.

Since Jung, the subject of counter-transference has been taken up by analytical psychologists like Stein, Fordham, Moody, Plaut, Strauss, Williams, Jackson, Gordon, Whitmont, Frantz, Lambert, Dieckmann and many others. A consistent originator of and contributor to such studies has always been Fordham. In 1957 he proposed a distinction that was very similar to, though independent of, Racker's, whose views (described above) were also published in the same year. Fordham designated the two types of counter-transference as illusory and syntonic (Fordham 1957). *Illusory* counter-transference, like Racker's neurotic counter-transference, refers to an analyst's response to his patient's transference whereby he projects his own infantile material on to his patient in such a way that his perception of his patient's nature is obscured if not illusory. This kind of distortion can be analysed and corrected. In *syntonic* counter-transference, the analyst reacts to the patient's transference as if he himself were that internal object (with all its feelings) which the patient has alienated from himself by transferring it on to his analyst. One of the indications that this is going on is that the analyst notes that he is feeling or behaving in a way that is alien to him and uncharacteristic of him. Fordham's well-known example was that of a situation in which he remained silent and unresponsive to a barrage of questions from the patient—questions that in fact were scarcely answerable. This was unlike his nature, and he discovered with the help of the patient that he was responding in feeling and even a little in action in exactly the same way as the patient's father—one of her internal objects—had done when she was a girl. Her transference had evoked syntonic counter-transference feelings in her analyst.

It seems clear that Fordham's and Racker's views are strikingly close, although Racker postulates a concordant and a complementary counter-transference with interactions of resolution going on between them. That process seems similar to the one implied in Fordham's resolution of the syntonic counter-transference. As a result of this resolution he returns to a state which is similar to the concordance returned to by Racker when he has learnt from his complementary counter-transference. One other implication with both authors is that concordant, complementary and syntonic counter-transferences may all be contaminated by neurotic or illusory elements in the response of analysts to their patients' transferences, whether positive or negative, and it is vital that consciousness of this is gained.

More recently Fordham (1978, p.93 and *passim*) has concentrated upon the actual unconscious mechanisms upon which counter-transference in general seems to be based. He holds that they are projective and introjective processes. The analyst projects on to the patient elements of his own experience, compares the two, withdraws the projection and offers an interpretation. Otherwise he introjects, i.e. discovers within himself emotional content belonging to the patient. Out of a comparison of this content with his own experiences he offers an interpretation. These transactions seem to arise out of situations where the analyst's emotions are powerful, unexpected, and noticeably alien; where elements looking as if belonging to the formation of object-relations on the part of the patient are to the fore; and where the analyst is reverberating to the powerful impact of parts of the patient's personality of which the latter is unconscious—namely internal archetypal objects. It may be regarded as a dramatic emotional situation that gradually transforms into quieter states of understanding—in Racker's words, the passage from complementariness to concordance.

In a later paper Fordham (1979) suggests that the time is coming when the term counter-transference may be limited once more to the illusory or neurotic counter-transference, so that the vigorous interplay of complementariness and concordance would no longer be regarded as counter-transference but understood as part of the normal therapeutic processes of projection and reprojection, of introjection and re-introjection. The advantage of Fordham's suggestion is that the word counter-transference is thus limited to the designation of processes of neurotic illusion in the analyst that hold up the ongoing analytical process and lose the positive value of the asymmetry whereby the analyst is able to be truly responsible for the treatment. In this case, perhaps, the notions of concordance and complementariness should be retained to describe certain dynamisms of an identificatory and de-identificatory sort in analysis.

A final word should be said about Fordham's elaboration of Jung's famous marriage quaternio figure in his description of the archetypal transference and counter-transference (Jung, 1978, p.87). It corrects Jung's implied notion that the analyst–patient relationship is symmetrical—a point we have already touched on. Fordham points out that the diagram may be modified for greater clarity. This is based upon the fact that within the relationship the analyst's ego is stronger and his or her relation to his or her anima or animus more firmly established. As a result of this, his perceptions of his patient can be deeper and more accurate and wider, while the projections and introjections are less so, more flexible and indeed *reversible*. This means he can use them for obtaining information. The patient by contrast begins analysis with resistances that interfere with the process of of withdrawing projections and with the process of becoming aware of the animus or anima and of the interaction between them. It should perhaps be stated, to avoid misunderstanding, that the asymmetry envisaged is not to be regarded as extreme. If it were, the question would arise as to the patient's suitability for analysis.

It must be clear that the modifications pointed out by Fordham are of crucial importance in the whole attitude of the analyst today: in the way he conducts an analysis, in the way that he views himself and his function and the responsibility he takes for the patient's treatment, whether in the analysis of regressed patients or in the handling of the archetypal transference and counter-transference.

It is thus that we come full circle in our discussion of (1) the interaction between transference and counter-transference, (2) the relationship of both to that between the patient and analyst as real persons, and (3) the long-term response of both patient and analyst to transference/counter-transference interpretative elucidations.

Conclusions

Much of analysis has turned out, despite some reluctance on the part of the pioneers, to require a great deal of work on the transference/counter-transferences that become uncovered in the analytic relationship. We have seen much agreement between psychoanalysis and analytical psychology over this. The infantile transference, the illusory transference and the delusional transference are all understood by both schools. Not so clearly perceived is the archetypal transference, though Anna Freud's "externalizations" (1936) are not far removed. In principle, however, there is agreement about the value of attending to transference and counter-transference, for three benefits appear to arise:

(1) Analysis of transference illusion and delusion can promote the patient's capacity to make better object relationships, beginning with the analyst as a real person. This benign result stems from the gradual withdrawal of frustrated infantile expectations from the analyst after enough symbolic parenting has been experienced. This is particularly the case with borderline patients with early narcissistic damage and with Fordham's heavy "defences of the self" (Fordham, 1974).

(2) Analysis of the infantile and child transference can facilitate the repair of things that went wrong in the early days and months of infancy and childhood as well as a release from the distortion of experience resulting from such damage. The most usual problems met are parent–infant and parent–child problems, sibling rivalry and oedipal problems.

(3) Aspects of the patient's personality that are unconscious or unrealized may be found transferred to the person of the analyst. When the almost inevitable envy of his analyst in whom these qualities are thought to reside has been analysed, it may be possible for the patient to own them and to experiment with them in his own person. For analytical psychology, of course,

these contents are archetypal in varying degrees, such as the shadow, animus, anima, *puer aeternus,* and wise old man or woman, and must be matched with elements in the analyst's personality in the first place and then assimilated. This implies that the more the complexities of the analyst's personality have been analysed and realized the more will this be possible.

Transference content and feeling have, however, been discovered to be much influenced by the concordant and complementary responses of the analyst. When, however, the counter-transference has been considerably neurotic or illusory and has thus lasted too long, the analysis may come to grief as the patient may be coming up against a real block in the analyst as a real person. Otherwise the agapaic complementary and concordant response of the analyst, when really appropriate and to the point, promotes gratification, gratitude and growth in the patient and is an expression of the soundness and therapeutic potency of the analyst as a real person.

The motive power that keeps the therapeutic encounter alive and moving is, as Jung has pointed out, incestuous love and in my view the agapaic capacities of the analyst. It often arises out of power struggles, out of fears of engulfment and swallowing, or out of periods of mutual gratification and gratitude, especially when the destructive aspects of talion law are sufficiently overcome on the analyst's part. In the patient a passion for autonomy, integration, individuation and a realization of the self may often be discovered to be behind the efforts made. For the analyst, empathic gifts, the need to repair, gratitude towards his own analyst and belief in the creative powers of the self supply much of the power. Above all, perhaps, it is his enhanced sense of life, as object relationships with the patient are promoted, that operates upon the treatment in a cumulative and energizing way.

It should be obvious that an analyst practising in the 1980s does so over against a rich historical development in the whole field of interaction and transference/counter-transference experience. If he comes from the Jungian background, he will know that in it, from the beginning, the interaction of the two real persons (the patient and the analyst) has always occupied a central position in therapy—sometimes in a way that seemed polar opposite to psychoanalysis, with its emphasis on technique and transference analysis. We know, however, that this is not really the case, as evidenced in the introduction to *The Psychology of the Transference* (Jung, 1946). We have found that his images in the area of personal interaction need further elucidation, and passages in the present chapter describing the work of Fordham and Racker show to some extent how in detail the interactional processes alluded to by Jung work themselves out. They may be described as:

(1) The dialectical procedure described by Jung may be further analysed as follows. The mutual influence of analyst and patient can promote a longitudinal process involving, for instance, the analyst's predisposition which evokes positive transference and, in response to this, further positive concordant counter-transference. Gradually the patient risks the expression of a negative transference which may evoke negative complementary counter-transference that gets transformed by the analyst into a deeper concordant counter-transference. Gratitude for this activates deeper positive transference leading to therapeutic advance.

(2) The image of the transformation of the two personalities, as if resulting from a mixture of two chemicals, may be analysed further. The analyst's personality is opened to reverberate to that of the patient in concordant and complementary ways. Through this his deepened knowledge of the patient enables him to make an interpretation that is creative within the patient's personality, while the potency of both patient and analyst is enhanced.

(3) Jung's dramatic image of the overcoming of the demon of sickness by the healthy therapist taking it over and subduing it by his powers can be partially elucidated by Racker's and Fordham's use of the concepts of identification, projection, introjection, and reprojection. The analyst takes into himself the painful inner problem of his patient, understands and assimilates it, and then can give it back to the patient in a repaired form whereby the latter can understand, assimilate and integrate it in himself in a creative way. It should, however, be added that this can only take place when transference illusions and delusions have been sufficiently analysed.

(4) The measure of therapeutic power of that sort is dependent upon a kind of wounding of the therapist. For Jung it is "not without impairing the well-being of the subduer" (Jung, 1929, p.72), cf. Adler's note on "the wounded healer" (Adler, 1961, p.117), that the demon of sickness is overcome. Racker has shown how the analyst, feeling the impact of the patient's love, greed, hate, aggression and destructiveness upon his own person, can overcome talion response and transform the energy aroused in it into therapeutic and analytic potency. In more general terms as well, the analyst is unlikely to be practising analysis if his own earlier wounds have not been dealt with in his own analysis.

(5) Jung's image of the marriage quaternity has been further elucidated by both Racker and Fordham. Racker's concept of the interplay between concordance and complementariness is clearly implicitly that between endogamous and exogamous relationships as

suggested in the diagram (Racker, 1968). Furthermore, Fordham (1978) has suggested modifications in the diagram to show the asymmetry that is proper to the analytic relationship under normal circumstances.

(6) Finally both Racker and Fordham have further explained the nature of the incest phantasies pointed out by Jung to be present in the analytical situation. It is because the patient seeks help from an analyst willing to try to meet his need, and especially because the very enterprise is likely to direct attention to childhood experiences, that both parties are inclined to be involved in mutual child – parent and parent – child wishes. It is only because the analyst has had so much more analytical experience of all sorts that a deadlock does not set in under such circumstances.

The considerations adduced in the last six paragraphs are intended to show how the vivid images employed by Jung in respect of the therapeutic interaction are only enhanced by the application to them of concepts derived from the developmental standpoint and some of the early mechanisms involved. This is not, however, to attempt to explain Jung's imagery away, but rather to acknowledge its place as part of the whole. In any case, imagery and the whole palpable, visual and emotional experience remain an essential part of the uniqueness and specificity of the personalities both of the patient and the analyst. It is this that makes of every analysis that succeeds a unique event, however much in common there may be with every other analysis that goes on in parallel.

A Case Fragment

The complexity of the subject of this chapter has left little space for a description of the detailed particularity of a case, save a fragment where transference and counter-transference is illustrated in some of its ramifications.

A professional woman operating a discipline that combined thought at a high level of abstraction with a close attention to a mass of statistical surveys was referred to me for depression. She presented as very feminine, combined with a devotion to social change, career, and feminism plus a wish to stabilize her relationship with her husband, to have a baby and to find a way of giving it good care. She was vivacious, an excellent verbalizer and an interesting raconteur of personal experiences. These were largely connected with her personal relationships, which she warmly enjoyed although she had trouble with odd misunderstandings and sometimes painful endings. She had a facility to describe and think clearly about these and to move into emotion and tears without much difficulty, though much more in terms of heartbreak than anger. Self-confessedly, she smoked too much.

Her family were involved in primary occupations in the main. Her father had been loved but had to be away from home for periods while he pursued his occupation, which was a dangerous one. Her mother, left to manage alone, developed fairly cast-iron and intrusively domineering animus defences of rigid principle, alternating with an infantile demandingness, one result of which was that she could be possessed by frightening and furious rages. She also disapproved of her daughter's way of life and accused her without justification of sexual promiscuity. My patient found consolation in the love of her siblings, both sisters, and in being extremely successful intellectually at school and university. In the larger world, in a different continent from where she was brought up, she pursued her career with success and single-mindedness and wrote a good deal, in the midst of a series of affectionate but stormy relationships with members of both sexes. Her husband was a patient and kind man of high intelligence. She combined, however, great dependence upon him with a fear of being intruded upon by him—a fear that would suddenly descend upon her with an irrational intensity of feeling. She suffered from quite deep depressions and had seen a psychiatrist on one occasion; he had touched on something he sensed as manipulative egotism and, according to her experience of him, had been downright critical of her. This must, almost certainly, have been about aspects of her omnipotence and omniscience resulting from her damaged narcissism.

In the therapy my responses were varied. She, with vivacity and charm, held my attention by the intelligence and humanity of her communications. Yet I could feel myself all the time distanced. On one occasion I felt angry over a piece of what was really a justified though seemingly egotistical demand originating in anxiety. I also noticed her apparently easy acceptance of my interpretations, the absence of any expression of the militancy over feminism and politics that she professed, and the lack of barriers arising out of the age-gap between us. Maybe, I thought, I was for her someone to consult on certain topics like a living book.

One day, after about a year of therapy, she came for the first session after a month's holiday break. She arrived in a terrible state—exhausted, physically agitated, feeling empty and paralysed over some pressing writing work. She felt absolutely and tearfully at the end of her tether and it was a long time before there would be a holiday from work. She had lost the capacity to concentrate. Something was missing. I pointed out that she had not come to me for a month and ascertained that her husband was far away at a university where he was teaching for a year and I said that she was feeling abandoned, unheld and unfed as a result of both our absences.

The next time she came, her mood was quite changed. Her husband had been able to visit her. She had been hugged and held and she said that I must have been right about her missing her husband. She had found all her energy again and could write and work. She said this with gratitude but did not take up the point about the break in the treatment.

The next time she came, she said that the good work was continuing and then that there was something she had to say but couldn't remember it. However, she went on to say that she had suddenly begun to notice two things about her behaviour with me. The first was that coming to me reminded her of the "show and talk" class at school, when she had to bring something to school, show it to the class and then talk about it. We agreed that she did this with me. She would show me her life, or a bit of it, and talk about it. She agreed that it was a useful accomplishment and that she earned her living showing and talking as a teacher, but she felt this got into the way of the therapy—as indeed it partly did. The second thing was that coming to me sometimes felt like coming home from school to her mother. The moment she arrived she began to entertain her mother, tell her stories with great vividness and detailed imagination. Then she said that this was actually a way of stopping her mother probing, asking questions and getting into rages! At that moment she looked at me with a wry smile. "Of course," she said, and thus recognized a similar aspect of her communications to me whereby her graphic and entertaining talk would, she hoped, ward off probing questions from me, however therapeutic my intentions might be. Once more something that served her in her teaching could be used to preserve her inviolability. I remembered to myself that she had once hinted that she had difficulty in talking about her sexual life to me. This whole set of incidents was therefore quite a discovery for her and an advance in communication and consciousness and went some way to explain my feelings in response to her. I was justified in my feeling of being distanced and eliminated. I had not yet realized enough, however, that one of her aims was to head off my "probing" therapeutic self. I was right in feeling entertained and held by her vivacity and eloquence which also carried a definite suggestion of intimacy and warmth about it. I was certainly right in feeling I was being shown things, perhaps as if to a teacher. I was being fobbed off by her entertaining and gratifying talk, and it was this that was producing complementariness in my responses as well as concordance. The concordance, however, arose naturally enough out of her making it easy for me to empathize and go along with and understand her situation, and it was not beyond my powers to learn from the complementariness and to deepen the concordance. My patient's transference was largely infantile and childlike underneath the high-grade adult mentality. It was not without archetypal content however—that of the terrible mother orgiastic in her rage. In so far as the father was concerned, my patient had learnt to cope with his absence by a stoical pride in being able to do without anything, so that, in a sense, he ceased subjectively to exist. My feeling response included a sense that affectionate feelings on her part were being held in check, thus suggesting that she had transferred on to me the "absent father" who, though loved, had to be done without.

This fragment demonstrates the coming into consciousness of a transference on to me of "distancing" experiences in connection with both mother and father, while some of the warmth must have been connected with her ability to establish good sibling feeling for me instead. That the transference experiences in question came in from the past had already been adumbrated by her when during the previous session she said that she had made a discovery when talking to her younger sister. They both suddenly realized that they were still treating each other as if it were ten years ago. She still saw her sister as a child while her sister still looked up to her as a smart, trendy "with it" undergraduate, though in fact the present situation was quite other. It was thus that my patient introduced the theme of the past still saturating her experience of the present.

The transference experience described in this fragment illustrates two of the uses of transference interpretation. The first is to demonstrate how the past can still be falsifying a patient's all-round experience of the present. The second is to release the patient into a more realistic object-relationship with me. This enables the patient to be more free from identification with the past and from horrific anticipations of the future. Thus the nourishing experience of living in a present span becomes a possibility and partially a reality.

In terms of Jung's diagram (see p.154), this process may be understood partially in terms of factors A, B, and D. Side by side with the relatively uncomplicated interpersonal and co-operative relationship (factor A), my patient could receive some anima projection from me of an inspiratory type and could project some animus insight upon me in finding herself able to make some use of my interpretations (factor B). As for factor D, although there was not much anima or animus identification either in myself or in my patient, I was well able to appreciate her animus, which was high-grade, while she did not have much overt difficulty with my anima aspects. The reconstruction analysis was able to elucidate aspects of the infantile and child transference. Thus she handled me as (*a*) the potentially dangerous and enraged mother by deflecting my attention and entertaining me with interesting talk and descriptions, and as (*b*) the helpful school teacher to whom she could "bring and show". She could tentatively try me out as a benign mother by making demands that were in fact reasonable. Nevertheless, she remained cautious. As for her "absent" father, affection for him was not fully admitted so that in childhood and early adolescence she had to deny that this absence mattered. This was transferred to me in my absence. The experience of her mother was a distinctly archetypal one—the demonic, furious and frightening one to be warded off. It was intensified by the anger against her father for his absences being directed against her mother with whom she was already furious. This fury was then reversed so that the mother was experienced as doubly dangerous and myself likewise.

Chapter Eight

Dreams and dreaming

No book on analysis, repair and individuation can avoid a consideration of the way in which analysts can use their patients' communication to them of their dreams and dreaming to increase their understanding of the dynamic process involved. They will be told dreams whether they ask for them or not, although the patients' motives for telling them are likely to be extremely varied. Indeed, considerable advances in the understanding of dreaming and the use made of it in their patients' communications are being made by analysts of all schools. Furthermore, outside the field of analysis, light is being shed by the sleep laboratory experimenters and by brain neurophysiologists on the nature and purpose of dreams and their possible function in the maintenance of psychological health, whether interpreted or not.

This chapter will sketch out changes in psychoanalytic thought about dreams and then try to bring out whatever seems relevant to analysts from the two sets of experimenters already mentioned. It will then describe the contribution of classical analytical psychology to the subject and show how more recent analytical psychology has modified and reslanted its earlier views and reconsidered ways of making use of dreams and dreaming in the analytical interpretation of their patients' situation. Two case-histories are presented to illustrate these new developments.

The Psychoanalytic Tradition

The action of Emmy von N. in presenting her dreams to Freud nearly eighty years ago led him towards a point where he could begin to talk of the dream as "the royal road to the knowledge of the unconscious activities of the mind". This was, on the whole, a revolutionary idea for a mind of his time, rationalist and scientifically orientated as it was, although a shade too topographical, static and fixed for present-day tastes. Much more dynamic was his theory that during sleep we experience a lessening of the tension that accompanies the daytime inhibition and control of primary-process-originated impulses to action. That tension is further lessened by giving such impulses some expression on the level of phantasy or dream. These drives are postulated to provide the latent content of the dream, obscured from consciousness by a manifest content that employs condensation, displacement and the language of signs and symbols—a sort of wish-fulfilling "under the counter" manoeuvre.

Such manoeuvres undoubtedly do take place, but as a general theory of dreams this is open to many criticisms and is of limited value only. Yet for all that, Freud did adumbrate for psychology the notion of an inner world within which protective and integrating processes can be furthered by dreaming, considered as an activity, apart from any interpretation of dream-content aimed at enlarging ego-consciousness.

In the history of psychoanalysis, however, the widespread supersession of topographical theory by structural theory and the rise of Hartmann and the ego-psychologists brought about a lessening of interest in dreams for quite some time (Altmann, 1975). More recently that process has been reversed, and the language, images and feelings of dreams are now being taken as valid and appropriate expressions of numerous aspects of the psyche such as: unconscious infantile phantasy; vicissitudes in the formation of object relations and internal objects; the interplay between the patients' inner figures understood as whole or part objects; and the interplay at deep levels between patient and analyst, both in terms of transference and counter-transference, and in terms of the analyst and patient as objects in their own right. In a word, the contemporary psychoanalytic approach is much nearer to that with which we are familiar as analytical psychologists.

Perhaps the most striking expression of the changed attitude of psychoanalysts towards dreams and dreaming is that of Charles Rycroft in his recent book *The Innocence of Dreams* (Rycroft, 1979). He elaborates a notion, similar to Jung's, that dreams are innocent in the sense that they are the language of primary process, imagination and the deeper parts of the self. They are relatively fleeting experiences made up of images, metaphors and symbols, intensely private, and communicable only with difficulty. They represent ways of communicating with oneself about the self or parts of the self. They are connected with poetry, though Rycroft points out certain differences. His attempt is to link Freud's view of dreaming with Coleridge's "poetic imagination", considered to be the "prime agent" of creative poets and writers. Thus Rycroft quotes from no less a person than Charles Darwin, who in turn quotes the poet Jean-Paul Richter's dictum: "The dream is an involuntary kind of poetry". Rycroft also quotes from David Tod Ray's book *Kuo Mo-Jo: The early years*: "The language of poetry is not a human effort to express emotions, but emotion's expression of itself". Thus, according to Rycroft's proposition, we can substitute the word "dream" for "poetry" in contexts like these. This refreshing book seems very near to much in contemporary Jungian thought about dreams and dreaming. Jung is examined in a way that focuses upon a particular interpretation of his views, though the later developments of analytical psychology are not mentioned. What is so remarkable about Rycroft's work is the extent to which it represents a radical revision of psychoanalytic attitudes on this subject.

Some Contributions of the Sleep Laboratories

However that may be, Freud certainly held the view that dreaming as such serves psychological health. It was implicit in his psychology of dreaming and anticipated by him to be a by-product of his way of interpreting dreams in analysis. A parallel view of their function is well known to have the support of workers in the sleep laboratories like Oswald (1966), Hartmann (1973) and many others, who have established the distinction between rapid eye movement sleep (REM, paradoxical or D), and slow-wave sleep (orthodox or S). Slow-wave sleep is relatively dreamless and mainly facilitates the restoration of worn-out and fatigued somatic processes (see Redfearn, 1975); REM sleep, as suggested by the dreaming process and its content, sorts out and orders both the sleeper's impressions of his previous waking days and his interactions with his environment, certainly outer and probably inner, to much of which he cannot give waking attention.

In addition, Hartmann thinks that other functions of REM sleep may include the repair of systems subserving attention, secondary process and self guidance. In general terms, Jones in *The New Psychology of Dreaming* (1978) sums up the five main psychological functions performed by REM sleep and dreaming in the preservation and development of the human organism as follows:

(1) The *neutralization* of periodic psycho-noxious aspects of repressed infantile wishes; (2) the *stimulation* (through the imagery and more bizarre content of dreams) and release of the psyche, which can be cramped by the conventional and over-controlled thought processes of

everyday rational life; (3) the *reorganization* of ego-functioning by increasing the cognitive grasp of the dreamer; (4) the maintenance of *optimal vigilance* in mammals, whether in terms of potential danger to life and limb or in more sophisticated terms within the network of relationships in which the organism is involved; (5) the maintenance of *perceptiveness in depth* particularly in relation to self-knowledge and development.

One obvious implication of all this independent work on dreaming is, as Scott (1975) has pointed out, that analysts can draw further encouragement to maintain interest in the relation of their patients to dreaming. The experimental subjects seemed willing to tell their dreams to the experimenters. Sometimes children, too, wake up in the middle of the night and want to tell their dreams to their parents. Are they told to go to sleep again as it is "only a dream"? Are they promised they will be listened to tomorrow? Are they listened to on the spot? What about parents who are over-intrusive and try to drag the dreams out of their children, who then clam up and refuse to tell? Their dreams become their secrets. The same questions can be asked in principle about analysts and their patients. Quite an important aspect of the analysis of a patient, it turns out, is the consideration, as an analytic point in its own right, of vicissitudes in his attitude towards his dreams and his presentation of them. Thus the fact of dreaming, in the light of the work of the dream laboratories (and also the neurophysiology of the brain, next to be considered) may be understood to be at least as significant as any other fact of experience. Indeed, it may turn out to be rooted in processes that are of primary importance in the growth and development of creative personality.

The Cerebral Hemispheres and Dreaming

Furthermore, analytical psychologists such as Rossi (1977) and psychoanalysts such as Stone (1977) and Jones (1978) have begun to draw the attention of analysts to the research carried out, over more than a decade, by neurophysiologists into the functioning of the cerebral hemispheres and the callosal bridge, which both separates and links them and facilitates the working together, as a whole, of the cerebral bases of the psyche. These studies arose out of work in the field of brain damage and the split brain, quite independently of any interest in analysis.

Stone has focused on the points, emerging from a mass of detail, that seem most relevant to the interests of analysts as follows (Stone, 1977). Usually there is a fairly clear differentiation between the type of capabilities based upon the left hemisphere and of those based on the right. The situation may, however, be one of reversal or random distribution. Preponderantly it is found that in the left hemisphere are grouped together a number of rational capabilities—particularly verbalization and language facility. Also included are: linear thinking; the use of propositional and mathematical logic; aim-directed planned action; analytic thinking; and an exact adaptation to clock-time. On the right hemisphere are based feeling and emotion, musical experience, and visual and spatial accuracy. It is the basis, in a way that is less available to the left, of relating to reality within or without by developing *holistic* imagery which sums up situations as a whole. The images may be beautiful, horrific, bizarre, humorous, cartoon-like, and may contain puns and playfulness of all sorts. Clock-time is scarcely heeded.

This description of the cerebral bases of human adaptation to and relationship with the environment, inner and outer, demonstrates the complementariness of the two hemispheres and how necessary both are for the organism to survive as a whole. It is bound to carry great interest for analysts of all schools.

Stone goes on to cite Cohen (1975), who found that REM dreaming, at each point of its emergence during the night, shows all the features of right hemispherical activity. He was also able to demonstrate that as the night wears on the left hemisphere seems to exert more and more control of REM dreaming so that more verbal activity comes into the dreams, suggesting a kind of growing co-operation between left and right. Stone also cites Bakan (1975), who, elaborating in greater detail, notes the similarities between dream experience and right hemispherical modes of expression. He reports electro-encephalographic evidence for relatively greater activity in the right hemisphere during REM sleep and concludes that REM sleep "provides an opportunity for the exercise of the right hemisphere system while it is functionally disconnected from the left as a result of reduced callosal transmission" (during early sleep especially). He adds that the "relative ascendance of the right hemisphere system during REM sleep confers physiological and psychological benefits on the organism" (Bakan, 1975).

The last two sections of this chapter have contributed to the main theme by extending the scope of the theory of dreaming with which analysts can work and enlarging the somatic underpinning of the psychological observations in Freud's description of primary and secondary process as well as Jung's description of the two languages of the psyche and the functions they serve. A further implication of the scientific work on sleep is that the problem of the interpretation of dreams and dreaming, an activity in which left-hemispherical processing is also involved, remains primarily a task for the analyst, reinforced in his interest in dreams as he is by the work of the sleep laboratories and helped as he is by neurophysiology, to sustain a connection with the "somatic" basis of his work, however "psychological" or "spiritual" it may often seem.

Analytical Psychology and Dreams

The approach to dreams which is characteristic of analytical psychology is a vast subject. A detailed elaboration of it has recently been published (Hall, 1978; Mattoon, 1979); I shall merely summarize the account of a classical Jungian understanding of dreams given in the chapter on dreams in Meier's *Jung's Analytical Psychology and Religion* republished in 1977. For Meier, as for Jung, the dream is to be understood as a spontaneous and natural product of the psyche-soma. It has a language of its own which can in principle be progressively mastered. It often emerges into consciousness when, in the dreamer, an *abaissement du niveau mental* has come about. As in a drama, four movements in it can often be discerned: the presentation of the dramatis personae, the exposition, the crisis, and the solution. Because the dramatis personae can be personifications or images of forces within the dreamer or in the outer world, the interpretation can be either objective or subjective. Furthermore, apart from personal figures, typical archetypal motifs may appear, such as that of the hero's journey, treasure in the cave, the crossing of the river, friendly animals, and the *circumambulatio*. The language of the dreamer is largely that of signs and symbols and the form includes condensation, contamination and other distortions. Various kinds of relations between conscious and unconscious figures are envisaged. Interpretation is related to a *circumambulatio* around associations of a personal and contextual nature, often taking a whole dream series into account, and mythological parallels are sought (Meier, 1977).

That this content-orientated approach to dreams is rich and impressive goes without saying; it both complements and is compensatory to the Freudian approach in a creative way; it enjoys a bonus of vindication from independent experimentalist work on dreaming. Problems arise, however, in the practical handling of their patients' dreams by analysts in the daily clinical situation, and the last quarter-century's experience has enlarged the analytic range of understanding, interpretation and practice in a number of ways, a selection of which can be grouped under four headings.

The first heading concerns itself with the eliciting of dreams from patients. This is a practice that has grown up amongst analytical psychologists, although, according to Jung (1929), at one time he only asked for dreams when all other clues and hints had failed. Whether he was right is secondary to the general analytical question of whether material of any sort should be demanded of their patients by analysts. Thus a request for dreams, or indeed for any other specific kind of material, represents a real action on the part of the analyst, suggests an interference with the spontaneous emergence of material and communication of whatever sort, and thus can run the risk of introducing an actual strain or resistance into the relationship. It can complicate the transference/counter-transference. It may encourage either compliance or rebellion in the patient rather than facilitate communication of his real concern at any moment of time to an analyst who is able to be open to receive it, with neither prejudice nor the imposition of his own preferences upon the patient.

The second heading concerns the fascination that Jung's discoveries about dreams can exercise upon intuitive and imaginative analysts who may also have benefited personally from dream analysis. It is possible for them to slip unconsciously into feeling themselves to be "dream interpreters" rather than analysts of their patients' dynamics. The dangers of this kind of over-subjective phantasizing about a patient's dream have long been recognized. It was hoped that the study of dream sequences would achieve greater objectivity. A further step towards concentrating upon the patient's personality as such is to take his dreams not to be necessarily central in significance, though sometimes this may turn out to be so, but to be simply part of the flow of communication, with a nodal core, understood as meaningful. Thus associations to a dream can sometimes be seen with hindsight to have begun in sessions before the dream is presented and to have gone on for sessions afterwards. In addition there is evidence that archetypal themes may be discovered in the patient's material in many forms other than in dream-imagery, i.e. in his reports of actions and events, in his descriptions of people, in slips of the tongue, in non-verbal communication and in the transference/counter-transference situation. In this way the interpretation of the dream becomes part of the analysis of the patient as a whole and is controlled by his material as a whole. This is not, of course, to deny that much dream-imagery can, in a striking and vividly experiential way, give the patient access to the emotional, spatial, non-temporal and holistic mode of the right hemisphere as part of the totality of his response to his situation.

The third heading concerns the transference/counter-transference, not so much in terms of its expression in the content of the dream, but more as it gets expressed in behavioural terms through the manner and mode of the patient's reporting of dreams to his analyst, together with the analyst's feeling-response to his patient's action—a response which may or may not be appropriate. An inappropriate response may be due to a bias arising out of the analyst's psychological type, as elaborated upon by Thomas Kirsch (1927) or out of a counter-transference that may be "neurotic" (Racker, 1968) or "illusory" (Fordham, 1957).

Let us first postulate a situation where that last consideration would not need much attention. In it, the analyst is really open. The patient knows it. The transference has been analysed sufficiently for the patient's use of his dreams to be relatively freed from transference distortions. When he remembers a dream, he will communicate it quite naturally as part of the flow of communication, and a useful interpretation, considerably influenced by the dream, can follow. Telling a dream represents an event in its own right. An action similar to that of Emmy von N. is taking place. The patient is performing an action towards his analyst and it is understood why.

Now let us envisage a distorted situation. Because most patients today know that dreams come into the work and interest of analysts, their transference can influence the way in which they present their dreams in therapy. The nature of his response when understood can indicate to the analyst what his patient really intends by his action. The following are examples:

(1) The patient presents regular dreams out of compliance and possibly a wish to divert the analyst's attention from his real and feared problem. The analyst may feel suspicious at the ease and smoothness of the process.

(2) The patient constantly brings a mass of dreams to each session—far too much dream material to deal with in fifty minutes. He is either telling the analyst or boasting to him how he, the patient, is the kind of man that produces wonderful dreams, or he is swamping the analyst with them into silence or out of existence in the service of a massively aggressive defence. The analyst will feel either left out and underestimated, or flooded, drowned and oppressed.

(3) The patient brings neither living material nor dreams. He is really saying, "I'm not giving you what you want. You only want to intrude on me and spy on me, as my mother did. I don't want anyone to know about how bad I am, or rob me of any good I have." The analyst then feels undeservedly starved and cold-shouldered.

(4) The patient brings scraps of dreams and emphasizes how incomplete they are, or he throws them at his analyst in isolation and without a word of association. The analyst feels tantalized and titillated, but his counter-transferential helplessness may tell him that his patient, by a reversal, is seeking relief from a helpless and lifeless depression and wishing to have his own psyche tantalized and titillated into a semblance of feeling alive.

(5) Then there is the patient who, flinging dreams at his analyst, makes sarcastic or destructively negative responses to his analyst's attempts to understand the dreams and the material as a whole. This can arise out of envy, contempt and defiance of the analyst as the richly endowed one, or it can represent a defence of the self against the terrifying power of the analyst (Fordham, 1974). The analyst on his part feels the sting of the envious or defensive attacks upon him and his skills, or that he is laying siege to an impregnable fortress as well.

In all these situations, the analyst needs to focus upon the patient's *behaviour* with his dreams, while the *content* of the dreams, even if relevant, may have to be used for the time being for the analyst's information alone.

The fourth heading concerns some of the contents and actions in the dream. Recent psychoanalytic advance enables us to increase our understanding of the part played in dreams by unconscious infantile phantasy about "part" as well as "whole" objects and how images of that sort jostle side by side with internal objects and archetypal imagery (see Chapter 4). The point is illustrated in some of the dream material I shall shortly present.

The considerations adduced above do not necessarily conflict with either Jung's or Rycroft's (1979) emphasis, both obviously running counter to classical psychoanalysis, upon the "innocence" of dreams which say what they mean though in the image-laden, metaphorical or symbolic language of the right cerebral hemisphere. I have, rather, been describing ways in which patients can manipulate their dreaming as part of an unconscious resistance to or defence against the feared intrusive or overwhelming presence or influence of their analysts. As, however, the polarity between the right and left hemispheres seldom amounts to an absolute split, the so-called "innocence" of the dreaming activity may be influenced, innocently enough, by the defensive considerations already adduced. The simple story of the dream on some occasions may contain within itself signs of camouflage that are more or less transparent to the keen observer. Furthermore, it should not be forgotten that Rycroft's emphasis upon the privacy of the dream experience means that it can only be partially, if at all, checked by another person and not very much even by the dreamer who, after all, created it but at the same time is having to rely upon his memory of a fleeting type of experience. Thus considerable distortion of the experience is likely to ensue when an attempt is made to communicate it to an analyst. This incidentally is but one of the considerations that justify analysts in treating their patient's dreams very much within the context of a wider web of communication.

Cases

I now propose to give two highly compressed accounts of cases that bear out my main points.

1. The Case of Robert

(a) Robert, an intelligent and gifted young doctor, described himself as the youngest son, by some seven years, compared with his older brother and sister, both artists, whom he experienced as fairly trendy and chaotic in their personal lives. He felt that they had been openly contemptuous of his little penis when he was a small boy and physically rough with it. They still were so today in respect of his social and medical position—so "bourgeois", from their point of view, compared with theirs. Robert's mother was a practical, ambitious, somewhat high-minded woman. She was well-meaning but not very tactful and certainly not openly demonstrative of her tenderness. Robert experienced her as somewhat cool and "nordic", but proud of her son, who so successfully used his educational opportunities to get him through to medical qualification.

The father seemed very different—a warm-hearted, sensitive, feeling type of man, rather dark and "southern". He was experienced by Robert as a decent man, successful in his life and work as a financier, although subtly self-denigratory and too passive at home in relation to his wife. Robert managed the medical rat-race, with its ups and downs, successfully enough in objective terms, but always combined this with literary, poetic and musical interests. He could be dreamy, though gifted therapeutically, and quite capable of exact practicality in his medical treatments. Subjectively, he had always felt somewhat unsure of himself with siblings because of the phantasized small penis, and to compensate had developed his natural charm to aid him on his way. He was also taken with the anthropological concept of "liminality" and felt himself to be perpetually in threshold situations, with few of the landmarks clear. He also entertained the neurophysiological notion that he was "right-hand hemispherically dominant", and, seemingly to himself, more imaginative, pattern-conscious and intuitive than practical, aim-directed and logically exact in thinking and speech.

(b) The context of the dream. At the time of the dream Robert had come to the end of a hospital appointment and found himself having to mobilize energy to secure a suitable new one as part of his career structure. He went to view a hospital post which was interesting medically but also involved a good deal of rather demanding administrative work. He was describing this to me the next morning when he mentioned the dream he had awoken with:

> I am in a house, maybe the parental home with a difference. I went to the top of the house, where there was a large attic with big windows. In the room I found a strongly built housemaid with a plain, if not ugly, face. To my surprise, she became very sexually aggressive and implored me to have intercourse with her, yelling and shrieking at me to do so and jeering at my supposed impotence. I was not provoked into action but replied that I was perfectly capable of intercourse but did not intend to have it with her.

The context of the dream was therefore his mobilizing energy, his bracing himself up to going all out for a job that demanded administrative clarity and decisiveness. The dream emerged after eighteen months' communication of the material I have already described. In addition, there was the theme of finding himself surprisingly competent when taking on jobs, despite the very considerable fear and uncertainty experienced by him in threshold situations. Thus, while he had been characteristically hesitant before entering upon analysis, he had feared—and that fear was aggravated by his friends—that he would be entering upon a really painful process of being held down to the grindstone with the minutiae of his life subjected to ruthless analysis. Indeed he had been half-influenced in choosing Jungian analysis by way of a phantasy that it would not be so obsessively rigorous as psychoanalysis. Again he had found himself, with some surprise, enjoying his analysis and finding himself able to cooperate satisfactorily.

My own counter-transference enabled me to be spontaneously open and acceptant of all the facets of his personality as they came up—not favouring the imaginative any more than the practical and not asking specifically for dreams. Robert's difficulties stemmed back to the primal scene where in his phantasy his parents' marriage had been made difficult by his mother and father being such different kinds of people. Furthermore the effective, practical, but cool attitudes of his mother were often experienced by him as unattractive and repellent, reinforced, indeed, by the contrast to them presented by the seemingly easy-going attitude of his father. It was this, coupled with the phantasized small penis, that rendered Robert's awareness of his practical abilities and, indeed, physical strength, less clear to him than it was to others, including myself. There are traces of all that distributed in the dream, such as the repellent features of the housemaid plus her vigour, his coolness, the taunting references to the impotence phantasy and his defensive reply. It is therefore arguable that the dream had emerged out of a mass of experiences already communicated to me and which may be taken as associations to the dream prior to its event. This made it easy for him to establish a holistic view of its significance within the whole context of his problems.

(c) The nodal point of the dream. The central point of the dream communication would seem to be that, faced with the demand of practical reality in the form of a post requiring administrative responsibility, i.e. head thinking among other things symbolized by the action taking place at the top of the house (his body), he found it ugly and unattractive and rather haughtily and coolly drew back from it. On the other hand, insistence of the ugly maid up there suggests that, deep down in him and despite his dislike of it, there was another factor, an anima-figure potential that was interested in, and desirous of, practical work and insistent upon being allowed participation in his life. That side of his anima had become to some extent an internal object as a result of his experience with his mother. When he married, the repellent aspect of that internal object modified. Indeed his wife was able, clever intellectually, practical and also attractive. That modification was further fostered in the homosexual transference to myself, in the sense that while appreciating his darker intuitive and feeling sides, I certainly did not despise the other.

He was beginning therefore to get hold of the way in which early traumata had knocked him into a cool and negative, rather grudging, relation to his practical administrative abilities in which, nevertheless, a good deal of libido was present. Really to grasp that fact needed something like the surprise element and emotional content that was beginning to emerge in previous sessions but was finally brought together and focused by the dream in a way that was vivid and striking to him. In later sessions, Robert began to consider the liminal experience in general from two angles, i.e. (1) the normal anxieties accompanying it, as such, and (2) the extent to which liminal anxieties in his case had been intensified in an over-determined and indeed crippling way through exposure to them at an early and tender age without adequate support and understanding by the family matrix.

in coming to relate to real people in external world archetype is modified.

2. *The Case of Charles*

My second case is that of a young man whose life took an opposite turning from Robert's during his adolescence.

(*a*) According to Charles's account of his history (he was referred at the age of twenty), his experience of his parents was of a beautiful but cool mother from a wealthy background, and of a father, from an old family, somewhat blustering and, in Charles' early days, brutal, but whose life had consisted of a series of failures in business, often at the expense of his wife's money.

Charles was the eldest child with a brother 1½ years younger and an even younger sister. Charles changed when his brother was born and became possessed by hatred and rage towards him, in a way that was noticed, right from the beginning, by the parents, and indeed experienced for much of his life according to his own consciousness. At school he did well at lessons and in addition became a good rugby player, although for long years he had wished he was a girl. He had a memory that, when young, he would get depressed and cling to the skirts of a marble statue of the madonna for comfort. At the age of eight he disobeyed warnings and was very nearly drowned while sea-bathing. At 14½ he had become a sort of leader of the rebels at his boarding school and at 16 he "dropped right out", smoked a lot of dope and lived away from home without working. A venture at a university failed after the first few weeks.

He began to discover in himself and to cultivate seriously transvestite phantasies, which he acted out so that he learned to dress and look like a beautiful girl and become the object of lust in the boys and admiration, at least, in the girls. He also married a girl who had been an *au pair* in his parent's house. She left him free with his transvestite activities but began to oppose him when he turned his attention to the idea of an actual change of sex. Before applying for the final operation, he was beginning to think that his wish was really unobtainable. He felt too much of a man, to his despair and chagrin, and so he applied for an analysis, which "had" to be Jungian, since it seemed to him to be more imaginative and feminine and to value dreams—important to him because he had good ones, of which he was proud.

(*b*) Charles's presentation of himself during the earlier part of the treatment was of himself as a feminized man—skilful in his command of girlish gestures. A leading feature that emerged in the course of the analysis was an intense envy of women. The wish to be a woman turned out to be really an attempt to fuse or be one with his cool mother who, he thought, had rejected him for his brother. Furthermore, he had wished to avoid the cruel, frightening world of men, in which his father had been so unsuccessful. The disappointment and frustration experienced at the heart of his existence had produced a nihilistic wish to turn everything upside down in bitter rage. He would choose sickness, impotence, evil, destructiveness and perversion. My acceptance of all that, together with my interpretations, started off a slow underground movement of change, which contrasted with both the nihilism and the self-destructive anger.

The treatment had been intensive and unbroken by anything save the standard holidays. It was not very long before Charles began more and more to reiterate that he was sure that he was thoroughly male and that he was angry and heartbroken about this. Soon, by smoking less dope, he began to compare the subjective experience of being on dope with that of not being on it. He found new experiences with his wife as she really was—an emotional woman—and primitive compared with his experience of her in a fusionary illusion of oneness when they smoked dope together. She, too, began to realize her disturbances and went into analysis, while his parents entered marital therapy.

After a year, during which he sat in a chair, keeping his eyes fixed upon me, he started to try ways of using the couch. This was symptomatic of a less negativistic transference to me as a parent figure, so that he could allow himself to feel more of a patient—more relaxed and less watchful.

After another year, at the age of 22, he decided to go to work, for the first time, in a regular job. It involved working with people in difficulties, and here he experienced considerable success. When he was 23, he secured a place in a university again, five years after dropping out at 18. He followed an honours course in philosophy. It turned out well and, to his encouragement, he started being awarded alphas for his essays. At the same time, albeit rather unwillingly, he agreed with his wife, who was keen that they should try for a child. She became pregnant and he was sufficiently in touch with his genital sexuality not to feel too badly about it. Thus by the time the baby was born, he was well on the way to being able to enjoy her as a father and to be something of a holding person for his wife and to support her tentative moves into maternal preoccupation. He was no longer gripped by his illness but could be conscious of conflict raging in him and could even tolerate the notion of repair. Accompanying changes in his physical appearance began to appear: his face began to show some strength; his manner became more open; he could laugh and talk more freely; and he decided to sit up and face me more often than to lie on the couch, while feeling free to do either with spontaneity.

(*c*) As time went on, the telling of his dreams, which at first, under the influence of reading Jung and in accordance with a certain gift of poetic imagination, he had both compliantly and with a pleasurable sense of achievement brought along as products of his imagination like poems, fell into the flow of communication in the midst of varied material. A group of four are striking and took place during a fortnight after four years of analysis:

(1) I go to a medieval castle on the top of a high steep pointed hill. It is cold and has no window panes. My family is there. It seems I had had an incestuous relationship with my sister about which my parents are angry with me. I fly into a rage over this and, to distract my parents' attention from the incest, hit out at a great sparkling chandelier. I smash half of it. We all, as a family, get down to picking up the pieces. I find that the sparkling glass is not shattered and disintegrated but rather is in its original tiny pieces. We gather them together to start re-assembling the chandelier.

(2) I am in a medieval city. There is a destructive man about. With his friends he rushes through the city spraying it everywhere with a poisonous substance. This will kill every living person in the city. I find rising within myself a surge of almost demonic energy. I feel it will be either him or the rest of the world for survival, so, with this demonic energy, I attack him with overwhelming strength and tear his eyes out.

(3) I am in the waiting room. There is a see-through wall between it and my analyst's consulting-room. I can see him treating a black girl. The scene changes and I am in a big tent, but I realise I am actually inside the skirts of a huge doll whose legs are near to trampling on me.

(4) I meet my woman philosophy teacher. She has become a beautiful rather golden girl and emphasizes that I am good at philosophy.

(*d*) If we take these dreams as a whole, we can hardly avoid noting the transference and counter-transference to be found in them and the extent to which by now Charles was involved in them—not as a somewhat schizoid participant or watcher. His emotions were aroused. Two of the dreams, being set in medieval times, could refer to adolescence; the other two are about youth anyway. In the first dream, he felt that the cold castle on the top of the hill represented his cool phallic home, so defensive (a fortress) and so vulnerable to the cold (no window panes), where incestuous feelings of warmth, in this case towards his sister, were condemned—according to his experience of it. He could acknowledge the fury this had aroused in him and how it made him want to destroy everything symbolized by the chandelier and in particular to smash up its many-faceted and sparkling light. And yet even that was not mere nihilistic rage against the light as such. He insisted that it was a strategy, a guilty manoeuvre, to distract his parents' attention from the incest that he was determined to act out. In fact this was now masked, as he hardly ever saw his sister. It had instead been lived out in the earlier part of his marriage after he had "dropped out". A more subjective interpretation would be to consider the incest motif to refer to an inner sister-anima side of his nature extremely important to his psychological development. He could not think that this aspect of his potential self would be truly sympathized with by his parents. As an image, his sister was loved by him but felt by him to be distant in age, seldom seen and perhaps, in his view, liable to be damaged by the parents as internal objects. He also thought that the cold castle and the cool chandelier light symbolized his feeling that my "cool" analytic interpretations had frustrated his loving feelings towards me and made him feel more angry and guiltily defensive than he had realized. For all that, according to the dream picture, he had only half-destroyed the chandelier, and furthermore it was not even shattered but had simply come to pieces—more a deintegration than a disintegration, and with the whole family involved in repair.

In the second dream, he felt his blood was up again. His associations were to his occasional violent attacks upon his own destructiveness. He felt he had to end the destructive activity, even to take the law into his own hands—very surprising, as he had been paranoid in a somewhat trendy way in connection with the police. He realized that he was conscious enough to experience how violent the conflict had started to become as he became more aware of the destructive elements in the nihilistic side of his nature. Sometimes the battle seemed to be for life itself, during which time there was no opportunity to weigh up and integrate what was valuable in his nihilism. There is in this material a hint of Oedipus blinding himself as a punishment for incest but, perhaps, too, it acted as a blinding realization of how deep down he really loved life. The transference element in the dream arose out of his sensing a certain ability in me to discern with some urgency crypto-destructive behaviour in both the inner and the outer world. There was an element of identification or at least a partial agreement with me in this, but at that moment in his development he was tending to be still too violently repressive of his nihilistic side and not yet sufficiently understanding of it. Not surprisingly, he was hardly mature enough yet to sustain within himself the tension of the opposites, shown as they are in the dream to be in a pathological condition of mutual destructiveness.

In the third dream, which is a direct representation of the transference, he sees me analyse a young black woman, that is, his black instinctual feelings—his real ones as against his nihilistic destructive impulses, but they are split off still and "in the next room". That contrasted with his old habit of wishing to dress like a woman, expressed in the next part of the dream as finding himself inside the great doll's dress, but at the risk of being trampled on. He had an association with the tent-like cover. He had been taking part in a newly formed large group. He had felt the male leader to be rather an old woman. He had sensed potential violence and repressiveness in the group and had himself remained rather wary and anonymous in it. As regards transference/counter-transference, the first part of the dream reflected the facts of the treatment. I did indeed steadily analyse all the time what was happening to his instinctual life and feelings as well as the signs of, and risks accompanying, his longing for the mother, the old woman, perhaps also myself, as discernible in the second part of the dream.

The last dream seemed a bonus one in the midst of his travail—the golden woman, associated by him with his philosophy tutor, and validating him in his studies. We are here dealing with the anima as an internal object and perhaps the next development of the image hitherto projected on to his sister and his wife. Thus, an inner predisposition to expect and to meet a woman of a validating and inspiratory type, together with an internal image of this aspect of the anima, are matched and met by an appropriate woman in the real world, namely a real female philosophy tutor who was encouraging him and, along with other teachers, awarding him alphas for his university essays. It also had a reference to transference and counter-transference interactions, as I had found myself, from early on, spontaneously believing in his potential and ability and had pointed out signs of it as they arose. I regarded these responses as partly originating from anima aspects of myself.

Later dreams showed how he was beginning to integrate his angry nihilistic feelings, by no longer needing to destroy them and by finding, in a new way, a more suitable place for them.

Of course, it would not be supposed that Charles's life was now to have a "happy ever after" quality about it. The child, a vigorous and lively girl, had been born. Charles's wife, under the strain of a brand new experience and not very far advanced in her analytic development, could, and not infrequently did, break down into an over-tired and unhappy infant herself. Charles needed to be on his mettle to hold things together in his little family, side by side with doing studies and being financially responsible. The old nihilistic impulses could arise when his wife got low and Charles was out of touch with the incipient father archetypal capacities within him. A dream illustrated the first problem:

> I am in swampy land with a lot of shallow water lying around. I myself am paddling about lying flat on my stomach and on a sort of board. My wife is near me also paddling on a sort of board. I see an older man who is in a boat. He seemed to be

paddling ahead as if he were leading me (or us) onwards. He seemed to have red hair and a round face, with a fringe of red hair right round the face, but with no moustache or beard. I say to my wife "This is the Wise Old Man" but I feel as if I am talking not quite directly to her—and, if anything, using the phrase to encourage her in the midst of these rather difficult circumstances.

When he brought me the dream, he said that he thought that the Wise Old Man referred to me as I tended his development and in a way led him on. He thought that his wife in the dream represented an aspect of him as well as herself in person, for he thought that he was in a phase where things were not quite clear and differentiated in his life. He and his wife were in fact finding it swampy and hard going. He felt that a lot depended on him to keep on to their arduous path over against the temptation to give up and become nihilistic. Of course there were a number of archetypal internal objects in the dream: the swamp; the journey very close to the water on the flat boards; the boatman leading the way across the water; the psychopomp with the red hairy fringe around his face—a sort of sun-god with just a hint of a head mandala image withal. That showed how, in the transference and also in the reality of my dealings with him, I was being able to meet an archetypal predisposition on his part to seek and accept a psychopompic guide with a level of illumination sufficient to help him along with his journey. It meant of course that, in his establishment of object relations with me as his analyst, the internal object that emerged was fairly heavily influenced by imagery of a traditional sort which was archetypal in nature and function. The dream quite well illustrates Stone's thesis (1977) in the following way. The holistic imagery of the right-hand cerebral hemisphere provided for Charles a feeling grasp of his situation as a whole. That coupled with his newly developing left-hand hemispherical capacities for verbalization and for representational logic (his philosophical studies) and aim-directed activity (in practical everyday survival) could free enough energy to help him through the testing circumstances of his life at this stage.

A second dream opens out even more clearly his relationship to fathering, to inaugurating action and to taking a lead:

I am with a Nigerian friend of mind. He could introduce me to a big black boss-man, but when he does so the big black boss-man takes no notice of me.

The Nigerian friend was a writer and publisher and had suggested to Charles that he might be able to help him with his writing. The man had turned out to be largely a rather dull parasite or sucker. Charles wondered what he was doing that the big black boss-man could find no time for him and he wondered whether he was not still in conflict over fully taking on his new-found masculinity and fatherhood with responsibility for family and career. Was there, he thought, something of the dull parasitic sucker in his attitude still. This image could symbolize a negative expression of dependance which he had always feared and disapproved of—no doubt in a defiant way. He had often told me about this and from time to time worried over the financial aid given him by his grandparents on the maternal side, even though his style of life was extremely modest. If he was thus parasitic, then the boss-man figure could be alienated from him and hold him to be of no account. The figure draws upon the archetypal image of the "natural man", i.e. "black" and "the boss". Charles had not had much experience of boss-men. There had been some authoritarian school masters in his life, though he dropped out before the completion of his school career. It left me as the object of a primitive archetypal transference, that of the black boss-man and obviously related to what he conceived of as my expectations for him and the possibility of my disappointment and alienation if he did not live up to them.

These later dreams contain themes that are only to be expected during the vicissitudes and ups and downs of Charles's new way of life. The experience of them and the interpretative process that went on between him and myself greatly assisted in an integrative way Charles's movement on towards a repair and enhancement of life. He was recovering from a serious illness that may be regarded as probably the sign of an immense vitality in coping with a strikingly non-facilitating environmental experience in infancy and childhood and in defending the self from serious danger from both within and without (Fordham, 1974). It should be added that, as part of the ongoing processes of his life, he gained, at the end of his university course, an excellent Honours Degree. The work for it was largely done while functioning reliably enough as a husband and the father of a child.

Conclusion

I have tried to demonstrate ways in which dreams emerge in a useful and striking fashion, whether interpreted or not, in the midst of a general flow of material under the circumstances of: (1) their not being specifically asked for by the analyst; (2) their being taken as one aspect of a wide range of communications on the part of the patient, out of which central or nodal points of meaning can be isolated and interpreted (in other words, the patient is being analysed rather than the dream); and (3) their being taken within the transference/counter-transference situation.

Produced to a greater or lesser extent by right-hemispherical activity, though seldom entirely uninfluenced by the left, dreams can often be understood by patient and analyst to sum up in a remarkable way the psychological situation of the dreamer—his blocks, his dynamisms, perhaps the direction to be taken in his life. Above all, perhaps, they not only express archetypal themes and patterns in terms of images and internal objects, but also can introduce the dreamer to the beginnings of an experience of emotional intensity hitherto only latent or not allowed to come into consciousness. They thus play an important part in the realization of the self and the individuation process.

Chapter Nine

The individuation process

The title of this book suggests the view that individuation, considered as process or end-product, is, for all its spontaneity, by no means free from hazard and potential damage. Furthermore, Jung's descriptions of it are not without complications and unsolved questions. Thus, while most analysts tend to find their patients to be very individual people, unusual indeed, perhaps complicated, even outstanding, in ways that are striking or quiet or deeply hidden, this does not mean that they are necessarily thereby individuated in Jung's sense of the term.

The Individuation Process in Jung

Jung's concept is a wide one and it can be conveniently considered under three main topics: the differentiation of the individual from the collective, the relationship of the individual to the collective, and the nature and conditions of the development of individuation as such.

First, Jung focuses on individuation as the process of forming and specializing the individual nature in a way that differentiates it from general collective psychology. This process he describes as a "natural necessity", but open to damage as much in the sphere of the psychological as of the physical or physiological. Because this individual aspect is not specially sought but has its *a priori* foundations in the psyche, he uses strong language about any frustrations it may encounter. Any levelling down to collective standards, he writes, can be "injurious to the vital activity of the individual" and "an artificial stunting" (Jung, 1921, p.448). On the other hand, although the collective may sometimes seem to pose a threat to the individual, the latter is much more concerned to *differentiate* from it rather than to oppose it—perhaps an optimistically stated aim when considered in the light of subsequent events in Europe.

188

Secondly, in defining individuation by reference to its relationship to the collective, Jung stresses its complementary nature and the mutual interdependence that is involved. The vitality of society depends upon the existence of healthy individuals within it. Contrariwise, the individual depends upon the support of the collective and needs to observe certain minimum collective standards. In support of this Jung (arguing no doubt from his Swiss experience) employs the homely simile that the plant "must be able to grow in the soil in which it is planted". He can, further, hold that individuation leads to a sense of intensive and universal solidarity—not to mere isolation. On the other hand, if an individual way is raised to a norm, an acute conflict with the collective norm takes place and what Jung called individualism becomes the order of the day. In the end, however, once it is granted that individuation leads to a natural appreciation of the collective norm, Jung then goes all out to say that "the more a man's life is shaped by the collective norm, the greater is his individual immorality". (Jung, 1921, p.449).

What we have described so far of Jung's concept of individuation stems from his statements in *Psychological Types*, a book the material for which took him the first two decades of this century to collect. Subsequent politico-social events have, of course, made his remarks on the relationship between the individual and the collective less applicable. For instance, the "soil" (in Jung's sense of the word) must often have been judged in the past to be poor indeed. Situations often recurred—and not only in primitive cultures—in which individuals have been oppressed by ideologically inspired pattern imposition that has not seemed to take account of their real developmental needs, especially in the case of children and young adults. Obviously, much depends on how far the needs of the immature are understood by those in positions of authority. For instance, authority may get exercised too much as a form of self-regarding control of others rather than in the service of the growth and enlargement of the true nature of the young in accordance with the original meaning of the word "authority". It is the old question of "the rubber stamp" rather than the fostering of personal relationships between individuals and the people involved in "holding" them, whether in the context of family, school, community, or psychotherapy, etc. A great deal depends upon the larger collective's willingness to be *open* enough to accommodate a wide variety of people and even to be able to maintain a certain dynamism and adaptation to change of the sort that can be promoted by the positive aspects of social critique (see Lambert, 1980).

A third group of ideas about individuation as such was generated by Jung as his thought developed through the years. He increasingly concentrated upon the idea of the psychological individual as "the individual, a separate in-divisible unity or whole" (Jung, 1963, p.352). This single, homogeneous and unique being was not to be thought of as isolated but as profoundly implicated in the human situation. It was to represent a unique expression in particular and personal terms of what is shared in common with the collective. Jung linked this with the unfolding of the original potential pattern of wholeness in a person. Phrases used by him to describe this included "the supreme realization of the innate idiosyncrasy of a living being" and "the optimum development of the whole individual human being" (Jung, 1934b). The concept could, of course, be misunderstood as an over-polarization of the personal and the collective within an individual as if two separate and abstract entities were in a state of mutual antagonism that somehow needed resolution, but I do not think that this was Jung's intention. The individual person possesses the psycho-somatic constituents and potentialities that are possessed in common by all the other human beings in the natural groups to which he belongs. This refers to the ever-widening circles of family, community, nation or race, and, in a general way, to mankind itself as a whole. At the same time, each one of these factors is expressible in a more or less individualized and personalized form. Above all, it is in the whole or integrated person that this individualized and personalized factor expresses itself at the highest degree of intensity. Furthermore, when it is asked how such an integration could be achieved, Jung's answer was that it is the function of an unconscious potential that, from within the personality, can spontaneously order the multitudinous instincts,tendencies and oppositions of the personality into a unique and meaningful whole. Jung considered that he had assembled enough evidence to suggest that this may be thought of as an innate power of the self rather than as a contrivance of ego-consciousness. For him the function of the latter was to come to terms with these unifying processes and, in a discriminating way, to cooperate with them as they emerged.

The result of this process of integration Jung designated as *individuation* in which the individual experiences a new equilibrium and a new centre which ensure for the personality a new and more solid foundation.

We have been describing what is a subjective experience for the individual. It is also possible for an outside observer to discern signs of this integrated individuation in another person. In such a case the person's behaviour is not felt to be fragmented by self-contradictory conflicts and splits. He feels to the observer to be in touch with himself as he really is, never a mere imitator of others, and psychologically able in principle to treat them as they really are. He seems genuine in what he does—as a whole person and hence neither too smoothly and obviously self-confident nor too diffidently unsure. He seems freed from a compulsive need to be highly "individual" and "outstanding". His confidence and faith do not seem to be based upon the repression of anxiety or doubt. Such persons have a solid feeling of survival capability and hence can feel relatively secure in a variety of situations or social contexts.

Later Developments in Individuation Theory

In the years since Jung's formulation of the theory of individuation, a good deal of work has been done in England (under the stimulus of Fordham, Redfearn and others) on the inevitable questions that are raised by the concept. These centre round the timing of individuation, phases in it, and the actual concrete psychological processes involved. Before describing the more recent work, it would be desirable to list some of the discrete bits of observation and theory used by Jung in the formulation of his theory. They are:

(1) There is an interaction of interdependence between the individual and the collective.

(2) Psychological qualities and potentials that are shared in common with others can nevertheless be made personal in a unique way by the individual.

(3) Two states of being may be observed in the self: a multiplicity of individual elements and drives looking like a chaos and a unifying pattern-forming process appearing in images like those of the mandala, the lotus-flower etc.

(4) The individuation process is (according to Jung) to be observed as part of a development from the first half of life on to the second. In the first half of life, the task of the individual is to learn to adapt to educational disciplines, to social requirements, to the demands of work and profession and to the establishment of family and community life. The second half of life demands integration of all the personality elements neglected by this one-sided effort of adaptation. The inclusion of and relationship with the shadow, animus, anima by the integrative processes of the self may lead to individuation and a certain wisdom and sense of the meaning of life as the individual grows older. In a way, according to this view, the self seems in the first half of life to be somewhat falsely adapted to outside influence, while in the second half the realization of its "truth" in individuation is never finally achieved.

(5) There are references on Jung's part to the process of the *realization* of the self in individuation. There is also his work done in the last years of his life on cultural development during which he was studying a process in European consciousness connected with a progressive integration of hitherto unrealized chthonic and somatic elements, e.g. as expressed in alchemy (Jung, 1951; see also Lambert, 1977). In a way that was parallel to Winnicott's interest in "satisfactory personalization" (1945), he seems to have been concerned with "incarnation" as exemplified in the last paragraphs of *Answer to Job*. Words like "realization" and "incarnation" suggest that during the individual's life span the self and its contents may undergo considerable change as the result of learning from experience and tangling with life in terms of flesh and blood and space and time, thus ending up in a condition quite different from that in which it started.

There can be no doubt about the stimulus provided by Jung's ideas on these five fronts. Indeed they have been freshly responded to by Fordham and others in a restatement of a Jungian theory of early development which modifies Jung's view in some ways and extends it in others. The first important consideration is that of the dating and span of the individuation process. Fordham has shown convincingly that recent work on infant development suggests that by as early as two years of age the infant can have acquired skills and psychological capacities as a result of which he fulfils in principle the fundamental criteria for individuation (Fordham, 1968). This view is based upon observation of infant development of the sort that can be judged as spontaneous and natural within a sufficiently facilitating environment. What is meant, of course, is that the individuation in question is appropriate to the stage of development arrived at by the infant. A further implication is that there are many other stages in a person's life where a suitable level of individuation may be achieved as well: early childhood, latency, puberty, the various stages of adolescence, early adulthood, starting work, marriage, parenthood and so on. The main differences lie within the range, complexity and intensity of each level of individuation reached. The comparable status of each level is not in question.

At this stage of the discussion the dating of the individuation process might be regarded by some as a rather academic question. That it is not really so is demonstrated by the fact that the earlier view envisages that the first half of a person's life should conform to social and educational requirements almost falsely and without much reference to inner feelings. The later view, on the other hand, envisages at least the possibility of true self experiences from the earliest years onwards and that these can be supported or facilitated by adequate parents, teachers and others. The implication is that infants, and children in general, have a psychology of their own which can be fostered. Whether this is so in any particular child or young person is quite another question, for training and pattern imposition on the one hand or permissive neglect on the other are still quite common. Under such circumstances the child does not so much develop in relationship with his parents as adapt to the circumstances in what is at bottom a rebellious or angry and impersonal way.

The idea that individuation is perhaps less a state to be reached near the end of life than something fully and appropriately realizable at each stage of development in a person's life is based upon a dynamic view of developmental change observable in the self. Fordham's work has enabled us to reconsider elements 1, 2, 3 and 5 of Jung's thought, as mentioned above, and see them in a different setting. The hypothesis is that at an early stage *in utero* and then, on another level, with the separation from the mother at birth, the individual self may be thought of as being in a state of undifferentiated potentiality. Fordham calls this the original self. Its components are archetypal predispositions or potentiality, a potential for the emergence of bits of ego-consciousness, and certain potentialities connected with self-realization. The most important of these latter potentialities is, for our purpose, the capacity to deintegrate and reintegrate (Fig. 1). By this is meant a capacity for the self to loosen sufficiently for some of its archetypal elements to separate out and be predisposed to relate to the bits of reality that fit them in the external world either in real or symbolic terms. This seems to happen at a time when it is essential for the individual's survival that the appropriate piece of external reality is presented and made available to the infant (Fig. 1). An obvious example is when, out of the original self, an archetypal predisposition to expect a breast and nipple deintegrates out of the whole and is met by the presentation to it of an actual breast or nipple. When this matching takes place satisfactorily and repeatedly enough, the self can reintegrate. It will as a result, however, have become different, for it now contains a deintegrate that has been matched by reality (Fig. 2). This can now become an internalized object based upon well-established memories of palpable experience and hence no mere idea or image. This deintegrative–reintegrative process repeats itself time and again as the self "unpacks" its archetypal potentialities and matches them with real objects—breast, nipple, white wall of the breast, the mother's shining eyes and teeth, i.e. part objects at first, then whole objects like mother, father, siblings, etc. All the time, by a kind of breathing process, the self deintegrates and reintegrates at appropriate times in the

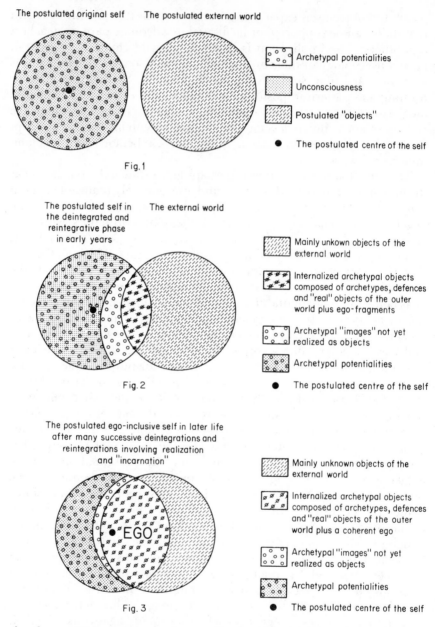

The postulated original self   The postulated external world

□ o o o Archetypal potentialities

▨ Unconsciousness

▨ Postulated "objects"

● The postulated centre of the self

Fig. 1

The postulated self in   The external world
the deintegrated and
reintegrative phase
in early years

▨ Mainly unkown objects of the
external world

▨ Internalized archetypal objects
composed of archetypes, defences
and "real" objects of the outer
world plus ego-fragments

□ o o o Archetypal "images" not yet
realized as objects

▨ Archetypal potentialities

● The postulated centre of the self

Fig. 2

The postulated ego-inclusive self in later life
after many successive deintegrations and
reintegrations involving realization
and "incarnation"

▨ Mainly unknown objects of the
external world

▨ Internalized archetypal objects
composed of archetypes, defences
and "real" objects of the outer
world plus a coherent ego

□ o o o Archetypal "images" not yet
realized as objects

▨ Archetypal potentialities

● The postulated centre of the self

EGO

Fig. 3

developmental process, and accordingly the reintegrated self contains
progressively more and more archetypal realized objects that have been
internalized—a very different matter from either formal potentialities
or even potentialities presenting themselves to the psyche as *images* only

and devoid of real experience. There is, for example, a world of difference between an image of a father originating out of an inner archetypal expectation, and an internal object which is a product of a matching of the expectation with an actual flesh and blood father-person. Thus the experience of the real father can give palpable reality to the archetypal father both as an inner reality and as a meeting of the expectation of an outside father. It seems also true that ritual and symbolic events provided by a culture can make effective for some individuals such inner archetypal processes as rebirth, initiation, inner marriage, death etc. (Fig. 3).

This capability of the self enables it to realize more and more of its potentiality by assimilating ever more newly presented, or, indeed, searched for, aspects of reality whether in the outer or the inner world. If we were to take views of the self at various phases of a person's life in terms of diagrams using a circle with contents, we would find the contents altering with each successive phase of deintegration and reintegration. The circle representing the original self would contain figures representing archetypal potentialities only. At later phases in the person's life the contents would be (1) unrealized archetypal potentiality; (2) unrealized archetypal imagery; (3) deintegrates taken back into the self containing experiences of the outer or the inner world to which elements of ego-consciousness have become attached; (4) an ego-complex or coherence, partially autonomous, but at the same time sensitive to the needs of the organism as a whole. The proportions between these four elements naturally shift as life goes on, and for a healthy and alive person the self-circles during the latter end of their lifetime would be likely to contain a larger proportion of archetypally originated internalized objects, probably less and less distorted by infantile defence systems, and a well-formed but flexible ego-organization.

It is, I hope, clear that the more the original elements of the self deintegrate and match up with the particularities of inner or outer reality, the more personalized or individualized they become and hence the more individuated the self as a whole.

Ego-Consciousness in Analytical Psychology

Furthermore, ego-consciousness is postulated to play an important part in this process. It arises at the point of impact between the archetypal expectation and the object meeting it—an impact containing in itself a greater or a smaller shock according to how clash-free the fit between these two entities is. It appears that increased ego-consciousness is activated by the clash so long as it is not unduly great, and it is the awareness of the particularity and "thusness" that the ego contributes that assists the process of individuation. The words "so long as it is not unduly great" are very important, for if the clash between the expectation and the object presented is continuous and unusually great, ego development is not promoted. Instead the infant becomes the battle ground of overwhelming feelings of rage, disappointment and isolation to the extent of being "shattered". He will grow up with what is called a weak ego, unable to consider, hold tension or postpone the immediate satisfaction of impulse. To protect himself from this, the individual has to build up artificial defences against real feeling. It will be obvious that some of the most intractable problems met by analysts centre round damage to the deintegrative–reintegrative process. These can range from a hold-up of the ongoingness of this process to states where the whole personality is best described as shattered though held together by cast-iron defences. It is to the study and therapy of this that Fordham's work on *The Self and Autism* (1976) is devoted.

Provided, however, that no such "shattering" has taken place, we may expect to find that a certain coherence of the fragments of ego-consciousness takes place and forms a complex. This has a centre and also a relative stability. It may be called *the ego*, so long as it is realized that the ego needs to be able to de-cohere and re-cohere in a way that is parallel to the deintegration and reintegration of the self when new content is being taken in.

Finally, to complete this account of the individuation and the ever richer complexity of the self as the deintegration–reintegration process takes place at significant points in the life span of an individual, it seems necessary to summarize the concept of ego-consciousness as it has developed in analytical psychology. Jung described consciousness by the use of a number of images. It is like a surface or skin upon a vast unconscious area. It is like a magnet attracting to itself impressions from the outer world and contents from the inner world. It is like a searchlight playing upon a more or less known area. On a somewhat more conceptual level Jung wrote of its constituents as: (1) a general awareness of the body and personal existence; and (2) a certain idea of having been in existence for some time and based upon a long series of memories. He also described the functions or tools of ego-consciousness. They are to meet the human need for orientation and are designed to deal with the ectopsychic data of the exterior world and to some extent the endopsychic data of the inner world. The first he dealt with by his famous theory of types and functions (Jung, 1921).

The endopsychic data he conceived of as composed of: (1) memory; (2) the subjective component of conscious functions; (3) emotions and affects and (4) invasions. Over (1) and (2) ego-consciousness could exercise control but much less so in the case of (3) and (4). At a later date Jung thought of ego-consciousness as originating in and arising out of the unconscious matrix of the personality. He wrote: "The self, like the unconscious, is an *a priori* existent, out of which the ego evolves. It is an unconscious prefiguration of the ego" (Jung, 1954).

Later analytical psychologists have, like Harding, distinguished between (1) low forms of awareness where nevertheless the word "I" is used as the subject of verbs and (2) developed ego-consciousness which combines awareness of what I do and who it is that does it with a sense of what the things done mean (Harding, 1965). A further description of ego-consciousness by Abenheimer (1968) emphasizes three modes of it in terms of (1) *awareness of frustration* arising at the *oral* stage and the discovery of restoring harmony through seeking help by crying etc., (2) *awareness of the power* to control bodily function activated at the *anal* stage, and (3) a notion of the ego as *pure will power and control* that gradually develops as the child learns to abstract himself to a certain extent from his needs. I have argued elsewhere (Lambert, 1980) that certain specificities of ego-awareness also emerge at the phallic oedipal and genital stage of development (see also Plaut, 1959) and that a further awareness of the ego as awareness of responsibility for the subject's actions emerges during the negotiation of the movement from the paranoid – schizoid position to the depressive position, according to Klein (1935). Finally, to these descriptions of the many-faceted aspects of ego-consciousness we may add that of Fordham. He lists the indications of the presence of mature ego-functioning as: (1) perception, (2) the organization of mental contents, (3) memory, (4) control over mobility, (5) reality-testing, (6) defence structures and (7) something very important—namely a capacity to relinquish controlling and organizing functions both in states of deintegration and when it needs to stand aside in favour of spontaneous creative functioning. (Fordham, 1969).

My description of ego-consciousness certainly suggests a quite complex and effective organization of libido with a centre and a shape and a degree of semi-autonomy that can nevertheless surrender some of its powers in the service of the self as a whole. The development of it is an impressive and enriching achievement, and the self in which, through many deintegrations and reintegrations, a sound ego-consciousness has developed is a very different entity from the original self and is well on the way to individuation.

Conclusions

One major implication of this book has been the belief that, though it is true that collective society can inflict damage upon the individuation potential of the persons it is composed of, much more damage is brought about within the patterns of relationship to objects personal and non-personal that come into being in the early phases of a person's development. The trouble often lies in distorted if not destructive interactions that arise between immature individuals and the often insufficiently mature persons who function for them *in loco parentis*.

In accordance with this view, Chapter 3 devoted attention to the basic personality and attitude of the analyst into whose hands the damaged patient seeks to entrust himself. Chapter 4 tackled the very important and complicated issues of resistance and counter-resistance in treatment. It certainly looks as if resistance always represents in some way an affirmation of the potential individuation of the patient, even when it is delusional or illusory. It is a safeguard against stalling over the issue of affirming one's individual and personal expression of the human situation. The danger is that of substituting for this the individuality of another person, the analyst. The problem of delusion and illusion when relating to another person was considered in Chapter 4, where the phenomenon of the full psychological experience of real objects in their suchness and particularity was examined. The individuation process is greatly furthered by the impact of the reality of another person as against a shadow-boxing contest with a phantasy being. Chapter 5 dealt with the reconstruction of situations in a person's history, generally to be found repeated in various guises, in the context of which habitual if not fixed patterns of interaction have developed. The individual may thus become both maladapted to and incapable of real experience in the here and now, thus missing the concrete experiences of the present that are so vital to individuation. One of the most important of such individual experiences is that of personal relationships. In Chapter 6 I turned to the complicated relationship between the interaction of two real persons on the one hand and problems connected with transference and counter-transference on the other. In particular I tried to show how the delusionary and illusionary experiences of transference and counter-transference can be sufficiently recognized and analysed to make room for the development of interpersonal experiences that are the more nourishing because of the improved object relations thus achieved. I also pointed out that, in the transference and counter-transference experience, the parties concerned, and in particular the patient, may learn more about themselves through the mirroring processes involved—provided that they can withdraw and integrate the projections they discover themselves to be focusing upon their analyst. All this provides content for the individuation process. Perhaps above all it is fostered in the confrontation with and impact of another particular living person, the analyst, in whom individuation has for long been a living issue. In Chapter 7 I considered the phenomenon of the dream and dreaming, and also the use of dreams by patients defensively for other purposes than those implied in working upon them as conveyors of meaning. The aim was to demonstrate the unique work of the dream in expressing, through visual and musical imagery etc., feeling significance of a holistic sort. By this I mean an intuitive-feeling sense of the central meaning of an individual's life in terms, in the first place, of imagery even if, through interpretation, the intellectual, aim-directed, logical thinking processes of the left hemisphere may be brought in for focusing purposes later. Every inner transaction of this sort may be regarded as working towards the realization of the unique individuality of the person in whom it is taking place.

Note added in proof: Self-experiences and self-representations

The subjective personal experience of the self seems to embrace at least successive feelings of togetherness, untogetherness and re-togetherness, though the underlying sense of wholeness and substance would often seem to be progressive when a long-term view of the individual's life-span is considered. These processes have been hinted at in more abstract terms in Figs 1 to 3. In this connection it must be remembered that the integrative experiences of the self so far described are enabled to become conscious by the growing ego-coherence that develops alongside the processes described above and which serves to implement their realization. Whether we consider the self in terms of one individual's history or in terms of its historical development in a culture, we must include in the diagrams those areas which denote both unrealized archetypal potential and as yet undiscovered and not yet penetrated aspects of the outer world. A third mode of self-representation emerges through the symbolic imagery with which Jung has familiarized us, particularly in *Collected Works*, Vols XI and IX. Through painting and sculpture, verse, drama and music, often in the service of religion, imagery emerges, symbolizing not only the inner unifying aspects of the self but also holistically hinting at its infinite possibility, richness and paradoxical nature. This imagery is no doubt originally based on the functioning of the right cerebral hemisphere, though in the developed religions it would seem to be compounded with, elaborated by and modified by the action of the left. Many analytical psychologists emphasize the *numinous* feelings that may accompany religious themes and ritual as well as self imagery experienced in dreams. The phenomenon of numinous feelings, conceptualized by Otto and further developed by Jung, must be taken with caution. Though, for instance, religious rituals have attempted to stimulate numinous feelings, it has generally been considered that the latter arise spontaneously and so cannot be required of the faithful. A much more complex task, is the clinical one raised by our increased knowledge of the representational imagery of the grandiose self that develops in narcissistic personality disorder. Attempts must be made to distinguish this from representations of the self as described by Jung. They probably often overlap, and discriminatory investigation is likely to benefit all parties concerned.

Postscript

I have attempted in this book to demonstrate a kind of logic that is inherent in the analytic, interpersonal and, finally, individuated development of the self. Such a description cannot, however, pretend to be anything more than a rough guiding framework, for the psychological movement in question proceeds, in practice, in a very higgledy-piggledy way. It includes regressions, temporary gains and rewards, and then, sometimes, quite deep further regressions into areas of disintegration, horror and grief.

The analytic development of patients depends upon an unhurried containing attitude on the part of their analysts quite as much as upon confrontation or a sense of urgency.

The emergence of the self requires a conscious going along with what is discerned to be happening. This is something that normally needs the support of a holding situation because of the powerful and frightening emotions involved—even more so when no adequate holding mother figure, or mother and father pair etc., have become introjected during infancy and childhood. We now think that a child thus deprived has to invest a great deal of libido into being his own mother, into holding together his environment, and even, in extreme cases, into holding together his own body. He is in an insecure position for growth. Achievements in plenty there may be, but personality growth, inner strength, wholeness and, it must be said, a capacity for personal relations in which a person is conscious enough of his own personality and of that of another's to be able to relate in truth—that is another story. It is, of course, considerations of this sort that force anyone aware of the perils inherent in the human situation in an era when the cohesion of the community and the religious symbolic systems, that bind it together and shape instinctual discharge, have begun to disintegrate, to acknowledge the achievements of Freud and Jung. It is common parlance to speak of their "heroic" self-analysis and almost too easy to speak of it thus. It was heroic in personal terms, although hardly so much based on defiance as upon necessity. It was heroic in cultural terms in the same way, for although both men could make use of a number of thinkers as part of their cultural heritage, they were operating during a period when the old unconsciously based orders and symbolical systems were being questioned and undermined. They had to do their work without much in the way of a holding culture. They therefore did what they could, each subject to the fears and doubts that appertained to their individual personality structure and psychopathology. Indeed they have provided something of a holding culture for later generations. As a result, those later generations have been able in turn to do much to improve the analytic setting with its own kind of holding and confrontations, and within which lost, disintegrated and damaged individuals can discover not only some fresh meaning in the old symbolisms but also their own personal way of analysis, repair and individuation. As the years go on and we learn more about the conditions of such development, I find myself more and more impressed by the quotation from John Gower's *Confessio Amantis* 57, II p.35 with which Jung opens his Introduction to *The Psychology of the Transference* (1946): *"Bellica pax, vulnus dulce, suave malum"* (A warring peace, a sweet wound, an agreeable evil). For those who can be enabled to risk an experience of the analytical relationship thus paradoxically described, there can arise the possibilities suggested by the title of this book.

Glossary

This glossary attempts to define at some length analytic terms as used in this book or in general analytic parlance—a selection, however, that is in no way exhaustive. In it there are three groups of topics: (1) topics related to analytical psychology, (2) topics connected with the defences and their psychopathology, and (3) other topics outside the two specialized ones. Some items are quotations from the glossary in *Dying and Creating* by Rosemary Gordon which is Volume IV of the Library of Analytical Psychology. They are marked (Gordon, 1978).

A. Analytical Psychology

(1) Anima and Animus

The *anima* may be defined as the aspect of male psychology that is concerned with relatedness, imagination and inspiration. In dreams and through projection on to actual women, it is often personified by female figures representing various levels of development in that whole area. Similarly the *animus* is referred to the aspect of female psychology that is concerned with conceptualization, discrimination, classification and cultural expression. In a way that is parallel to the anima it is often personified in dreams and in projection upon actual men by male figures also at various levels of development or discrimination. These projections can cause trouble owing to the fact that confusions arise between the anima and actual women and between the animus and actual men, and between both and internalized familial figures of the opposite sex, like father, mother, brother and sister.

In his later work, Jung seems to have related anima and animus to the Eros and Logos principles respectively—two archetypal elements to be found in the members of both sexes in varying combinations and forms of expression according to the varying cultural determinants of race, location and history—to say nothing of the personal somatic basis of contrasexuality in men and women.

(2) Archetypes

(a) The archetype *an sich* is a theoretical postulate or entity found useful in handling psychological phenomena. The postulate is that there is an innate readiness to handle experience in terms of certain well-known and often repeated patterns.

(b) The archetype is postulated to express itself in typical *thematic patterns* like those of movement, change and; transformation on the one hand and specific *forms of human functioning* on the other.

(c) These themes get expressed in *imagery*—varied, but transparent enough to those who are at home with imagination—such as crossing the threshold, initiation, the journey, death and rebirth, and confrontation by meaningful figures, like the mother, the father, in a wide variety of rather stereotypical expression—distillations, perhaps, of innumerable experiences that are, roughly speaking, similar, though not of course identical.

The concreteness of the archetypal imagery derives from a meeting of and a union between real situations and an archetypal predisposition in people to attend to them. We are dealing here with instinctually based forms which, while nourishing the personality, yet carry the danger of stereotypification in such personalities as lack integration or where ego-functioning is weak. Areas for investigation in the field of archetypal forms include (1) the psychogeneses in infancy and early childhood of the particular combination of archetypal determinants that dominates the life of any particular individual; (2) ways in which a person's familial and cultural environment supports a certain selection of archetypally based personality factors at the expense of others; and (3) the formation and internalization of archetypal objects (see pp. 133-135).

In general, archetypal theory may be said to adduce considerations of a structuralist kind which run counter to the *tabula rasa* views of the human mind that seem to be implied in much of the socio-political thought of today with its strong emphasis upon manipulation of people from outside.

(3) The Conscious

That area of experience which is available for knowledge and awareness. 'To be conscious' has really two connotations:

(1) The state in which one is awake and aware: in other words one is not asleep or anaesthetized or in a coma.

(2) The state in which one is self-aware. This can be further sub-divided into:

(a) Primary self-awareness, which means that one knows and is aware of what one does and experiences;

(b) Reflective self-awareness. This means that one's own mental processes are the object of one's attention and reflection. (Gordon, 1978, p.173).

(4) Ego

"That part of the psyche which evolves out of the original self through maturational processes in relation to inner and outer reality. Its primary goal and function is the making and the preserving of consciousness, and of the sense of personal identity and continuity. It also mediates between drives and affects on the one hand, and reality and its testing on the other" (Gordon, 1978, p.174).

(5) Enantiodromia and the Theory of Opposites

Jung was not left untouched by the influence of Hegel upon European thought and was therefore impressed by the dialectic and the idea of the opposites coming together into synthesis as a result of their essentially complementary nature. He developed the idea of a number of different types of oppositeness. For instance, he found ambivalence and relativity in objects to which adjectival qualification has been attached. Such objects tend to turn into their opposite. Jung applied the ancient notion of *enantiodromia* to this, i.e. "the drive into the opposite". For instance, the virtue of the "good" mother could reach a point where good loving support turns into something as negative as destruction of the autonomy of her child by rendering him over-dependent and by robbing him of his initiative with, of course, an underlay of impotent rage. On the contrary, small doses of "bad" mothering may have the "good" result of stimulating her child's aggression, rebellion and enterprise. If the "badness" intensifies beyond a certain point, however, the effects of the "bad" mother are more likely to be destructive as such, although her libido may begin to flow into reparative efforts after that. The point at issue is that in these adjectivally qualified situations, too great an intensification of libido in one direction will cause a flow into its opposite. In the case of the mother the two attributes coexist whether looked at from the objective point of view of what constitutes sound mothering or from the subjective view of the child and indeed of herself. A creative solution will be found in a marriage of the opposites rather than mutual annihilation, a constant alteration of swings, or a defensive maintenance of a split. Every archetypal figure appears to have positive and negative aspects and a kind of conjunctio within the dynamism of every day life represents emotional health.

Another set of complementary opposites is inherent within many human relationships, e.g. in those of man and woman, husband and wife, parent and child. Another is found in adjectival descriptions like good and bad, high and low, black and white, where each requires the other for the purposes of definition. Yet another is found in certain principles like life and death, Eros and Logos, conscious and unconscious, individual and collective, order and freedom, rationalism and romanticism, etc., where the maintenance of fixed oppositions would go counter to observation and perforce be defensive in motivation. Again the fostering of a mutual facing and confrontation, an *Auseinandersetzung*, a conjunctio, a marriage, carries the promise of a creative and fruitful issue.

The infantile and primitive origins of the mature capacity to discern the oppositeness that is inherent in human existence almost certainly lies in the early defensive manoeuvres of "splitting", to be defined later. Defensiveness apart, however, Jung's thesis is that much of the dynamics behind individual, group and social life arise out of the play of opposites at all levels.

(6) Image

"The perception of sensory data like forms, colours, sounds, smells, movements, objects, etc., in the absence of an actual external stimulus which could have caused such a perception. It is the representation of a sensuous and individual, and sometimes collective, experience. External stimuli may, of course, have been present in the past, and the image is practically always dependent on such past experiences" (Gordon, 1978, p.175).

(7) Imagination

"The coalescence of images into a dramatic form so that they tell a story with cognitive content and emotional urgency and meaning. We may agree to say that an image is like a still picture while imagination is like a moving film" (Gordon, 1978, p.175).

(8) Libido

"Jung uses the concept 'libido' as synonymous with 'psychic energy', irrespective of the particular area or channel into which it happens to have been drawn. This contrasts with Freud's use of the term libido. In his first formulation he thought of libido as the energy attached specifically to the sexual instincts; in his second formulation he distinguished ego-libido from object-libido; in his third formulation he defined libido as the energy of Eros or the life of instinct, while another form of energy was thought to be attached to Thanatos or the death instinct" (Gordon, 1978, p.175).

(9) The Original Self

The original state of undifferentiated wholeness that is postulated to characterize the psychic life, probably, of the foetus in the early weeks (but see Liley, 1972) and, at the most, during the first few days of the neonate's life, prior to the long process that will set in of deintegrations and reintegrations, whereby more and more both of the inner world and the outer world is being experienced with consciousness and built into the self. Thus the early simple form of the original self becomes a much more complex whole. The original self links with experiences of fusion. The later developing institution favours ever greater complexity of integration through separateness and discrimination.

(10) Participation Mystique

A term employed by the anthropologist, Levy-Bruhl to denote "the peculiar kind of psychological connection between a subject and an object in which the identities of the two are confused if not fused" (Gordon, 1978, p.176). Jung found the concept relevant and it has connections with Klein's concept of projective identification. See p.212.

(11) The Persona

The aspect of the human psyche in society designated by Jung the *persona* was named so after the masks worn by classical actors to represent the characters they were to portray. An element of contrivance and selection must be considered inevitable in establishing a range of suitable psychological adaptations to the requirements of a person's function both in its own right and in the eyes of society. It needs to be appropriate and not too far from the truth and yet it is understood that it is not the whole story. In terms of the imagery of clothes, so frequent in dreams, there are clothes (or no clothes) that are suitable for each and every occasion and they emphasize varied aspects of a person's functioning. This is useful for being understood on a functional level in social co-operative work and it can help a person to limit his personality sufficiently to perform a specialist function. A judge, for instance, wears clothes, maintains a demeanour, and uses legal terms and criteria that no doubt assist him to perform his duties and which help others to know what he is talking about. It would not, however, be supposed possible, let alone desirable, that the whole range of his personality could be expressed through his judicial persona.

Persona functions are, no doubt, to be regarded as a normal part of life, but pathological developments are possible too. A person's persona may be widely deviant from his real nature in a way that may be gross and obvious or subtly secret in the extreme—to the confusion and pain of all concerned. Or he may be identified with or glued to his persona to the crippling if not the loss of the rest of his nature. Or his understanding of the true nature of the persona may be nil, so that naked indiscretion becomes the order of the day. Such psychopathology stems from schizoid and obsessional tendencies or defensive "innocence" respectively.

In the situation of the flight from "inner reality", the persona becomes a system of attitudes developed through imitative identification with external authority, modes and manners, feared or admired. Its aim under such circumstances is to use capacities, no doubt quite genuine, to give a spurious sense of substance to an individual who feels weak, vulnerable, withdrawn—even destroyed at the core or centre of his real personality. This misleading use of persona allies it very closely indeed to Winnicott's "false self" which protects a weak true self felt to be reclusive, non-operative, even unrealizable.

(12) The Shadow

The unevenness of development that is usual in infants and children, as well as that one-sidedness of development that is often fostered by the support given by families, communities and whole cultures to certain systems of valuation as against others, naturally leads towards the neglect of certain human capacities for survival or creativity. These tend to remain primitive, underdeveloped and underadapted even under conditions of mere lack of encouragement. If for any particular individual they become important for fulfilment or even survival and yet remain suppressed, they seem to become destructively disturbed and sometimes appear in dreams personified as threatening, even psychotic, figures. These neglected bits have been designated by Jung as the *shadow*. Aspects of the shadow are probably discernible in most individuals and cultures and feature in most of the more advanced religions. Though such features seldom present themselves in an attractive form, it was strongly emphasized by Jung that they need recognition in a confrontation and then differentiation, assimilation or integration as an essential element of individuation.

The unlovely forms taken by the shadow provoke the question of whether the shadow as such is a pathological phenomenon. The answer seems to be certainly not, although it can develop a pathology if it is neglected or actively persecuted. In other words it can turn nasty if ill-treated. It certainly needs to be distinguished from the psycho-pathology that stems from serious early and cumulative trauma. In such a case the individual can be overwhelmed by states of violent destructive rage in response to neglect, premature stress or isolation. These get countered by cast-iron defence systems that are more destructive in the long run than protective. For such cases, therapy is much more a matter of repair within a sound holding situation combined with the analysis of the early infantile states including traumata and defences within the transference. In cases, however, where the assimilation of the shadow constitutes the main problem, the therapy needs much more to be confrontative and challenging to the patient in the here and now of the transference situation. This is particularly so when the patient projects his shadow factors on to his environment almost completely and in a very unconscious way.

(13) The Self

Several aspects of the self have been dealt with in Chapter 8. The following is a summary of the concept. The self is a theoretical entity used to encompass the idea of the personality as a whole in all its aspects. It is a psycho-somatic unity composed of consciousness and unconsciousness both personal and collective. It includes ego-consciousness and largely depends upon it for its suitable realization. It is an entity in which the whole is greater than the sum of the parts, in which a series of opposites can come together and form completely new synthesis, in which self-righting capacities come into play if one-sided development goes too far. It is capable of loosening into its components by deintegration in order to admit new experiences, and then, as and when this has been done, to reintegrate. It is conceived of as if possessing as a libidinal source a centre that seeks realization and reinforcement at the circumference in terms of flesh and blood relationships within space and time. Out of it, with the aid of ego-consciousness, images appear, sometimes in dreams and noticeably in religions and mythological systems, which may be understood as self-representations. These can appear in more or less abstract geometrical form like squares and circles, sometimes in impersonal objects like a large animal or a city or a house, and sometimes in human type form.

There seem to be times, especially in infancy, when the self appears to be in danger from disintegrative hostile states of rage. Under these circumstances a blind defensive system can develop which effectively isolates the individual involved and which has been given the special term "defences of the self" by Fordham.

(14) Symbol

Etymologically, symbol derives from the notion of throwing together and so according to Stein embraces the action of "throwing together such things as have something in common" (Stein, 1957). According to Hauser (1959), "Symbol brings the idea and the image into an indivisible unity, so that the transformation of the image also implies the metamorphosis of the idea. The symbol can only be interpreted, it cannot be solved." A symbol "links the strange to the familiar, conscious to unconscious, here-and-now to general and abstract, soma to psyche, fragment to whole and reason to passion. In a symbol form is intimately relevant to content" (Gordon, 1978, p.178).

(15) Symbolic Attitude

This is "the 'as-if' attitude which ensures that that which does the signifying is not confused with that which is signified". (Gordon, 1978, p.178).

(16) Symbolic Equation

This occurs when in someone's mind "the symbol and the object symbolized are felt and treated as though they were identical; in other words the existence and characteristics of one of them is denied or not yet recognized, because it has been totally assimilated in the other". (Gordon, 1978, p.178).

(17) The Symbolic Function

This is "also named the 'transcendent function' by Jung. It refers to that process which links the conscious to the unconscious and the strange to the familiar; its form is intimately relevant to its content. It is characterized by the 'as-if' attitude and so facilitates the experience of representation, not identification; consequently it involves the recognition of similarities in objects that are, at the same time, known to be separate and distinct. This then enables men to relate to unobservable realities in terms of observable phenomena and so mediate the experience of the world as having meaning and significance." (Gordon, 1978, p.179).

(18) The Unconscious

Jung's concept of the unconscious turns out upon long-term reflection to be, despite its structuralist features, not so grossly but only subtly different from Freud's. It remains, however, that his well-known distinction between the *personal* and the *collective* unconscious permits a wider range of discriminatory and detailed observation.

The *personal unconscious* consists of, on the one hand, a number of personal experiences of oneself and one's capacities and of other people that for various reasons have been repressed in the Freudian sense of the word. On the other hand it is postulated that within it are personal and individual potentials that have not yet been realized. The *collective unconscious* is conceived of as the source of archetypal potential structures that, until they are realized, remain more or less stereotypical and impersonal because in principle belonging to all men, or at least to human nature as such. Reflection shows, however, that the distinction cannot be maintained as sharply as that. For instance, the image of the internalized mother of the personal unconscious, while without doubt heavily influenced by personal experience of the actual mother, nevertheless bears the mark of archetypal material. Aspects of the personal mother are shared by all men collectively, and it is indeed a matter of degree as to how personal the original relationship and experience was or, on the contrary, how collective impersonal and stereotypical it really was as a result of insufficiently and inadequately sustained personal contact with her.

From within the collective unconscious, libido activates archetypal potential in terms of imagery. This is also increasingly activated by outside objects corresponding to it and which are sought out often with the aid of ego-consciousness. From within this area also two movements towards integration are postulated. The first is towards integration of archetypal and personal potential, often emerging in various states of mutual opposition. These oppositions are not thought of as irreconcilable in principle even in the case of such basic contraries as Eros and Logos. The second integrative movement seems to be between ego-consciousness and the contents of the personal and the collective unconscious. It is as if the latter seek personalization through the individual or, in other words, "incarnation" in terms of flesh and blood in space and time.

For both Freud and Jung there is a dynamic interplay of various kinds between the two—between ego and id and between ego-consciousness and the more impersonal structures of the collective unconscious. Perhaps Freud by temperament and out of his personal history hoped for mastery of the id by the ego. By comparison, almost certainly, Jung considered the collective unconscious to be the prime mover and the ego-personality to be involved in allowing itself to be "lived" by it, despite the fact that, in his old age, he more and more revered the miracle of ego-consciousness. The whole issue of these, perhaps, temperamental variations in emphasis has been most sympathetically dealt with by Rycroft and expanded upon with reference to both Freud and Jung and illustrated by the work of Coleridge and Gerard Manley Hopkins in *Dreams and the Literary Imagination* (Rycroft, 1980).

B. The Defence Systems

Frustration, pain, rage, hate and fears about survival, especially in objectively unfavourable circumstances, seem to be part of the life of infancy—alongside of, or alternating with, gratification, bliss, peaceful security, hope and love. Sometimes the former greatly outbalance the latter, so that then very intensive defences spring spontaneously into being to cope with the miseries involved. Although the distinction is by no means absolute, it is still possible to distinguish between a kind of half-blind defence against annihilation of the personality as such and defences that are involved in protecting ego-consciousness from the experience of pain of all sorts.

(1) Defences of the Self against Disintegration or Death

In extreme cases of early environmental failure, *defences of the self* (Fordham, 1974) and those that are a function of *narcissistic personality disorder* arise. (Kohut, 1971; Kernberg, 1974). They attempt protection against the pain and horror and danger of helplessness, isolation and the disappointment connected with unmet expectations, as well as the shattering experiences of boundless rage that ensue. A grandiose do-it-yourself psychology masks an inner emptiness. An impossibly perfectionist expectation of good parental responses to the infant or child, let alone adult, on the part of other people issues into the feeling that they are all full of demonic ill-will and totally untrustworthy. As a result life is reduced to a continued obsession with minimal levels of survival, for the defence turns out to be cripplingly expensive. It should perhaps be pointed out we are dealing here, among other things, with fears about *disintegration*.

Disintegration is a condition clearly to be differentiated from Fordham's concept of deintegration and one in which not a coming apart into its constituents but a large-scale smash up of the self takes place. It originates in overwhelming stress in early infancy arising out of abandonment, or lack of holding and skin contact by the mother, remaining for long periods unattended to when needing to be fed, cleaned up and made comfortable in terms of temperature or positions in the cot or pram. Alongside of this, there is an absolute need to be in familiar surroundings, to be secure with a central mother figure, to have company but not too much impingement, to be protected from sudden loud noises or bright lights, etc. The overwhelming stress already alluded to leads to paroxysms of rage and a shattering of confidence. If this becomes a cumulative process spread over a long period, it seems likely that a condition of serious weakness may get established. Defences against disintegration are likely to be strong and coupled with an inflated fear of any deintegrative–reintegrative processes that may be activated by developmental and other changes both from within a person and in his relationships with the outer world of people, things and general conditions.

(2) Defences against Consciousness of Pain and Anxiety

(a) *Identification, projection, introjection, and projective and introjective identification*   Pains and anxiety that arise in connection with the fundamental human aim of separation from the mother and the achievement of unit status give rise to defensive states like *identification, projection* and *introjection* and also a special combination of them originally described by Melanie Klein as *projective* or *introjective identification*. This is a "psychological mechanism which aims to re-establish the experience of fusion; it involves the mixing and muddling up of subject and object, inner world and outer world and hence the undoing of boundaries" (Gordon, 1978, p.177-178).

(b) *Envy, contempt and defiance*   The defences already listed seek to maximize feelings of identity and minimize those of separateness and seek to obliterate consciousness of bad or painful feelings connected with separateness. At a later point, the anxiety and rage connected with feelings of lack, weakness and dependence, in a situation of nevertheless some degree of separateness, often combine to establish another and very important trio of defences—namely *envy, contempt* and *defiance*. These are specialized infantile experiences that are to be distinguished in the main from the adult connotations of the words involved. Adult envy, for instance, is generally not so compulsive that it may not be mastered and move into emulation. To experience contempt for certain types of adult behaviour is, though painful, nevertheless often quite justifiable. Defiance has sometimes saved individuals, groups and nations from annihilation by enemies. All this, however, is not to say that adult envy, contempt and defiance are not sometimes saturated by the rageful and self-defeating feelings so central to the infant experience of these emotions. The infantile experience of envy rests upon the feeling that the breast or the mother is full of a goodness that is being withheld from him. The rage accompanying this is destructive and would destroy the breast and all its goodness—a serious matter subjectively when we remember that there is only a minimal distinction in the infant's mind between feeling or wish and action or deed. Though the fear of separation is thus defended against, the relief is filled with delusion, for a new alarm, horror and depression set in over survival, since all that is left to the infant is a destroyed breast. So awful is this consequence that the destructive attacks get turned in upon the infant himself in order to protect the breast/mother from them. Now, however, the infant becomes depressed as a result of the attacks turned against himself. The mechanism is also transparent enough to the observer of adults regressed within the transference or in other intimate relationships where parent–child psychology is dominant.

Further steps in this bleak set of defences issue into *contempt* or scorn. The withholding breast is denigrated by contempt. It is no use anyway and hence not worth striving for.

As a result, by a kind of inexorable infantile logic, *defiance* sets in with the desperate thought that anyway the infant can do without the breast/mother very well after all. Plainly such defences are desperate ones, based upon delusion and a symptom of serious disturbances. Indeed in their extreme form, the child may consequently become unable to use the breast/mother in any satisfactory way whatsoever. The pathological content can be high indeed and abounds in malignant destructivity noticeably alternating with depressive inactivity.

It is sometimes wondered whether it is really possible for an infant not yet arrived at unit status to be capable of envy, contempt and defiance, for the latter states rather assume a sense of "otherness" or not-self. The objection is partially modified when it is remembered that envy, contempt and defiance are highly delusion-filled and are not based upon a realistic sense of the other but only a rudimentary awareness of something not exactly "me" upon which, or whom, some sort of dependence is experienced. We are using "as-if" language to suggest attitudes in the infant that cannot fully be verified.

(3) Splitting

Splitting arises out of intense anxiety over the discovery of love and hate within one's own psyche and operates particularly towards the same person – mother. The defensive solution is to split. Now there are two mes and two mothers. One is good. The other is bad. The two are not allowed to meet. While this defence may be useful for a while, in the longer run and especially if it persists into adult life, it can cause endless instability and misery in personal relationships. Nevertheless, like most defences, it carries something positive for the growing and developing infant. It can be behind the fostering of a primitive *discriminatory* awareness and an understanding of the bi-polar nature of existence so emphasized by Jung and already touched on in this glossary. It is also true that it is a most important development in infancy to become able to tolerate the fact that the "good", that is to say gratified, loving and happy, me and the "bad", that is to say pain-filled, enraged and hating, me are one and the same person, and likewise the "good" mother and the "bad" mother.

(4) Fusion

Splitting processes and defences arise out of an earlier process which itself is partially defensive. This earlier process is the wish for fusion, or oneness with the breast or mother. Of course the "fusion" involved is a psychological feeling and not literally a physical fact. We are dealing here with a benign illusion which the instinctual mother empathically "plays in" with. The illusion affords the infant that feeling of omnipotence which gives him or her a good start in life—after which the surrender of the feeling of omnipotence at the right time can lead to experiences of sound dependency that are appropriate and realistic. The illusion of fusion involves a certain amount of denial of bad feelings, and for this to be possible there must be an adequate holding mother who can meet needs quickly so that the infant can feel that his wish has only to be experienced to be met.

If this benign illusion of fusion fails to get itself established satisfactorily, the longing for it is known to persist all through a person's life and it can render a person unable to stomach any experiences of separateness or otherness. Naturally his wish is destructive of relationship potential in later life for, in this, autonomy and separateness are as important as temporary states of identification and oneness. The wish for fusion in this case partakes of defensive idealization.

(5) Manic Defence

Melanie Klein has developed the notion of a manic defence against various types of depression. As the paradoxically grey deadness of depression is not only painful but disapproved of socially and culturally, substitute activities, representing a false but exciting way of being alive, come into being. The pursuit of excited states in play, danger, games, jokiness, non-stop work activity as a way of life, and even intellectual and artistic activity, can all be used as a manic defence against depression. However, when this is happening, something of genuineness and spontaneity is missing. Nevertheless, activity quite sound in itself can be used for this purpose.

(b) Idealization

Idealization comes in as a defence mechanism as a way of dealing with the pain of lack of food, mother, validation, love, etc. It consists in building up in phantasy an ideally perfect person to aid one or a perfect situation. Thus the fairy godmother, the perfect meal, the perfect attainment, the perfect environment are the creation of idealization in phantasy. The defence serves to keep the deprived infant or the starving man going a little longer before it fails, as it must, and the subject sinks into despairing apathy. Idealizations falsify life by phantasizing that it could be better than it could possibly be. The defence is expensive: when it fails, despair and disillusion set in and any help available seems worse than useless and cannot be accepted.

The defence of idealization has very little to do with setting up normal aims and ideals of improvement in the achievements and skills of life. Such are legitimate—unless the standards are set so high as to paralyse all achievement.

(7) Perfectionism

Perfectionism represents, of course, a kind of idealization but tends to be more all-embracing so that it gets built into the character structure. The alarming plight of the perfectionist is that he embraces unreal absolutes. If things are not good then they are impossibly awful. Anyway, perfection is hardly ever possible. If, however, it is approached, the perfectionist is not defeated. He can set up a *sliding scale of perfection*. Every time an ideal seems reachable, or something satisfactory or good enough is realized, the scale of measurement is advanced further so that the present achievement is felt as worse than useless. Adults in some societies tease children by removing ever further from their reach that which they stretch out with their hands to grasp—an action that always appears funnier to the adult than to the child.

(8) Anna Freud's List of Defences of the Ego

Anna Freud (1937) described defences that seem clearly neurotic in the main and apply more fully to individuals who have achieved unit status to a degree. These defences represent ways of avoiding consciousness of anxiety and pain produced by bad experiences. They have been designated as *regression, repression, reaction-formation, isolation, undoing, projection, introjection, turning against the self* and *reversal*, to which may be added *denial* and possibly *sublimation*. As it took a book to describe these defences of the ego, they can perhaps only be hinted at here by showing how I might deploy them if for example there was urgent work to finish that was important, but, for all that, irksome and becoming painful as a result of increasing fatigue on my part. I might *regress* into a childish state and simply give up. On the other hand, I might *repress* all consciousness of painful fatigue. By *reaction formation* I carry on saying how fresh and good I feel. By *isolation* I do not let myself perceive the fatigue and I draw no logical conclusions from the state in terms of action or thought. In *undoing* I act as though the consciousness of fatigue had never happened. In *projection* I get rid of the feeling and see that someone else is fatigued—not myself. In *introjection* I notice someone else as fresh and vigorous and take it into myself. By *turning against the self*, I turn my anger about feeling so tired against myself and upbraid myself for laziness. In *reversal* I pretend to myself that I am fresh and free from fatigue and force myself to believe it. In *denial*, I simply say "I'm not tired—not me!" In *sublimation* I raise the experience of fatigue into ennobling self-sacrifice.

It must be amply clear that most of the defences thus listed, when used, so to speak, piecemeal and *ad hoc* can become enabling factors in maintaining action that requires courage, pertinacity and effectiveness. They may be used to extract the "last ounce of energy" that makes all the difference between achievement and failure. As thoroughly built-in parts of the character structure in a continuing sense, however, they display a negative aspect, for they can falsify one's sense of reality or truth and may play havoc with personal relationships. It has perhaps been this aspect of this type of defence that has caused people to misuse the idea. In itself neutral, the word defence has sometimes been used as a term of abuse in character assassination and the capacity to defend oneself against dangerous attacks denigrated—a mistaken view with dubious motivation. Negatively speaking, however, these defences can be expensive like the others to the degree that they distort cognition and thought, warp the emotions and feelings and interfere with true perception.

C. Allied Topics

In this section I have quoted at length from the Glossary in *Dying and Creating* by Rosemary Gordon (1978) (Volume IV of the Library of Analytical Psychology).

(1) Ethology

This is "a term, originally employed by J. S. Mill to designate the 'Science of Character'. In modern times, Tinbergen, a follower of Konrad Lorenz, has used this term for the new science, the 'scientific study of animal behaviour'. This is essentially concerned with the experimental investigation of the bio-physiology of instinct" (Gordon, 1978, p.175).

(2) Innate Fixed Pattern

"A concept evolved by the science [of] ethology. A hierarchical organized nervous mechanism which is susceptible to certain primary releasing and directing impulses of internal as well as of external origin, and which responds to these impulses by co-ordinated movements that contribute to the maintenance of the individual and the species" (Gordon, 1978, p.176).

(3) Innate Release Mechanism (I.R.M.)

"A concept evolved by the . . . science [of] ethology. A selective neuro-sensory mechanism that releases on reaction and is responsible for its selective susceptibility to a particular special combination of sign-stimuli. The existence of I.R.M. is suggested by the strict dependence of a reaction upon a specific set of sign-stimuli" (Gordon, 1978, p.176).

(4) Instinct

"That correlate of structural physiological, behavioural and experiental features, established by heredity which is activated in a co-ordinated manner when the organism encounters the relevant or matching situation in its environment. It is then composed of a congenital impulse plus specific emotional excitement" (Gordon, 1978, p.176). For Jung the "archetypal images represent the goals of the instincts" (Gordon, 1978, p.172) or, again, the mental expressions of the psychosomatic entity of which the instinctual activities are the physical expression (Gordon, 1978, p.173).

References

Abenheimer, K. (1968). The ego as subject. *In* "The Reality of the Psyche", (ed. J. B. Wheelright London). Barrie and Rockliff for the C. G. Jung Foundation for Analytical Psychology.

Adler, G. (1961). "The Living Symbol", London, Routledge and Kegan Paul.

Altmann, L. L. (1975). "The Dream in Psychoanalysis" (Rev. edn.), New York, International Universities Press.

Bakan, D. (1958). "Sigmund Freud and the Jewish Mystical Tradition", Boston, Beacon Press.

Bakan, P. (1975). Dreaming, R.E.M. sleep and the right hemisphere. Comments on D. Cohen's paper presented at the 15th annual APSS meeting, Edinburgh, 1975.

Balint, M. (1968). "The Basic Fault", London, Tavistock.

Bion, W. R. (1962). "Learning from Experience", London, Heinemann.

Bion, W. R. (1962). "Elements of Psychoanalysis", London, Heinemann.

Bion, W. R. (1965). Transformations. London, Heinemann.

Bion, W. R. (1970). "Attention and interpretation", London, Tavistock.

Blum, H. P. (1980). The value of reconstruction in adult psychoanalysis. *Int. J. Psycho-anal.* **61**, 1.

Brenman, E. (1980). The value of reconstruction in adult psychoanalysis. *Int. J. Psycho-anal.* **61**, 1.

Boss, M. (1979). "Existential foundations of medicine and psychology", New York, Jason Aaronson.

Cohen, D. B. (1975). Lateralisation of functioning in the cortex during R.E.M. sleep: preliminary evidence from dream content. Presented 15th annual APSS meeting, Edinburgh.

Colonna, M. T. (1981). Lilith and the black moon. *J. analyt. Psychol.* **26**, 1.

Copans, S. and Singer, T. (1979). "Who's the Patient Here? Portraits of the Young Psychotherapist", New York, Oxford University Press.

Deutsch, H. (1939). A discussion of certain forms of resistance. *Int. J. Psycho-anal.* **20**, 72-83.

Dieckmann, H. (1971). Die Konstellierung der Gegenübertragung beim Auftauchen archetypischer Traüme: Untersuchungs methoden und Ergebnisse. *Z. anal. Psychol.* **3**, 1.

Edwards, A. (1976). Review of Volkan, V. D. "Primitive internalized object relations". *J. analyt. Psychol.* **22**, 2.

218

Edwards, A. (1978). Review of Kohut, H. "The restoration of the self". *J. analyt. Psychol.* **23**, 3.

Fairbairn, W. R. (1952). "Psychoanalytic Studies of the Personality", London, Tavistock.

Fenichel, O. (1945). "The Psychoanalytic Theory of Neurosis", London, Routledge and Kegan Paul.

Fordham, M. (1957). Notes on the transference. *In* "Technique in Jungian Analysis" L.A.P, Vol. 2, London, Heinemann.

Fordham, M. (1957) "New developments in Analytical Psychology", London, Routledge and Kegan Paul.

Fordham, M. (1962). Uses and abuses of interpretation in the dialectical relationship. Unpublished.

Fordham, M. (1966). The limits of analysis. Unpublished.

Fordham, M. (1968). Individuation in childhood *In* "The Reality of the Psyche", (ed. Wheelwright, J. B.). London, Barrie and Rockliff for the C. G. Jung Foundation for Analytical Psychology.

Fordham, M. (1969). "Children as Individuals", London, Hodder and Stoughton.

Fordham, M. (1969). Technique and counter-transference *In* "Technique in Jungian Analysis", L.A.P vol.2, London, Heinemann.

Fordham, M. (1971). Failure in analysis. Not yet published.

Fordham, M. (1971). Ending phase as an indicator of the success or failure of psychotherapy. Not yet published.

Fordham, M. (1971). Interpretation. Not yet published.

Fordham, M. (1974). Defences of the self. *J. analyt. Psychol.* **19**, 2.

Fordham, M. (1976). "The Self and Autism", L.A.P. Vol.3, London, Heinemann.

Fordham, M. (1978). "Jungian Psychotherapy: A study in analytical psychology", Chichester, John Wiley & Sons.

Fordham, M. (1979). Analytical psychology and counter-transference. *In* "Countertransference" (ed. L. Epstein and A. H. Finer), New York and London, Jason Aronson.

Freud, Anna (1936). "The Ego and Mechanisms of Defence", London, Hogarth.

Freud, S. (1893-5). Studies in hysteria. *Std. edn.* **20**.

Freud, S. (1900). The interpretation of dreams. *Std. edn.* **4**, 5.

Freud, S. (1909). Notes on a case of obsessional neurosis. *Std. edn.* **10**.

Freud, S. (1910). The future prospects of psychoanalytic therapy. *Std. edn.* **11**.

Freud, S. (1912). The dynamics of the transference. *Std. edn.* **12**.

Freud, S. (1915). Observations on transference love. *Std. edn.* **12**.

Freud, S. (1926). The question of lay analysis. *Std. edn.* **20**.

Freud, S. (1937). Constructions in analysis. *Std. edn.* **23**.

Glover, E. (1955). "The Technique of Psychoanalysis", London, Bailliere, Tindall and Cox.

Gopaleen, M. na (1968). "The Best of Myles", London, Picador.

Gordon, R. (1978). "Dying and Creating: a search for meaning" L.A.P. vol. 4, London, Heinemann.

Gordon, R. (1980). Narcissism and the self; who am I that I love? *J. analyt. Psychol.* **25**, 3.

Greenson, R. R. (1978). "Explorations in Psychoanalysis", New York, International University Press.

Greenson, R. R. (1965). The working alliance and the transference neurosis. *Psycho-anal. R.* **34**, 155-181.

Guntrip, H. (1961). "Personality Structure and Human Interaction", London, Hogarth.

Hall, J. A. (1978). "Clinical Uses of Dreams: Jungian Interpretations and Enactments", New York, Grane and Stratton.

Hann-Kende, F. (1936). Zur Überstragung und Gegenübertragung in der Psychoanalyse. *Int. Z. Psychoanal,* **22**.

Harding, E. (1965). "The 'I' and the not 'I'". Princeton, Princeton University Press.

Hartmann, E. L. (1973). "The Functions of Sleep". New Haven, Yale University Press.

Hartmann, H. (1951). Technical implications of ego-psychology *Psychoanal. Q.* **20**, 31–43.

Hauser, A. (1959). "The Philosophy of Art", London, Routledge and Kegan Paul.

Henry, J. P. (1977). Comment on Rossi, E. The cerebral hemispheres in analytical psychology. *J. analyt. Psychol.* **22**, 1.

Hesse, H. (1979). "Steppenwolf", London, Penguin Books.

Hillman, J. (1971). "Schism as Differing Visions", Pamphlet No. 162, London Guide of Pastoral Psychology, c/o 56 Milner Road, London SW9 3AA.

Hillman, J. (1972). Three ways of failure and analysis. *J. analyt. Psychol.* **17**, 1.

Hillman, J. (1975). "Revisioning Psychology", London and New York, Harper and Row.

Home, H. J. H. (unpublished).

Hubback, J. (1972). Envy and the shadow. *J. analyt. Psychol.* **17**, 2.

Jacobson, E. (1964). "The self and the object world", New York, Int. Univ. Press.

Jones, R. M. (1978). "The New Psychology of Dreaming", London, Pelican Books.

Jung, C. G. (1913a). Crucial points in psychoanalysis, *Coll. wks.* **4**. London, Routledge and Kegan Paul.

Jung, C. G. (1913b). The theory of psychoanalysis. *Coll. wks.* **14**. London, Routledge and Kegan Paul.

Jung, C. G. (1921). Psychological types. *Coll. wks.* **6**. London, Routledge and Kegan Paul.

Jung, C. G. (1921–28). The therapeutic value of abreaction. *Coll. wks.* **16**. London, Routledge and Kegan Paul.

Jung, C. G. (1924). Analytical psychology and education. *Coll. wks.* **17**. London, Routledge and Kegan Paul.

Jung, C. G. (1925). The significance of the unconscious in individual education, *Coll. wks.* **17**. London, Routledge and Kegan Paul.

Jung, C. G. (1929). Two essays on analytical psychology, *Coll. wks.* **7**. London, Routledge and Kegan Paul.

Jung, C. G. (1930–31). The stages of life. *Coll. wks.* **8**. London, Routledge and Kegan Paul.

Jung, C. G. (1931a). Problems of modern psychotherapy. *Coll. wks.* **16**. London, Routledge and Kegan Paul.

Jung, C. G. (1931b). The aims of psychotherapy, *Coll. wks.* **16**. London, Routledge and Kegan Paul.

Jung, C. G. (1934a). 'The practical use of dream analysis', *Coll. wks.* **16**. London, Routledge and Kegan Paul.

Jung, C. G. (1934b). The development of personality, *Coll. wks.* **17**. London, Routledge and Kegan Paul.

Jung, C. G. (1934c). The state of psychotherapy. *Coll. wks.* **17**. London, Routledge and Kegan Paul.

Jung, C. G. (1935). Principles of practical psychotherapy. *Coll. wks.* **16**. London, Routledge and Kegan Paul.

Jung, C. G. (1935). The Tavistock lectures on the theory and practice of analytical psychology *Coll. wks.* **18**. London, Routledge and Kegan Paul.

Jung, C. G. (1939). Archetypes and the collective unconscious. *Coll. wks.* **9**. London, Routledge and Kegan Paul.

Jung, C. G. (1942). A psychological approach to the dogma of the Trinity. *Coll. wks.* **11**. London, Routledge and Kegan Paul.

Jung, C. G. (1946). The psychology of the transference. *Coll. wks.* **16**. London, Routledge and Kegan Paul.

Jung, C. G. (1951). Fundamental questions of psychotherapy. *Coll. wks.* **16**.

Jung, C. G. (1951). Fundamental questions of psychotherapy. *Coll. wks.* **16**. London, Routledge and Kegan Paul.

Jung, C. G. (1951). Aion. *Coll. wks.* **9**, Part II. London, Routledge and Kegan Paul.

Jung, C. G. (1954). Transformation symbolism in the mass. *Coll. wks.* **11**. London, Routledge and Kegan Paul.

Jung, C. G. (1954). Answer to Job. *Coll. wks.* **11**. London, Routledge and Kegan Paul.

Jung, C. G. (1976). "C. G. Jung Letters" Vol. II (ed. G. Adler). London, Routledge and Kegan Paul.

Jung, C. G. (1963)."Memories, Dreams, Reflexions", London, Routledge and Kegan Paul.

Kerenyi, C. and Jung, C. G. (1949). "Essays on a science of mythology" (*trans.* Hull, R.F.C.), New York, Bollingen Series XXII.

Kernberg, O. F. (1974). Further contributions to the treatment of narcissistic personalities. *Int. J. Psycho-anal.* **55**, 2.

Khan, M. M. R. (1974). Silence as communication *In* "The privacy of the self", London, Hogarth.

Khan, M. M. R. (1975). Introduction to D. W. Winnicott's "Through Paediatrics to Psychoanalysis", London, Hogarth.

Kirsch, T. (1927). Dreams and psychological types. Paper given at the 7th International Congress of Analytical Psychology, Rome, 1977.

Klauber, J. (1968). On the dual use of historical and scientific method in psychoanalysis. *Int. J. Psycho-anal,* **49**, 1.

Klein, M. (1932). "The Psychoanalysis of Children", London, Hogarth.

Klein, M. (1935). "Contributions to Psychoanalysis, 1921-45", London, Hogarth.

Klein, M. (1957). "Envy and Gratitude", London, Tavistock.

Kohut, A. (1971). "The analysis of the self", New York, Int. Univ. Press.

Kohut, A. (1977). "The Restoration of the Self", New York, Int. Univ. Press.

Lambert, K. (1973). Jung's later work: historical studies. *Brit. J. med. Psychol.* **35**, 3.

Lambert, K. (1973). The problem of authority in the early development of the individual. Pamphlet No. 170, London Guild of Pastoral Psychology, c/o 56 Milner Road, London, SW19, 3AA.

Lambert, K. (1974). Some notes on the process of reconstruction. *In* "Technique in Jungian Analysis", L.A.P. Vol. 2. London, Heinemann.

Lambert, K. (1977). Analytical psychology and the development of western consciousness. *J. analyt-psychol.* **22**, 2.

Lambert, K. (1981). Emerging consciousness. *J. analyt. psychol.* **26**, 1.

Ledermann, R. (1979). The narcissistic roots of personality disorder. *J. analyt. Psychol.* **24**, 2.

Liley, A. N. (1972). The foetus as a personality. *Aust. N.Z. J. Psychiat.* **6**, 99.

McLuhan, M. (1967). "The Medium as the Message", London, Penguin Books.

Mattoon, M. A. (1979). "Applied Dream Analysis—a Jungian approach", New York, Winston & Wiley.

Meier, C. A. (1977). "Jung's Analytical Psychology and Religion", reprinted Urbana, Illinois University Press.

Meltzer, D. (1967). "The Psychoanalytical Process", London, Heinemann.

Meltzer, D. (1973). "Sexual States of Mind", Ballinluig, Clunie Press.

Moore, N. (1972). Counter-transference, anxiety and change. *J. analyt. Psychol.* **17**, 1.

Neumann, E. (1954). "The Origins of Consciousness", London, Routledge and Kegan Paul.

Novey, S. (1964). The significance of the actual historical event in psychiatry and psychoanalysis. *Brit. J. med. Psychol.* **00**, 374.

Novey, S. (1968). "The Second Look", Baltimore, the Johns Hopkins Press.

Oswald, I. (1966). "Sleep", London, Pelican Books.

Partridge, E. (1958). "Origins", London, Routledge and Kegan Paul.

Plaut, A. J. P. (1966). Reflections on not being able to imagine. *J. analyt. Psychol.* **15**, 1.

Plaut, A. J. P. (1971). Myself as an instrument. Unpublished.

Plaut, A. J. P. (1972). Unpublished.

Plaut, A. J. P. (1975). A note on object constancy or constant object, *J. analyt. Psychol,* **20**, 2.

Plaut, A. J. P. (1959). Aspects of consciousness in Jungian Psychology *Brit. J. med. Psychol.* **32**, 4.

Popper, K. (1959). "The Logic of Scientific Discovery", London, Hutchinson.

Racker, H. (1968). "Transference and Counter-transference", London, Hogarth.

Redfearn, J. W. T. (1969). Several views of the self. *J. analyt. Psychol.* **14**, 1.

Redfearn, J. W. T. (1975). Review of E. L. Hartmann's "The functions of sleep". *J. analyt. Psychol.* **20**, 1.

Redfearn, J. W. T. (1977). The self and individuation, *J. analyt. Psychol.* **22**, 20.

Reich, W. (1928). Character analysis, *In* "The Psychoanalytic Reader" (ed. R. Fliess), London, Hogarth.

Rhodes, J. M. and Feather, B. W. (1972). Transference and resistance observed in behaviour therapy. *Br. J. med. Psychol.* **45**, 99.

Rosenfeld, H. A. (1965). "Psychotic States: A Psychoanalytic Approach", London, Hogarth.

Rossi, E. (1977). The cerebral hemisphere in analytical psychology. *J. analyt. Psychol.* **22**, 1.

Rubinfine, D. L. (1967). Notes on a theory of reconstruction. *Brit. J. med. Psychol.* **40**, 3.

Rycroft, C. (1968). "Imagination and Reality", London, Hogarth.

Rycroft, C. (1979). "The Innocence of Dreams", London, Hogarth.

Sanday, W. and Headlam, A. C. (1908). "A Critical and Exegetical Commentary on the Epistle to the Romans", Edinburgh, T. and T. Clark.

Sandler, J., Dare, C. and Holder, A. (1973). "The Patient and the Analyst", London, Allen and Unwin.

Schafer, R. (1973). The idea of resistance. *Int. J. Psychoanal.* **54**, 3.

Scott, W. C. M. (1975). Remembering sleep and dreams. *Int. Rev. Psychoanal.* **2**, 253.

Stein, L. (1957). What is a symbol supposed to be? *J. analyt. Psychol.*, **2**, 1.

Stein, L. (1958). Analytical psychology: a modern science. *In* "Analytical Psychology: a modern science" L.A.P. Vol. 1, London and New York, Academic Press.

Stein, L. (1962). An entity named ego. *J. analyt. Psychol*, **7**, 1.

Stone, M. (1977). Dreams, free association and the non-dominant hemisphere; an integration of psychoanalytical neurophysiological and historical data, *J. Amer. Acad. Psychoanal.* **5** (2).

Strachey, S. (1934). The nature of the therapeutic action of psychoanalysis. *Int. J. Psycho-anal.* **15**, 1.

Truax, C. G. and Carkhuff, R. R. (1967). "Towards Effective Counselling and Psychotherapy", Chicago, Aldine.

Volkan, V. D. (1976). "Primitive Internalized Object Relations", New York, International Universities Press.

Williams, M. (1963). The indivisibility of the personal and the collective unconscious. *J. analyt. Psychol*, **8**, 1.

Williams, M. (1972). Success and failure in analysis: primary envy and the fate of the good, *J. analyt. Psychol.* **17**, 1.

Winnicott, D. W. (1941). Observations of infants in a set situation. *In* "Through Paediatrics to Psychoanalysis", No. 100 International Psycho-analytical Library (ed. M. M. R. Khan) 1975 Edn. London, Hogarth.

Winnicott, D. W. (1945). Primitive emotional development. *In* "Through Paediatrics to Psychoanalysis", London, Hogarth.

Winnicott, D. W. (1947). "Hate in the Counter-transference", London, Hogarth.

Winnicott, D. W. (1950). Aggression in relation to emotional development. *In* "Through Paediatrics to Psychoanalysis", London, Hogarth.

Winnicott, D. W. (1951). Transitional objects and transitional phenomena. *In* "From Paediatrics to Psychoanalysis" No. 100, International Psycho-analytical Library (ed. M. M. R. Khan) 1975 edition, London, Hogarth.

Winnicott, D. W. (1956). Primary maternal preoccupation. In "From Paediatrics to Psychoanalysis". No. 100 Internationl Psycho-analytical Library (ed. M. M. R. Khan) 1975 edition, London, Hogarth.

Winnicott, D. W. (1958). The capacity to be alone. *In* "The Maturational Process and the Facilitating Environment", London, Hogarth.

Winnicott, D. W. (1963). The capacity for concern. *In* "The Maturational Process and the Facilitating Environment", London, Hogarth.

Winnicott, D. W. (1964). Review of *Memories, Dreams, Reflexions* by Jung, C. G. *Int. J. Psycho-anal.* **45**, 450-455.

Winnicott, D. W. (1965). "The Maturational Process and the Facilitating Environment", London, Hogarth.

Winnicott, D. W. (1969). The use of an object and relating through identification. *In* "Playing and Reality", London, Tavistock.

Winnicott, D. W. (1971). "Playing and Reality", London, Tavistock.

Zinkin, L. (1978). Person to Person. The search for the human dimension in psychotherapy. *Brit. J. med. Psychol.* **51**, 25-34.

Index

Abenheimer, K., 197
"Acting-out" therapies, 25, 26
Adler, A., 31, 64
Adler, G., 16, 162
Agape, 22
    and analyst, 9, 37–9, 40–45, 48, 49,
        51, 134, 135, 152, 153, 161
    and eros, 39–40
    and Hippocratic Oath, 36–7
    and image of feast, 42
    in classical Greek, 39
    in Hebrew–Christian tradition, 39–40
    Pauline concept of, 20, 22, 34, 35–9,
        51
    in Septuagint, 39
    in Fourth Gospel, 39
    in Epistles of St John, 39
    in The Apocalypse, 39
    range of meaning of, 40
Agape-factor, 24, 41
    delimitation of, in analysis, 42–3, 51
Alchemical thought, 192
    and transference/counter-
        transference, 154–5, 156
Altmann, L. L., 10, 169
Analysis
    and catharsis, 29–30
    and history, 113, 115–16, 123–4
    and problems of false self, 61–3, 68,
        85, 86
    and psychotherapy, 25–6
    and synthesis, 126–7
    continuity in, 43–4, 51
    failure of/in, 22, 23, 27, 78–9
    fatigue in, 135
    faulty procedures and attitudes in,
        and resistance, 58, 64, 69
    formation of internal objects in, 97–8
    history of interpretation in, 45–8
    incestuous love as motive power in,
        161
    interdiction on types of behaviour in,
        145
    number and frequency of sessions,
        43, 97, 98, 125, 144

rebirth in, 66
reductive, 118, 119, 126
ritual in, 44–5 51, 135
setting and background for, 51, *see
    also* Therapeutic set-up
termination of unsuccessful, 79
unsuitability for, 79
Analyst
    analogous to priest, 44, 45
    analysis and training of future, 12,
        26, 27, 28, 37–8, 42, 44–5, 82,
        135, 148, 152, 154, 156, 162
    anxiety of beginner, 81
    as psycho-historian, 123–4
    compared with archaeologist, 114, 123
    counter-resistance of, *see* Counter-
        resistance
    counter-transference of, *see* Counter-
        transference
    historical antecedents of, 20
    holding work of, 28, 125, 135
    interaction with patient, and
        personality of, 20–21, 34, 50, 51
    interpretation, and authority of, 60
    listening ability of, 41–2
    modifications in traditional models of
        function of, 6–7
    motivation of, 28, 135–6, 148, 152,
        161
    patient's envy of, 23, 27, 70–71, 153,
        160
    patient's idealization of, 71
    personality of, and contemporary
        analytical psychology, 22–4, *see
        also* Jung
    personality of, and contemporary
        psychoanalysis, 126–8
    reconstructive response of, 120–23
    reliability of, 43, 51
    resistance of and towards, *see*
        Resistance, Counter-resistance
    screening by, and interactional
        processes, 6, 7, 8–9, 41
    stresses of practice as, 136
    "wounding" of, 162

225

"Analyst–parenting", 51
Analytical psychology
  and dreams, 173–7
  counter–transference in, 154–60,
    160–63
  debate on ego in, 6
  ego–consciousness in, 196–7
  function of analyst in, 7, 21
  individuation in, 188–97
  investigations into self, 6, 11–12,
    193–7
  modifications in traditional models of,
    5–12
  personal factor in contemporary, 22–4
  reconstruction in, 117–19, 120
  traditional models of attitudes in, 2–4
  training in child analysis, 7
  transference in, 141–2, 160–63
Anima, 141, 142, 154–6, 159, 161, 191
Animus, 141, 142, 154–6, 159, 161, 191
Answer to Job (Jung), 17, 39, 40, 66, 67,
    79, 192
Anxiety
  defence mechanisms against, in
    infancy, 148
  of beginner analyst, 81
Apparent resistance, Winnicott's work
    on, 61–3, 68, 85, 86
Archetypal counter–transference, 156,
    159
Archetypal image, 90–91, 176
Archetypal motifs and themes, in
    dreams, 173, 187
Archetypal objects, 91, 95, 96, 97, 194,
    203
Archetypal phantasy, infantile, 11
Archetypal predisposition/expectation,
    and object relations, 90–91, 92, 93,
    95, 96, 131, 193–5
Archetypal transference, 65, 86, 141–2,
    156, 159, 160
Archetypes, 78
  and object–relations, 88, 89–93, 95,
    96, 193–5
  and ritual/symbolic events, 195
  in childhood, and reconstruction, 131
  Jung's views on, 90
  working definition of, 90
Armour–plated character structure,
    Reich's concept of, 57

Asymmetry, in therapeutic relationship,
    137, 144, 159, 163
Autism, normal in Kernberg, 89
Auto–eroticism, 89

Bakan, D., 20
Bakan, P., 172
Balint, M., 6, 50
Bartlett, F. C., 115, 119
Behaviour therapy, 25–6
Bion, W. R., 7, 12, 23, 27, 40, 41, 43,
    70, 74
  work on interpretation in analysis, 45,
    47–8, 83
Blum, H. P., 8, 116
Bosanquet, C., 23
Boss, M., 106
Brain, neurophysiology of, and dreams,
    11, 171–2, 176, 186
Brenman, E., 116

Callosal bridge, 171, 172
"Capacity to be alone, The"
    (Winnicott), 95
Carkhuff, R. R., 25
Cathartic confession, 29–30, 31
Cathartic experiences, and
    psychotherapy, 25, 26
Cerebral hemispheres, 18, 171–3, 174,
    176, 186
Chair versus couch, and recent
    developments in analysis, 9–10
Child analysis, training in, 7
Child, as symbol of emergent self, 66,
    72, 86
Children as Individuals (Fordham), 148
Children of nature, Freud's concept of,
    140
Cohen, D. B., 172
Coleridge, S. T., 169
Collingwood, R. G., 115
Colonna, M. T., 18
Complementary counter–transference in
    psychoanalysis, 149–50, 153, 159,
    161
Complementary experience, of mother
    and child, 94

Concordant counter–transference, in psychoanalysis, 147–9, 153, 159, 161

Confessio Amantis (Gower), 201

Confession, Jung's concept of, 9, 29–30

Constructions, in analysis, Freud's concept of, 46

Continuity, in analysis, 43–4, 51

Copans, S., 81

Corinthians I, text on agape, 35

Couch
  and work of reconstruction, 115, 118, 119
  versus chair, 9–10

Counter–resistance, 52, 79–87
  and hesitation in interpretation, 83–4
  and individuation, 87
  complementary, 80, 82
  concordant, 83
  neurotic, 80, 81–2
  non-neurotic, 80–81
  Racker's work on, 60–61, 68, 80, 81
  reactive, 82
  subjective experience of, 83–4

"Counter–resistance and interpretation" (Racker), 53

Counter–transference, 7, 8, 97, 134, 143–67, 169, 174
  and dreams, 174–6, 186
  and talion law, 150–52
  archetypal, 156, 159
  complementary, 24, 27, 28, 147, 149–50, 153, 159, 161
  concordant, 27, 28, 147–9, 153, 159, 161
  distortion, 135
  illusory, 158, 159, 161, 175
  in analytical psychology, 154–60
  in psychoanalysis, 143–53
  Jung's views on, 154–7
  neurotic, 145–7, 149, 150, 153, 158, 159, 161, 175
  syntonic, 158
  therapeutic benefits from 160–61

Counter–transference/transference interaction
  case–fragment illustrating, 163–7
  in psychoanalysis, 143–5

Croce, B., 115

Dare, C., 55, 58, 64

Darwin, Charles, 170

Defences
  against anxiety in infancy, 148
  and problems of false self, 61
  and reconstruction, 126
  and resistance, 56, 57, 69, 85
  of ego, Anna Freud's list of, 57

Defences of the Self (Fordham), 17

Deintegration, 12

Deintegrative processes, in original self, 91, 193

Deintegrative–reintegrative process, of the self, 89, 132, 193, 194–5, 196, 197

Delusion
  and patient–therapist relationship, 133
  vicious circle of, 151, 152

Delusional transference, 140, 142, 160

Depression, experience of time in deep, 113

Deutsch, Helen, 57, 68

Dieckmann, H., 53, 82, 157

Disintegration, 12, 121
  experience of time in states of, 113

Distortions of perception, and patient–therapist relationship, 133

Divine Child archetype, 7

"Do-it-yourself" psychology, 136

Dreams, dreaming, 168–87
  about the analyst, 44
  and analytical psychology, 173–7
  and clinical practice, 173–7
  and neurophysiology of brain, 11, 168, 171–3, 176, 186
  and transference/counter–transference, 174–6, 186
  archetypal motifs and themes in, 173, 187
  as language of primary process, 169
  case histories involving, 177–87
  contents and actions in, 176
  eliciting of, 174, 186
  Freud's work on, 168–9, 170
  in psychoanalytic tradition, 168–70
  interpretation of, 175
  modifications in classic theory and, 10–11
  seen as behaviour, 11
  sleep laboratory work on, 11, 168, 170–71

Drive theory, and object–relations, 89
Duration, experience of, 106, 112–14, 127, 181

Early life
  and developments in analytical psychology, 7, 8
  and developments in psychoanalysis, 8
  and individuation, 192, 193–5
  and psycho–cultural patterns, 131
  and reconstruction, 118–19, 124–5
  defence mechanism against anxiety in, 148
  experience of space and time in, 112–13
  See also Object–relations, formation of
Education, Jung's concept of, 9, 29, 31
Edwards, A., 6
Ego, 5, 6
  and recent work on the self, 11, 195–7
  and reconstruction, 116–17, 119
  defences, Anna Freud's list of, 57
  identification, in concordant counter-transference, 147
Ego–consciousness, 11, 19, 67, 169, 193
  and individuation, 190, 195–6
  and object–relations, 195–6
  in analytical psychology, 196–7
Ego organization, false, 61
Ego–orgasm, 96
Ego psychologists, 5, 169
Elemental passionateness, Freud's concept of, 140
Elucidation, Jung's concept of, 9, 29, 30–31
Environment–mother, 93
Envy and Gratitude (Klein), 114
Envy of analyst, patient's, 23, 27, 70–71, 153, 160
Eros, and agape, 39–40
Externalization, Anna Freud's concept of, 138, 142, 160
Extraversion, Jung's concept of, 131

"Failure in analysis" (Fordham), 22
Fairbairn, W. R., 8, 88, 89

False ego organization, 61
False self, problems of, 61–3, 68, 85, 86
Fatigue, in analysis, 135
Feather, B. W., 26
Feeling, Jung's concept of, 131
Fenichel, O., 46–7
Fordham, M, 6, 8, 11, 12, 16, 17, 22, 23, 27, 40, 46, 49, 53, 61, 74, 78, 79, 85, 89, 91, 92, 93, 95, 96, 121, 148, 149, 160, 161, 162, 163, 175, 176, 186, 191, 196
  description of mechanisms of defence in infancy, 148
  work on counter–transference, 157–9
  work on deintegration–reintegration process, 6, 91, 92, 193–195
  work on ego – consciousness, 197
  work on individuation, 192, 193
  work on original self, 6, 91, 92, 193–195
  work on reconstruction, 118–19, 120
  work on transference, 142
Freud, A., 56, 57, 68, 137–8, 142, 160
Freud, S., 9, 30, 31, 64, 69, 119, 123, 140, 143, 154, 172, 200–201
  and interaction in analysis, 20, 21
  and interpretation in analysis, 46
  and resistance, 54, 55–6
  and transference, 137
  clash with Jung, 2
  study of the Rat Man, 114
  work on dreams, 168–9, 170
Fusionary wish, 148

Gitelson, M., 143
Glover, E., 57–8, 68
Gopaleen, M. na, 15
Gordon, R., 6, 157
Gower, John, 201
Grandiose self, image of, 17, 88
Gratitude, in analysis, 28, 135, 152–3, 161
Greenson, R. R., 116, 139
Group therapy, non-analytical, 25
Guilt, and failure in analysis, 79
Guntrip, H., 8, 11

Hall, J. A., 173

Hann-Kende, F., 143
Harding, E., 197
Harlow experiments, 91
Hartmann, H., 5, 57, 169, 170
Headlam, A. C., 39
Heimann, P., 143
Henry, J. P., 11
Hero stories, 17
Hesse, H., 17
Hillman, J., 6, 23, 27, 40, 41
Hippocratic Oath, 20, 22, 34
    and Pauline concept of agape, 36–7,
        38
    and the analyst, 37, 51
    text of, 35
History, and analysis, 113, 115–16,
    123–4
Holder, A., 55, 58, 64
Holding work, of analyst, 28, 125, 135
Holidays, of patient and analyst, 43, 44,
    144
Home, J., 44
Homeostasis, in the psyche, 65
Hubback, J., 23, 40

Id, 11
    identification, in concordant counter-
        transference, 147
    resistance, Freud's concept of, 56, 66
Id-impulse, 96
Idealization
    as defence mechanism in infancy, 148
    of analyst by patient, 71
"Idea of resistance, The" (Schafer), 53
Identification
    as defence mechanism in infancy,
        148, 162
    in concordant counter-transference,
        147
Illusion, and patient–therapist
    relationship, 133
Illusional transference, 142, 160
Illusory counter-transference, 158, 159,
    161, 175
Imagination, 14–16, 27
    language of, 16–19
Incest phantasies and
    transference/counter-transference,
    154, 163

Incestuous love as motive power in
    analysis, 161
Individualism, Jung's concept of, 189
Individuation, 33, 51, 161, 188–99
    and dreams, 187
    and ego-consciousness, 195–6
    and object–relations, 105, 193–6, 198
    and reconstruction, 132
    and resistance/counter–resistance, 87
    dating and span of, 192
    developments in theory of, since
        Jung, 191–5
    in work of Jung, 188–92
Infancy, *see* Early life
Infantile archetypal phantasy, 11
Infantile transference, 141, 142, 160
Innate release mechanism, 91
Innocence of Dreams, The (Rycroft), 10,
    169
Integration, 33, 34, 51, 161, 190
Intellect, language of, 16–19
Interaction, in patient–analyst
    relationship, 8–9, 20–21, 34, 134
Intercrossing transference relationship,
    154
Internal object, objects, 8, 10, 11, 27,
    28, 72, 82, 88, 91, 95, 96, 147,
    169, 176, 193–5
    and archetypes, 159, 187, 193–5
    archetypal, 91, 95, 96, 97, 194, 203
    ego-supportive mother as, 96
    formation of bad, 97
    formation of, in analysis, 97–8
    in complementary
        counter–transference, 149–50
    in syntonic counter–transference, 158
    in transference, 138
International Psycho–Analytical
    Library, 143
Interpretation
    and authority of analyst, 60
    and constructions in analysis, 46
    and problems of false self, 63
    and psychopathology, 49–50
    and reconstruction of, 116, 117
    etymology, history and definitions of,
        in analysis, 45–8
    hesitation in, and resistance/counter
        resistance, 83–4
    mutative, 125
    of dreams, 174

part-object psychology in, 48–9
patient's blocking of, 50
timing and language of, 50, 83
Introjection, 33, 96, 159
 as defence mechanism in infancy,
  148, 162
 in counter–transference, 147, 158
Introversion, Jung's concept of, 131
Intuition, Jung's concept of, 131

Jackson, M., 157
Jacobson, E., 5, 6, 11
Jones, R. M., 170, 171
Journal of Analytical Psychology, 21, 23,
 142
Jung, C. G., 9, 12, 14, 17, 18, 19, 22,
 28, 39, 40, 41, 60, 79, 86, 132,
 146, 148, 151, 161, 162, 163, 169,
 170, 172, 173, 174, 176, 193,
 200–201
 and personal factor in analysis, 28–34
 clash with Freud, 2
 formulation of stages in work of
  psychotherapy, 9, 29–34
 formulation of typology and
  functions, 131, 196
 imagery for therapeutic relationship,
  157, 163
 individuation in work of, 188–92
 on analyst's function, 21
 on archetypes, 90
 on counter–transference, 154–7
 on ego-consciousness, 196–7
 on reconstruction, 117–18, 120, 126,
  127, 130
 on resistance, 63–7, 69
 on transference, 31, 65, 66, 141–2
Jung's Analytical Psychology and Religion
 (Meier), 173

K factor, 27
Kerenyi, C., 17
Kernberg, O. F., 5, 6, 11, 88, 89
Khan, M. M. R., 63, 84, 140
King, T., 113
Kirsch, T., 175
Kitchin, K., 16
Klauber, J., 115–16, 119
Klein, M., Kleinian psychology, 8, 10,
 17, 48, 60, 68, 70, 88, 89, 91, 93,
 114, 119, 135, 138, 152, 197
Kohut, A. V., 5, 6, 7, 11, 28, 88
Kraemer, William, 1
Krantz, K. E., 157
Kuo Mo-Jo: The early years (Ray), 170

Lambert, K., 8, 17, 41, 60, 67, 119,
 120, 157, 189, 197
Language
 of imagination, 16–19
 of interpretation, 50
Ledermann, R., 6, 17
Libido
 and ego-consciousness, 197
 in object–relations formation, 92
 in therapeutic interaction, 157
Liley, A. W., 206
Little, M., 140, 143
Lorand, S., 143
Lotus-flower image, 191

MacDougal, W., 26
McLuhan, M., 123
Mandala image, 191
Manic states, experience of time in, 113
Marriage quaternity figure, 154, 156,
 159, 162
Mattoon, M. A., 173
Meier, C. A., 173
Meltzer, D., 9, 17, 44, 66
Memories, Dreams, Reflections (Jung), 2
Memory, Bartlett's theory of, 115, 119
Money-Kyrle, R., 143
Moody, R., 157
Moore, N., 24, 41
Mother, as object and environment, 93
Motivation
 of analyst/therapist, 28, 135–6, 152,
  161
 of patient, 135, 161
Mourning process, and reconstruction,
 112, 127
Mutative interpretation, 125
Mythology, 17–18

Narcissistic personality damage/disorder,
 16, 49, 88, 138, 160
Negative capability, 23
Neumann, E., 67, 92

Neurophysiology of brain, and dreams, 11, 171–2, 176, 186
Neurotic counter–transference in psychoanalysis, 145–7, 149, 150, 153, 158, 159, 161, 175
Neurotic resistance, 53, 81–2
Neurotic sub–transference, 145
Neurotic transference, 139
New Psychology of Dreaming, The (Jones), 170
Novey, S., 115, 119
Nunberg, H., 140

Object–constancy, 93
"Object constancy or constant object" (Plaut), 93
Objectivity, in analysis, 20, 21
Object–mother, 93
Object–relating, and object–usage, 94
Object–relations, formation of, 8, 41–2, 62–3, 68, 86, 88–105, 159, 161, 169
    and aloneness, 95–6
    and archetypes, 88, 89–93, 95, 96
    and complementary counter–transference, 149–50
    and ego–consciousness, 195–6
    and individuation, 105, 193–6, 198
    and experience of duration, 106
    and reconstruction, 126, 128, 132, 138
    and schizoid patients, 97
    and transference, 138, 160
    case history concerning, 98–105
    child's contribution to, 93–4
    function of mother in, 93
    libido in, 92
    splitting process and, 93
    Winnicott's work on, 92–6
    See also Internal objects, Part objects, Whole objects
Objects, transitional, 94–5
Oedipal problems, 160
Original self, Fordham's concept of, 193
Origins (Partridge), 45
Oswald, I., 170
Over-impingement, 62–3, 93

Paranoid–schizoid position, 49

Part-objects, part-object psychology, 60, 68, 70, 91, 169, 176, 193
    in interpretation, 48–9
    in transference, 138
Partridge, E., 45, 54
Patient, motivation of, 135, 161
Persecutory anxiety, 49
Plaut, A. J. P., 9, 23, 41, 43, 44, 93, 157, 197
Postulated true self, 61, 62
Power drives, in transference, 141
Priest, analogous to analyst, 44, 45
Primal scene, 66, 72
    phantasies, 17, 19
Primary process, dreams as language of, 169
"Primitive emotional development" (Winnicott), 94
Problems of Modern Psychotherapy (Jung), 22, 28, 66
Projection, 33, 138, 159
    and transference in analytical psychology, 141–2
    as defence mechanism in infancy, 148, 162
    in counter–transference, 147, 158
'Psi' phenomenon, Bion's concept of, 48, 83–4
Psychic concealment, 29
Psychoanalysis
    and dreams, 168–70
    complementary counter–transference in, 147, 149–50, 153, 161, 162
    concordant counter–transference in, 147–9, 153, 161, 162
    function of analyst in, 6–7, 20–21
    modifications in traditional models of, 5–12
    neurotic counter–transference in, 145–7
    personal factor and contemporary, 26–8
    reconstruction in, 114–17, 19–20
    resistance in, 55–63, 67–8
    scientific preconceptions and interaction in, 20–21
    talion law in, 150–52
    traditional models of attitudes of, 2–4
    topographical and structural theory in, 169
    transference in, 137–41, 160–63

transference/counter–transference
  interaction in, 143–5
"Psychoanalysis as a human activity"
  (Meltzer), 44
Psychological Types (Jung), 189
Psychology of the Transference, The (Jung),
  34, 65, 154, 161, 201
Psychopathology, and interpretation,
  49–50
Psychotherapists, personal factor and
  contemporary, 25–6
Psychotic patients, and stance of
  analyst, 7
Psychotic transference, 140
Puer aeternus, archetype of, 161

Racker, H., 6, 8, 12, 22, 26, 27, 49,
  50, 53, 59, 66, 157, 161, 175
  work on resistance and
    counter–resistance, 60–61, 68,
    80, 81
  work on transference and
    counter–transference, 143–53
    passim, 158, 159, 161–2
Rapid eye movement sleep, 170–71, 172
Rappaport, 140
Rat Man, Freud's study of, 114
Ray, D. T., 170
Reconstruction, 8, 29, 46, 47, 106, 156
  and archetypes in childhood, 131
  and early environment of patient,
    124–5
  and experience of duration, 127, 131
  and individuation, 132
  and interpretation, 116, 117
  and Jung's formulation of typology
    and functions, 131
  and Kleinian analysis, 114, 119
  and mourning process, 112, 127, 130
  and object–relations, 126, 128, 132, 138
  and patient's defensive systems, 126
  and regressed/disintegrated patients,
    121
  and self, 132
  and synthesis, 126–7
  and transference, 107, 116, 130
  and traumata in middle life, 128
  as aid to analyst, 121
  case histories concerning, 107–12,
    122–3

clinical indication for use of, 120–21
dangers from neglect of, 128
first and revised, 118
function of, in analysis, 125
in analytical psychology, 117–19, 120
in psychoanalysis, 114–17, 119–20
limitations of, in individual analysis,
  130–31
objections to use of, 129–30
process of, 121–5
resistance of patients to, 129
resistance of psychotherapists to,
  129–30
therapeutic results of, 125–8
Redfearn, J. W. T., 6, 170, 191
Regression, 7, 121
  and preverbal communication in
    analysis, 119
  and problems of false self, 61, 62 63
Reich, A., 143
Reich, W., 57, 58
Reintrojection, 159
Reliability, in analysis, 43, 51
Repression, 29
  analysis of, and reconstruction, 118
  resistances, 56, 58–9
Reprojection, 159, 162
Resistance, 6, 7, 52–79, 159
  and defences, 56, 57, 69, 85
  and eliciting of dreams, 174
  and failure in analysis, 78–9
  and faulty procedures in analysis, 58,
    64
  and fear of damage by analyst, 74–8
  and fear of penetration, 73–4
  and hesitation in interpretation, 83
  and incapacity to change, 58
  and individuation, 87
  and patient's envy of analyst, 70–71
  and transference in work of Jung, 65,
    66, 69
  apparent, Winnicott's work on, 61–3,
    68, 85, 86
  etymology of, 54–5
  Freud's work on, 55–6
  Deutsch's list of, 57
  Glover's work on, 57–8
  in instinctual communities, 80
  in psychoanalysis, 55–63, 67–8
  in work of Schafer, 59–60, 66
  Jung's views on, 63–7, 69

Resistance—*cont.*
neurotic, 53
neurotic, of analyst, 81–2
non-neurotic, of analyst, 80–81
phallic ecstatic element in, 84–5
primary, 72–3, 74, 86
Racker's work on, 60–61, 68
repression, 56, 58–9
Sandler, Dare and Holder's work on, 58
secondary, 72–3, 74, 86
to infantile regressive material, 82
to reconstruction, 129–30
transference, 56, 57, 58, 68, 69, 72
Rhodes, J. M., 26
Richter, Jean-Paul, 170
Ritual, in analysis, 44–5, 51, 135
Rosarium Philosophorum, 154
Rosenfeld, H. A., 139, 140
Rossi, E., 171
"Royal marriage" motif, in work of Jung, 65, 66
Rubinfine, D. L., 9, 115, 118, 119
Rycroft, C., 6, 8, 10, 12, 22, 26, 27, 28, 45–6, 89
work on dreams, 169–70, 176

St Paul, 20, 22, 34, 35, 38, 39
Sanday, W., 39
Sandler, J., 46, 47, 55, 58, 64, 140
Schafer, R., 7, 8, 22, 26, 28, 53, 66
resistance in work of, 59–60, 66, 68
"Schism as differing visions" (Hillman), 40
Schizoid patients, and formation of object relations, 97
Scott, W. C. M., 171
Screening, by analyst, 6, 7, 8–9, 41
Searles, H., 140
Secondary personalization, 92
Secrets, conscious and unconscious, 29
Self, 6, 11–12, 33, 65, 93, 161
and dreams, 169, 187
and reconstruction, 132
child as symbol of emergent, 66, 72, 86
deintegrative–reintegrative process of, 89, 132, 193, 194–5, 196, 197
diagrams of development of, 194
dynamic view of developmental

change in, 193
integrative potentiality of, 116–17, 190, 191
original, Fordham's concept of, 193
"postulated true", 61, 62
problems of false, 61–3, 68, 85, 86
transitional object as symbol of, 95
Self and Autism, The (Fordham), 196
Self-representations, establishment of, 88, 89
Sensation, Jung's concept of, 131
"Sentiment", concept of, 26, 27, 28
Shadow, 141, 161, 191
Sibling rivalry, 160
Singer, T., 81
Sleep
rapid eye movement, 170–71, 172
slow-wave, 170
Sleep laboratories, work on dreams, 11, 168, 170–71
Society of Analytical Psychology, 1, 14, 40, 47
Somatic processes, restoration of in sleep, 170
Spock, B., 113
Stein, L., 18, 55, 90, 157
Steppenwolf (Hesse), 17
Stone, M., 171, 172, 185
Strachey, J., 47, 48, 139
Strauss, R., 23, 157
Sub-transference, neurotic of analyst, 145
Superego, 11
identification, in concordant counter–transference, 147
resistances, Freud's concept of, 56
Synthesis, and reconstruction, 126–7
Syntonic counter–transference, 158

Talion law, 6, 12, 24, 28, 41, 49, 82, 150–52, 161, 162
Therapeutic set-up, facilitating conditions in 42–5, 51, 144–5
"Therapeutic value of abreaction, The" (Jung), 117
Thinking, Jung's concept of, 131
Time, *see* Duration
Training/analysis
of future analysts, 12, 26, 27, 32,

37–8, 42, 44–5, 82, 135, 148, 152, 154, 156, 162
training in child analysis, 7
of psychotherapists, 25
Transference, 7, 8, 9, 10, 27, 28, 86, 97, 134–67, 169, 174
  and dreams, 174–6, 186
  and object–relations, 138, 160
  and psychoanalysis, 137–41, 160–63
  and reconstruction, 107, 116, 130
  and talion law, 150–52
  archetypal, 65, 86, 141–2, 156, 159, 160
  delusional, 140, 142, 160
  distortion, 135, 137, 175–6
  Fordham's work on, 142
  idealizing, 88
  illusional, 142, 160
  in analytical psychology, 141–2, 160–63
  infantile, 141, 142, 160
  in narcissistic personality disorder, 138
  internal objects in, 138
  interpretations, timing of, 50
  Jung's views on, 31, 65, 69, 141–2
  mirror, 88
  neurotic, 139
  psychotic or delusional, 140
  reconstruction in, 139, *see also* Reconstruction
  resistance, 56, 57, 58, 68, 72
  resistance to, 69
  therapeutic benefits from, 160–61

Transference and Counter–Transference (Racker), 143
Transference/counter–transference interaction
  case-fragment illustrating, 163–7
  in psychoanalysis, 143–5
Transformation, Jung's concept of, 9, 29, 32–4
Transformations (Bion), 41n.
Transitional objects, 63, 94–5
Truax, C. G., 25

Unconscious infantile phantasy, 8, 10, 89, 91, 93, 114, 169, 176

Volkan, V. D., 5, 6, 11

Weigert, 143
Whitmont, E. C., 157
Whole objects, whole object psychology, 60, 169, 176, 193
Williams, M., 23, 40, 67, 157
Winnicott, D. W., 2, 5, 6, 8, 11, 22, 26, 28, 59, 66, 68, 78, 88, 89, 124, 140, 143, 192
  work on apparent "resistance" and false self, 61–3, 68, 85, 86
  work on formation of object–relations, 92–6
Wise old man, wise old woman, archetypes of, 161

Yeats, W. B., 15

Zinkin, L., 96